INTRODUCTION TO SOVIET ETHNOGRAPHY

Edited by

Stephen P. Dunn and Ethel Dunn

VOLUME II

TABLE OF CONTENTS

Ianovskii, V.
1969 "Man in the North," SS, VII, No. 4, 16-26.

Il'inykh, N. I.
1972 "Peculiarities of the Organization and Activity of Mennonite Congregations," SS, XI, 145-159.

Iusupov, G. V.
1968 "Survivals of Totemism in the Ancestor Cult of the Kazan Tatars," In Diószegi, 1968a, 193-204.

Kalits, V. Ia.
1962 "New Features in the Life of the Peasants of Kihnu Island," SA&A, I, No. 1, 27-36.

Kálman, B.
1968 "Two Purification Rites in the Bear Cult of the Ob-Ugrians," In Diószegi, 1968a, 85-92.

Kaloev, B. A.
1969 "M. M. Kovalevskii (On the 50th Anniversary of His Death)," SA&A, VIII, 145-167.

Kapustin, N. S.
1971 "Specific Features of Certain Survivals of Religion in Everyday Life," SA&A, X, 37-56.

Katunskii, A. E.
1964 "The Reactionary Nature of the Contemporary Old Believer Ideology," SS, III, No. 2, 39-43.

Kharchev, A. G.
1967 "Marriage in the USSR," SS, V, No. 4, 3-25.

Kholmogorov, A. I.
1973 "International Traits of Soviet Nations," SS, XI, 211-327; XII, 3-33, *et seq.*

Klibanov, A. I.
1965 "The Dissident Denominations in the Past and Today," SS, III, No. 4, 44-60.

1970a "Fifty Years of Scientific Study of Religious Sectarianism," SS, VIII, 239-278.

1970b "Sectarianism and the Socialist Reconstruction of the Countryside," SS, VIII, 383-411.

1971 "Problems in the Psychology of Religious Sectarianism," SS, IX, 505-566.

Kobychev, V. P., and Robakidze, A. I.
1969 "Basic Typology and Mapping of Dwellings of the Caucasian Peoples (Materials for the Caucasian Historical-

PART IV

FOLKLORE STUDIES

PART IV. FOLKLORE STUDIES

Introductory Note

The two essays translated in this section continue the classical tradition of European folklore studies. Since they are largely free of any trace of Marxist methodology in a formal or technical sense, they will cause no difficulties for Western readers accustomed to this type of study. Accordingly, we will dispense with detailed commentary, and merely state that the tradition of folklore studies continues in full vigor, represented both by such eminent scholars as K. V. Chistov, B. N. Putilov, and V. K. Sokolova, and by a small army of student collectors (Sokolova 1970; Putilov and Sokolova, eds. 1972; Chistov 1967; Putilov 1969; Kolpakova 1962; Tudorovskaia 1967*; Chistov 1963; Mozheiko 1971; Zemtsovskii 1967, 1973; Luk'ianova 1972; Kravtsov, ed. 1972).

The pieces translated here cannot claim to be fully representative of the current state of the art; they are included both as examples of traditional techniques still in use and for their intrinsic interest. It should be noted that the tradition represented by Propp, although fundamentally ethnographic, is to some degree separate from that of current Russian ethnography, while Zhirmunskii operates largely in the categories used by literary scholars, except that he happens to be working with traditional materials.

Viktor Maksimovich Zhirmunskii, who died in 1970, was by original training and specialty a Germanic philologist. He began his professional life before the Revolution with a series of articles on German romanticism, and even in the 1920s published important detailed studies on the relationship between Byron and Pushkin, and on Goethe's influence on Russian literature. During the same period, he also directed and helped to carry out extensive ethnographic investigations, including a collection of folklore and dialectological materials among various groups of German colonists (Zhirmunskii 1928; 1931) — some Mennonite, others Catholic — living in the Ukraine. As a folklorist, he was considered by his Soviet colleagues and students to be the founder of the comparative method in its new and more sophisticated form. During the last two decades of his life, he was largely occupied with questions of the Turkic folk epos (particularly the Uzbek epic *Alpamysh*, which describes the resistance of the Uzbek people to the invasion by Genghis Khan's army, but includes much earlier epic material). Zhirmunskii was able to discover in the Turkic folk epos many elements common to Western epic poetry as well, such as the motif of the slaying of the suitors, from the final book of the *Odyssey* (Putilov 1962-1963; Meletinskii 1971).

Vladimir Iakovlevich Propp, born in 1895, graduated in 1918 from Petrograd University's section of Russian and Slavic philology. After graduation, he taught in secondary schools, and in 1926 began teaching German in the higher educational institutions of Leningrad while working with various scholarly institutions such as the Russian Geographical Society and the Institute of Art History. From 1932 on he taught at Leningrad University, first in the Department of Romance and Germanic Philology, then in the Department of Folklore, and still later, and until 1969, in the Department of Russian Literature. In 1938, he was made professor, and in 1939 defended his doctoral dissertation. "V. Ia. Propp was a convinced adherent of the comparative-historical method in the study of folklore. While he was sensitive and attentive to the ethnic peculiarities of folklore and strove to reveal the concrete ethnic traits in the artistic content of folklore items, he nevertheless believed that folklore creativity is conditioned by a number of general regularities which lead to the development of similar phenomena among various peoples and that the historical process of folklore itself always occurring within concrete ethnic boundaries reveals repetitive, similar, and analogous interethnic features" (Putilov 1971: 179). Propp was one of the few literary scholars or social scientists well known in the West, and many of his works have been translated. The piece translated here, however, shows him in a more specifically Russian context and provides entrée to a large body of ethnographic information not otherwise available in English.

* * *

REFERENCES CITED

Chistov, K. V.
  1963   "Folklore Studies and the Present Day," SA&A, Vol. I, No. 4, 37-48.

  1967 Russkie narodnie sotsial'no-utopicheskie legendy [Russian Folk Social-Utopian Legends]. Moscow.

Kolpakova, N. P.
  1962 Russkaia narodnaia bytovaia pesnia [The Russian Household Folk Song]. Moscow-Leningrad.

Kravtsov, N. I., ed.
  1972 Voprosy zhanrov russkogo fol'klora [Questions of the Genres of Russian Folklore]. Moscow State University.

Luk'ianova, T. P.
  1972 "O nekotorykh starinnykh obriadakh na Brianshchine (iz dnevnika fol'klorista)" ["On some old rituals in the Briansk area (from a folklorist's notebook)"], SE, No. 2, 85-87.

Meletinskii, E. M.
  1971 "Obituary for Viktor Maksimovich Zhirmunskii," SE, No. 3, 160-163.

Mozheiko, Z.
  1971 Pesennaia kul'tura belorusskogo Poles'ia: Selo Tonezh [The Folksong Repetoire of the Belorussian Poles'ia: The Village of Tonezh]. Minsk.

Putilov, B. N.
  1962-1963   "V. M. Zhirmunskii as Folklorist," SA&A, Vol. I, No. 3, 56-60.

  1969 "Russian and south Slavic epic songs about contests with serpents," SA&A Vol. 8, 43-69, 168-184.

  1971 "Obituary for Vladimir Iakovlevich Propp," SE, No. 1, 178-180.

Putilov, B. N., and Sokolova, V. K., eds.
1972   *Slavianskii fol'klor* [Slavic Folklore]. Moscow.

Sokolova, V. K.
1970   *Russkie istoricheskie predaniia* [Russian Historical
Legends]. Moscow.

Zemtsovskii, I.
1967   *Toropetskiye pesni* [Songs from Toropetsk]. Leningrad.

1973   "Pesni, ispolniavshiesia vo vremiia kalendarnykh
obkhodov dvorov u russkikh" ["Songs sung during calendrical
processions around farmsteads among the Russians"], SE,
No. 1, 38-47.

Zhirmunskii, V. M.
1928   *Die deutschen Kolonien in der Ukraine: Geschichte,
Mundarten, Volkslied, Volkskunde.* Khar'kov.

1931   *Volkslieder aus der bayrischen Kolonie Jamburg am
Dniepr.* Wien.

THE HISTORICAL BASES OF SOME
RUSSIAN RELIGIOUS FESTIVALS

V. Ia. Propp

I

By studying the Russian religious holidays of the
past, we can establish that some of them are of very
ancient date. They already existed before the introduction
of Christianity, and were connected with the major intervals of the solar calendar — the solstices and equinoxes. In
ethnography and folklore studies, the rituals and songs
which accompanied these holidays have received the not-
altogether-apt designation of calendrical ritual poetry, and
the holidays themselves — that of calendrical holidays. The
chief of these are Yuletide, Carnival, Pentecost[a], and the
Feast of Ivan Kupala.[b] These festivals were once of a
pronounced agrarian character: the work of the farmer
was determined by the succession of the seasons. The
church embarked upon a stubborn struggle with these festivals, and prohibited the ancient and merry customs and
rites connected with them as being "devilish" and "Greek"
— i.e., pagan. But it was not able to destroy the people's
merrymaking. Another means of struggle with these
ancient festivals was that the church timed them to fit
the new Christian cult. Thus, for example, the festival of
the winter solstice, the festival of the birth of the sun,
was transformed into the festival of the birth of Christ;
the festival of the summer solstice, connected with the
blossoming of vegetation on the earth, became the festival
of John the Baptist — or, in popular language, Ivan

Kupala. To these festivals, interpreted in ecclesiastical terms, the church added its own, connected with New Testament traditions; such, for example, are the feasts of the Transfiguration, the Ascension, the Holy Virgin [October 1], Assumption, and others unconnected with any folk festivals of pre-Christian origin.

Study of the pre-Christian strata of Russian religio-customary — the so-called calendrical — festivals is of very great importance. It reveals the pagan basis of these festivals, and thereby deprives them of their aura of sacredness and divinity. But this is not all. As we shall see below, study of these festivals throws light on the origin of some of the bases of church dogma and reveals their dependence on pre-Christian — i.e., purely pagan — concepts.

The pagan elements of Christian festivals constituted a survival; on the other hand, the church cult as such, which constituted the state religion, was not a survival in the eyes of believers. In our day, the situation has changed. Church festivals and the concepts connected with them have become a survival in their totality, and a harmful one at that. Determination of the pagan bases of some of these festivals helps us to reveal the pagan roots of Christian dogma as a whole, and thereby shakes and destroys faith in the divine origin and divine essence of church prescriptions and doctrines. At the present time, historical science has at its disposal material sufficient to carry out this task. We can sketch out a more or less accurate, although perhaps not exhaustive, picture of the celebration of the so-called calendrical festivals, chiefly according to reports from the 19th century, and give a scientific explanation of them. Some details of the festivals can be reconstructed in earlier forms from various indirect sources: the data of chronicles, church homilies and sermons, legislative acts, and certain other ancient Russian texts.

The number of works devoted to the festivals we have mentioned is rather considerable. Nevertheless, there are no generally accepted conclusions; there are theories and hypotheses which do not prove anything. Below we will have occasion to become acquainted with some of these theories.

The cause of this situation lies partly in the general speculative character of 19th- and 20th-century scholarship. Conclusions were drawn, not by means of rigorous comparison of facts but by more or less arbitrary guesses of an entirely abstract nature. Festivals were studied without relation to the economic life and activity of the farmer, although this is precisely where the solution to the riddle of his psychology and the roots of his concepts and ritual activities are to be found. We will see that the so-called calendrical festivals constitute agrarian festivals.

There was another reason, however, why the study of these holidays did not yield correct conclusions: the fact that the festivals were studied in isolation from each other. Thus, for example, Vsevolod Miller studied only Carnival; Potebnia, only Ivan Kupala; Anichkov, only the spring festivals — Trinity and the greeting of spring (Miller 1884; Potebnia 1914 [1867]; Anichkov 1903-1905), etc.

However, each festival in itself can be well studied only when the entire yearly cycle is studied.

On the basis of such a study we discover that these festivals consist, in part, of identical elements that repeat themselves in different forms. This observation is of primary significance for us. Thus, ritual remembrance of the dead took place at Yuletide, Carnival, Trinity, and Radunitsa[c], and at various other religious holidays. Another example: the burning or, in general, destruction of a doll took place not only at Carnival, of which it was considered characteristic, but also on Trinity, Ivan Kupala, St. Peter's Day, and at other times. Hence the conclusion that any ritual must not be studied within the limits of one festival and in isolation from the study of it on other religious holidays. Attention must also be paid to the form of these rituals on all days when they are carried out. The same must be done with all other repeated elements out of which the religious festivals are built up. This conclusion can be generalized: the calendrical festivals should be studied not so much by intervals as by their component elements throughout all the intervals. True, this method does not eliminate the danger of leveling out the peculiarities of these festivals. However, this difficulty is not a fundamental one, but a question of scientific technique: by studying, in disassembled form, the component elements from which the festivals in question are built up, we can easily reassemble them and show how Yuletide, Carnival, or other festivals were celebrated, how they ran their course, what they had in common, and what their specific differences were.

It is quite obvious that a full treatment of every Russian religious festival that is called calendrical, and of the rituals carried out during them, cannot be given in a short article. This requires a work of broader scope. But some of their elements can be considered as preliminary observations.

For the present article, we choose, out of all the elements, funerals — i.e., the burning, drowning, or tearing-up of a doll, an effigy, or some other object. This is the most universal and widespread of all rituals at Russian calendrical festivals. Its study is not only specific in character but also allows us to draw certain more general conclusions concerning the character, origin, and significance of the festivals where this ceremony was executed.

The presence of funerary rituals, which are present in various forms at all holidays of the agrarian-calendrical cycle, shows their homogeneity. One of the peculiarities of these rituals lies in the fact that the funerals are carried out in a comic, not a tragic, spirit. The mimicking of grief partakes of the character of parody and farce, and the funeral sometimes ended in a wild carouse.

We will set forth the material beginning with Yuletide, and then pass on to the subsequent festivals.

II

The usual church funerals were parodied at Yuletide. The funeral game was at one time part of the Yuletide sports. This game is called "dead man," "corpse" [in various dialectical forms], or "death." The game consisted of bringing into the house a man dressed as a corpse and, amid general laughter, mourning him and performing a funeral service over him, parodying the church ritual and mimicking grief.

We have the following description from Kostroma Gubernia. One of the players is dressed as a corpse. "The man puts on a white blouse, white trousers, white puttees, new *lapti* with thongs crossed as for a living man, and a homespun sash. The face is covered with a cloth, or a mask is put on of carved wood or of birchbark, horrible and unsightly. The 'dead man' is laid either on a hand sled, which is brought in by two children to the house where the girls are, or on a board carried by several people, amid the weeping and wailing of the accompanying parents, brothers, and sisters. In the house, the pretended relatives of the dead man call the girls or merely drag them in and compel them to kiss the dead man" (Zavoiko 1917: 24).

There were cases in which actual corpses were disturbed for this game. The priest of the Church of the Veil at Rakulo-Koksha, Vel'sk Uyezd, Vologda Gubernia, reported that during the performance of "Mavrukh" (of which more below) and other games, "they sometimes took out of the coffin whatever corpse they found there, stuck a splinter between its teeth and set it in a corner for light" (Zelenin 1914: 198).

The fullest description, developed from the reports of several correspondents, is given by S. V. Maksimov. The part of the dead man is played by a youth dressed all in white; his face is spread with oat flour. Long teeth made from turnips project from his mouth. He is laid in a coffin or on a bench, and tied down. "After him comes a priest in a hempen veil, with a priest's headdress made of blue wrapping paper, and a censer in which hot coals, moss, and dried chicken manure were smoking." A deacon follows, along with relatives carrying meat pies for the funeral feast. There begins a travestied funeral service, with sobbing by professional mourners, and so forth. The girls are compelled to kiss the dead man on the lips. Some of the young men go out to bury the corpse, while others remain in the house. A youth dressed as a girl offers the other girls *shan'gi* — pieces of frozen horse manure (Maksimov 1903: 300-301).

How widespread was this custom? Does it not constitute some local peculiarity? In this regard, Maksimov writes: "The custom of dressing up as corpses is still very widespread in the whole northern part of our country, and in Nikol'sk Uyezd, Vologda Gubernia, which we have mentioned, those who dress as corpses are not only the youths, but also married men, and, furthermore, several persons at a time, so that a whole *artel'*[d] of corpses sometimes breaks into the house for the *posidelka*[e]" (Maksimov 1903: 302).

In this connection, we may recall also the soldiers' comedy *Mavrukh* (a corruption of "Mal'bruk" [i.e., Marlborough in the French form]), the full text of which was published by Onchukov (1911: 135-136). The essence of the game consists in the fact that the dead Mavrukh is carried onto the stage on a bench, after which a funeral service begins. Various songs, some of them indecent, are sung to church tunes, without any particular connection. One is struck by the first four lines of this comedy:

> *The dead man, the queer fellow,*
> *He died on Tuesday;*
> *They came to bury him,*
> *He was looking out of the window.*

The following riddle was current in Vologda Gubernia: "Dead man, dead man, died on Tuesday; the priest came to cense him, and he's looking into the window." The answer to the riddle is "Grain."[1] This riddle will occupy us a little later.

In *Mavrukh*, we have a mixture of elements of the late soldiers' comedy, with elements of the Yuletide games, consisting of a comic funeral for a corpse.

The first thing which strikes one, in considering the Yuletide funeral games, is their pronounced anticlerical tendency. P. N. Berkov is correct when he writes that such games "reflect an ironical attitude toward church ritual" (Berkov 1953: 321), but this does not explain why this ironic attitude manifested itself precisely at Yuletide in the period of the winter solstice. V. I. Chicherov attempts to explain the presence of funeral motifs by the fact that the "theme of death" in the popular agricultural calendar represents the "winter death of nature and the extinguishing of the sun" (Chicherov 1957: 202). The influence of the so-called solar theory is clearly evident here. In this case, it is not justified, since at the winter solstice there takes place not the extinction of the sun but precisely the reverse: the renewal of solar energy, the turn toward light, toward spring.

In another part of this book, Chicherov writes: "Belief in the significance of the relation of the dead to life leads to the effort to enlist his help and protection, which are particularly important at the beginning of a given calendar period" (Chicherov 1957: 203). But if this is an expression of the attempt to enlist the help of the dead, why is the funeral of the dead man transformed into farce?

We will not advance other explanations for the moment. We will consider funeral motifs in other festivals. after which it will be possible to return to Yuletide.

III

The next large popular festival after Yuletide was Carnival. The central feature of the carnival festivities was the greeting and farewell to Carnival.

On Thursday of Carnival Week, an image of Carnival was made in the form of a doll or effigy, which was carried all over the village with laughter and jokes. This was called "greeting Carnival." The aspect of the effigy was not uniform. It could be depicted either as a man or woman. Here are several vivid descriptions:

Sakharov describes this feature as follows: "In some places I happened to see how the children in the morning prepared a straw figure — Carnival. Carnival was dressed in a kaftan and a hat, belted with a sash, and shod with *lapti*. This carnival doll was carried up a hill on a hand sled with welcoming lamentations" (Sakharov 1849: 72).

Maksimov gives a similar description: "It (Carnival) usually begins on Thursday of Carnival Week. The young men and girls make a doll of straw, dress it in a woman's outfit, bought by going shares, and place in one hand a bottle of vodka and in the other a pancake. This is 'Lady Carnival,' the heroine of the Russian carnival" (Maksimov 1903: 368).

Makarenko reports from Siberia: The "children,"

having made a "straw effigy" with male attributes and dressed it in masculine attire, set it in a special carriage made from two or three sleighs tied together; a horse was harnessed to each of them; an empty barrel was placed in the front of the sleigh and beside it a table with refreshments, empty bottles, and wineglasses. In the middle a pole was raised (nine or ten arshins[f] in height); a wheel was mounted on it at a certain height, and the effigy was tied to this in a sitting position, with a piece of butter and a bottle and glass attached; a trough was also laid in the carriage (Makarenko 1913: 146).

The greeting of Carnival was described in the Soviet period. A. B. Zernova reports from Dmitrov Raion, Moscow Oblast: "On Monday, in families which have young people, they make out of rags a female figure with a long braid, dressed in the clothing worn by unmarried women. The figure represents a girl; a pastry brush and a pancake are placed in its hands" (Zernova 1932: 18). Meanwhile, the crowd makes merry, sings, dances, and laughs.

How are we to understand this ritual, the ritual of Carnival?

No matter how carefully we study the forms and types of effigies, a descriptive typology will not reveal to us the meaning of this festival. The attempts which have been made to interpret the appearance of Carnival and the processions of greeting and farewell to it are various. On the basis of the fact that the effigy is destroyed, some have drawn the conclusion that an undesirable person was being destroyed. Carnival has been considered as a personification of winter. The destruction of Carnival signifies the departure of winter (see, e.g., Chicherov 1959: 372). Vsevolod Miller (1884) considered it a personification of the old year, which is destroyed before the onset of the new. Anichkov saw in it a personification of death. This theory is close to the purification (lustration) theories which reduce Carnival to an embodiment not only of death but also of the plague or, in general, of diseases, ailments, and ill-health, which is driven away in order to secure health for mankind.

We will approach the question differently. Without

prejudging the question of what Carnival "means," let us consider what is done with the effigy.

During Thursday, Friday, and Saturday, the doll was kept in the village. It might be placed at the top of a hill at the point from which coasting began. This circumstance is found most frequently. It might also remain at any point in the village, or it might be locked at night in some barn and kept there until the end of Carnival Week, when the farewell to Carnival took place.

The farewell to Carnival was held with as much noise as the greeting of it. Again the sleighs were hitched up; again the effigy was set up on them, and the gaily dressed merry throng accompanied the procession, running or riding on sleighs. This procession represented the funeral of Carnival.

One of the most detailed accounts was set down in Kaluga Gubernia and communicated by Shein: "On Pardon Sunday — that is, the last day of Carnival — the women and girls gather after dinner and perform the ceremony of Carnival's funeral in the following way: they make of straw a doll with hands, dress it in a woman's blouse and sarafan[9], and tie a kerchief around its head. In this form, the doll represents Carnival. Then they dress one woman as a priest and put over her head a burlap bag in place of a veil, and in her hand a pair of old lapti tied to a rope, in place of a censer. Two of the participants in the ceremony take Carnival by the arms and, accompanied by the crowd and led by the priest, proceed from one end of the village to the other, while various songs are sung. When the procession starts on its way back, Carnival is laid on a stick in place of a bier and covered with a shroud. Having come to the end of the village, the procession stops. Here the Carnival doll is undressed, torn apart, and entirely destroyed. During the procession with Carnival, the priest swinging the censer cries 'Hallelujah!' and after her the whole crowd shouts and raises a tumult, each one as he wishes: some cry, some wail, some laugh, etc. And while they are burying Carnival, they sing songs. In conclusion, we must note that the Carnival dolls are made in many houses in the village, but only one is buried" (Shein 1895: 333).

The first thing that strikes us is the remarkable similarity with the game of "dead man" or "death," which is played at Yuletide. At Yuletide the funeral service was held in the house, and at Carnival there took place, as it were, the carrying-out of the dead and his burial. The procession is clearly pre-Christian. Let us note meanwhile that the burial of Carnival is a burial accompanied by laughter. The participation of the "clergy" reinforces the comic element and is at the same time testimony to the struggle between the old paganism and the later church religion. The funeral did not take the form prescribed by the church. It was reduced to the tearing apart of the effigy; there was no commitment to the earth. The observation that the funeral was held to the accompaniment of laughter will be considered below.

In the materials cited, nothing is said about precisely where the destruction of the effigy took place, while for us this is important. The sources say vaguely: "Having come to the end of the village . . ." A second question, also left unanswered in our sources, is connected with this: what became of the pieces into which the carnival doll was torn, and what was done with them? The answer to the question which interests us may be found in other accounts.

One of the most precise descriptions of this ceremony was made by Zernova in Moscow Oblast during the Soviet period: "In Fedorovskoe, on the evening of Pardon Sunday, young people of both sexes decorate a sled and team with ribbons and braid. On the harnessed horse they seat a man-sized Carnival, dressed in the holiday costume of an unmarried woman. The young people sit in the sleigh and go around the village singing until dark. Late in the evening, the carnival procession rides out into the winter plantings, where a bonfire for the burning of Carnival has already been prepared" (Zernova 1932: 20).

In this case, we are told precisely that the doll is taken not merely outside the village but into the winter plantings — i.e., into a *sown field*. This circumstance cannot be accidental. Those ethnographers who reported that Carnival is burned "on the outskirts," or in general outside the boundaries of the village, paid no attention to the fact that Carnival was destroyed not just anywhere, but precisely in a field.

Afterward, the following took place: "When the bonfire begins to burn out, the participants in the burning take flaming brands and scatter them over all the adjoining winter plantings" (Zernova 1932: 21).

It is entirely obvious to us that the scattering of parts of Carnival over the sown fields was intended to ensure the successful growth of these plantings. This was the original meaning of this ceremony. Considering that all the interests of the peasant are concentrated on the land, and that his whole life depends on the harvest, such an explanation of Carnival is more probable than one which connects it with the old year, last year's sun, death, the plague, or the like. It is not yet clear why this ceremony was conducted precisely in these forms and not in others. Below we will see that the destruction of an effigy took place in other festivals as well, and then we can consider this question in more detail. At this point it is sufficient to indicate that certain details of the Carnival ceremony confirm the guess that this was a fertility rite. Shein indicates in passing that in Kaluga Gubernia "Carnival dolls were made in many houses, but only one was buried." This is confirmed by other indications. Zernova reports that Carnival dolls, which were attached to the rooftrees, were made in the houses. While the effigy for the whole village was destroyed on the fields planted to winter crops, the dolls for the families were taken down from the rooftrees, carried into the houses, and there burned in the stove — i.e., as it were, united with the domestic hearth — or else torn to pieces and thrown into the yard for the livestock (Zernova 1932: 21). The scattering of parts of the Carnival for the livestock had the same purpose as scattering them on the fields. Whereas the first was intended to secure the fertility of the fields, the second was supposed to ensure the fertility of animals. What is more, the Carnival doll was credited with influence on human fertility. On Carnival it was customary for sons-in-law and their wives to visit their mothers-in-law and be entertained by them, concerning which many humorous songs were composed. In Dmitrov Raion, the image of Carnival on the rooftree was supposed to be the first thing the bridegroom saw when he rode up. This was done so that the young couple would have children (Zernova 1932: 18).

The combination of details of the celebration of Carnival which we have considered gives us the right to draw the preliminary conclusion that this festival had an agrarian-magical character and was intended to further the fertility of the earth and the multiplication of all life. Why the effigy was destroyed at this time, why the ceremony was accompanied by a gay funeral, and why during this festival people gave themselves up to revelry — all this is not yet clear, but will be explained below when we consider the subsequent festivals.

IV

The next great festival, into which the themes we are studying enter, is the so-called "Rusalka[h] Week," preceding the ecclesiastical Trinity.[2] This celebration had a dual form: birch branches were distributed and placed in the houses. In addition, one birch tree was chosen in the forest and was then decorated and solemnly brought into the village. This festival was considered one of the greatest holy days in the year.

Among the Great Russians, the ritual celebration involved only the birch, but not other trees. The song runs:

> *Do not rejoice, oaks;*
> *Do not rejoice, green ones.*
> *Not to you the girls come;*
> *Not to you the beautiful ones;*
> *Not you they bring meat-pies,*
> *Pancakes, omelets.*
>
> *Io, io, Semik and Trinity!*

. . .

Rejoice, birches;
Rejoice green ones.
To you the girls come,
To you the beautiful ones;
To you they bring meat-pies,
Pancakes, omelets.

Io, io, Semik and Trinity (Tereshchenko 1848:
VI, 164).

The special position which belongs to the birch tree
is explained, apparently, by the fact that the birch is the
first and earliest tree to clothe itself in bright and festive
green, while the other trees are only just putting forth
buds. This gave rise to the idea that birch trees are endow-
ed with a special power of growth. The focus of this
power is considered to be in the growing points in the
branches: growth proceeds from them, and consequently
the power is located in them. This power must be utilized.
Such is the very simple train of thought which led to the
various ceremonies connected with birch trees.

Birch branches or young birch trees were brought
from the forest and distributed to the houses without any
particular ritual acts. Doors, houses, parlors, and gates
were decorated with birch trees, so that the village took
on a festive appearance. For this holiday, everything was
washed and cleaned, and the houses were whitewashed. In
Smolensk Oblast, and in some other places, these days
were called "the green Yuletide" (Shein 1887: 184-185).

Apparently, at the beginning of the 19th century, the
birches were dedicated in the churches. During the church
service on Trinity Sunday (Ascension) the people stood
with birch trees; these birch trees, like the palm fronds
dedicated on Palm Sunday, were considered to have special power for healing and various other purposes. Shein
reports from Smolensk Oblast: "On the day of the spirits,
the peasants have a custom of bringing flowers and grasses
into the church to be sprinkled with holy water, and
keeping them for the rest of the year. With them, the
peasants fumigate their houses and their livestock, and
when thunder clouds appear, they burn them in a slow
fire to avert the thunder" (Shein, 1887: 185).

The rites connected with the choice of a single young birch tree in the forest represent a more complex phenomenon. The following elements enter into this complex: selection and notching of a tree, its decoration, a common meal under it, the plaiting of wreaths, ritual adoption, the cutting down of the tree and its solemn transportation into the village, choral games and dances under the tree (before it is cut down in the forest or after it is brought into the village), destruction of the tree, and divination from the leaves thrown into the water.

Each of these elements must be studied in various and manysided connections. Here we will consider briefly the selection of the tree, its decoration, and the bringing of it into the village, so that we can then study the feature of its destruction.

By what indication the tree is chosen, the ethnographers do not tell us, but it is rather obvious that the birch tree chosen is a young and juicy one, in a place where there is room to dance around it. If the tree was chosen ahead of time, it is bent to mark it.

To celebrate the festival, the girls walk to the forest. The chosen birch tree was "tied up" — i.e., the ends of the branches were bent in a ring and tied so as to form a wreath which seemed to have grown on the tree. The Siberian custom of bending the top of the tree over into the grass, and making a "braid" by tying the top to the grass, is of special interest to us (Makarenko 1913: 168). In other places the tops of two birches were tied together so as to form a kind of arch. The wreaths might be plaited from branches of other birches, intertwined with grasses and flowers, and hung on the chosen tree. The tied birch was decorated. "One of the girls had a silk sash with which the birch was tied below at the root" (Shein 1895: 344). Ribbons, threads, and rags of various colors were hung on the birch tree, which was also sometimes decorated with flowers (Makarenko 1913: 171). The birch tree might also be hung with wreaths made of dough (Sakharov 1849: 84).

What is the ancient meaning of this ritual? Proceeding on the assumption that in popular conceptions the power of growth is contained in the ends of branches and in growing points, we may consider the bending in a ring and the tying as a means of somehow catching and retaining this power. The power must be carried out of the woods and given to the earth and to people. Below, where we consider the destruction of the birch tree, we will see that the tied-up birch tree was chopped up and thrown into the rye. Bending the top to the ground and intertwining it with the grasses represents an attempt to transmit the vegetative power of the birch to the earth. If these suppositions are correct, they explain a song for Trinity, transcribed in Smolensk Gubernia:

> Let us go, girls,
> To the meadows, the meadows,
> To plait the wreaths.
> We plait the wreaths
> For good years,
> For dense zhito[i],
> For barley in ears,
> For the bearded oats,
> For the black buckwheat,
> For the white cabbage (Shein 1887: 185).

The materials we have cited give us the right to conclude that the bringing of a decorated tree from the forest into the dwelling and onto the fields represented an attempt to use the vegetative power of trees for agricultural purposes, to transmit this power from the trees to the earth and to grains.

Study of the ceremony of destroying the birch tree confirms this observation. . . . In a number of places, the birch tree was dressed in male or female costume — i.e., it was turned into something like a doll. This doll, like the one at Carnival, was called *"gosteika"* [little guest]. Snegirev (1838: 134; on this point see Sakharov 1849: 88; Makarenko 1913: 167) reports: "In Minusinsk Okrug of Enisei Gubernia, the townspeople, having dressed a birch tree, which they call *'gosteika'*, in the best dress, place it in the shed until Trinity Day."

Similar information comes from a number of other places. The decoration of the birch tree, the procession with it, and the keeping of it until Trinity are very reminiscent of the Carnival ceremony, with the single difference that there is none of the revelry and merrymaking that are observed during Carnival.

The second feature was the destruction of the birch tree. Many of those who have recorded the Trinity ceremonies are silent on this point, but nevertheless a general picture can be reconstructed. The birch tree was "untied" — i.e., the wreaths and decorations were cut or lifted from it. Divination was afterward carried out with these wreaths. The birch tree itself was destroyed, and two forms of the destruction may be quite clearly distinguished: the birch tree was either thrown into the field or submerged in water. . . .

We have a number of proofs that the birch tree was placed in the rye. Maksimov reports that near Uglich the dismantled birch tree was placed in the rye, and that parts of the omelet and whole eggs were thrown around the field "so that it, our provider, should yield better" (Maksimov 1903: 464).

In Smolensk Gubernia, the procession was accompanied by a song:

> *Oi, where the girls walked, there the*
> > *rye grows thick;*
> *Oi, where the widows walked, there*
> > *grows the grass,*
> *The grass so high and green*
> *And where the young girls walked,*
> > *there bloom the flowers;*
> *The flowers are blooming all along the street,*
> *Along the street and by the birch tree,*
> *By the birch tree under the bushes*
> > (Shein 1887: 191).

What was the meaning of the fact that the *semik* birch tree was thrown into or placed in a rye field? If it is true that the birch tree was regarded as a kind of repository of vegetative power, then apparently there was an attempt by this means to transmit this vegetative power, brought from the forest, to the earth. This explains certain facts that are strange at first glance — for example, that "Trinity flowers were laid in the first cartload of manure" (Zernova 1932: 39). In this case, an entirely rational means of increasing the harvest did not replace a magical means: Trinity flowers, like the Trinity birch, give the earth fertility. This also explains to us why "the birch in certain cases is considered the guardian of the household" (Zernova 1932: 39).

Another form of the destruction of the birch consisted in submerging it in water.

Zernova reports from Dmitrov Raion: "in the evening the birch tree is dismantled, and either taken out to the rye field and left there or thrown into the village pond (1932: 30).

Zernova's report that the birch was submerged is by no means a unique case. Makarenko reports from Siberia: "On the evening of the day of the spirits, having taken away the decoration, they threw the birch into the Angara" (1913: 170). G. S. Vinogradov says the same: "In the evening, they go to the river. They take the clothes from the birch tree and submerge the tree; the flowers and branches are thrown into the water" (Vinogradov 1918: 42). He also reports several analogous cases from a number of sources.

According to Shein's data, in Vladimir Gubernia the birch tree was thrown into a spring from which a river rose (Shein 1895: 345). Also from Vladimir Gubernia, we have a more complete and very colorful description of the submerging of the birch tree. After it was brought into the garden, "the girls gather every evening around the white one and look at it as at some mystery, and sing and play until nightfall, and so it continues until Trinity Day. After supper on Trinity Day, they gather at the birch tree and sing, removing the ribbons from the tree and each breaking off a branch, which is called skinning the white one, and then they pull it out of the earth and drag it to the river like a criminal, to drown it; they carry it along the street in a whole crowd, each one holding some branch, and, having come to the bank, throw it in the water with the cry: 'Drown, *semik;* drown the angry husbands!' The poor birch, which previously was a toy and is now thrown into the water with contempt, floats where the water carries it." After this, the participants in the ceremony return home and make merry — i.e., the submerging of the birch tree is considered a festival (Shein 1895: 346). In this case, in addition to drowning, we also have the tearing into pieces, which accompanies the destruction of Carnival as well.

What did the drowning of the birch tree mean? Zernova (1932: 30) says: "The birch tree thrown into the pond is supposed to secure adequate moisture for the entire summer."

This interpretation comes from the participants in the ceremony themselves. Such "folk etymologies" are not always accurate, but this ceremony is connected with numerous other agricultural ceremonies dedicated to water, and particularly with the rituals of Kupala and with the whole circle of concepts about *rusalki*, which cannot be included in the present study.

Zernova's observations place the submerging of the birch tree on the same plane with other ceremonies connected with the destruction of a doll, and do not contradict them.

The data we have considered lead us to conclude that the Trinity ritual, like the rituals preceding it, expresses the farmer's efforts to influence the fertility of the earth. For this reason, we cannot agree with the theory of Kalinskii, who believes that the totality of the Trinity ceremonies was derived from the "deification" of the old trees and groves, in whose shade festivities were celebrated and sacrifices offered (Kalinskii 1877: 207).

This theory was essentially repeated by Anichkov. Citing very extensive foreign material, very broadly chosen but not mastered in detail, Anichkov came to the conclusion that the Trinity rituals derive from the cult of sacred trees, and represent survivals of it (Anichkov 1905: 158 ff.).

V

The Kupala ritual, with its traditional lighting of huge bonfires and jumping across them, would not seem to have anything in common with ritual burials or with the destruction of a tree, a doll, or an effigy. However, this picture changes when we pay attention to the details sometimes reported by collectors.

In many cases the celebration was confined, apparently, to the lighting of huge bonfires and jumping across them. However, more detailed consideration of this ritual shows that it was the Trinity birch or some other tree which was burned. In many cases an effigy was also made, which was subsequently destroyed. Shein reports from Kobrino Uyezd, Grodno Gubernia, that the fire there was lit on the side of the *"zhito* stubble." Here the peasants bring the "May" — i.e., the small trees which have stood in their houses since Trinity — and throw them on the bonfire (Shein 1887: 219).

There are similar reports from Slonim Uyezd. Here a harrow and the Trinity birch were taken three times around the village. The procession stopped at the end of the pasture, beyond the edge of town. "Here the harrow is first thrown on the ground, and on it the birch tree, and everything immediately burned" (Shein 1887: 223).

Another case belongs to the same category of phenomena: the bonfire is lighted "on the fallow field. This place, by custom, must be near a large tree standing on an elevation. . . . Under such a tree, a fire is laid, and brushwood is collected for it, if it is there in the forest; otherwise, firewood is brought for this purpose from the house" (Shein 1887: 222).[3] In this case, a live tree burns, as it were.

In Minsk Gubernia, several green trees were stuck into the ground near the bonfire — i.e., a kind of artificial grove was erected, within which the fire was lit (Shein 1887: 215).

Tereshchenko reports that in Malakhovo Uyezd, Kiev Gubernia, the girls on the evening of Kupala stuck a tree into the ground, which they decorated with wreaths of flowers and, while singing, lit a fire aound the tree (Tereshchenko 1848: V, 80).

According to Snegirev, "In the Ukraine, the Podol'e and Volhynia, the unmarried girls at sundown on Kupailo gather in one place and bring a willow branch decorated with flowers; fixing it in the ground, they walk around this tree, which they call Kupailo, and sing mournful songs in honor of it. This continues for over an hour; then the young men, who have been standing aside, throw themselves on the branch and, despite the defense of the girls, tear it up and carry it away; this ends this ritual" (Snegirev 1838: 30). In this case, the tree is torn to pieces, as was done with the effigy of Carnival. This was done independently of the ceremony of lighting the fire.

The data cited relate to Belorussia and the Ukraine. However, it is hardly possible that we have here a local form. The Kupala ritual among the Great Russians was in general poorly preserved. The burning of a tree, the lighting of fires under trees or around them, or the artificial placing of trees around a fire — are these not a local but a primeval form of the Kupala fires? This thought is prompted by an indication in the Gustyna Chronicle (entry for 1670), where it is said that in honor of Ivan Kupala "in the evening the simple people of both sexes gather and plait for themselves wreaths of edible greens or roots and, girding themselves with grass, light a fire in which they place a green branch."

Two details are important for us in this excerpt. The first is the words "in which they place a green branch. . ." The second detail to which we must draw attention consists in the fact that they walked or danced around the fire, wearing wreaths "of edible greens or roots" and "girding themselves with grass" — i.e., wearing around their waists some sort of grasses or grains. All this shows that the St. John's Eve bonfires are connected with agricultural interests and concepts, and not with some other kind. This was understood by the chronicler, and his "theory" is not worse but actually better than many later ones. The chronicler assumes that "Kupalo, as I think, is a god of plenty like Ceres among the Hellenes; and the ignorant people bring him gifts in gratitude for plenty at the time when the harvest comes." The chronicler is mistaken in thinking that the celebration of Kupalo is a ritual of thanksgiving, and that Kupalo is a deity similar to the "Hellene" (i.e., Roman) Ceres. But he is right when he assumes that the celebration of Kupalo is connected with the harvest. His error lies in the fact that the celebration is connected, not with the harvest just past, for which thanks are supposedly being given (in the agricultural zone of Russia, the harvest could not have been completed on the 24th of June), but with the coming one, whose success the people wishes to assure. Furthermore, we will be able to explain the lighting of bonfires and the burning of a tree in themselves only when we consider the entire cycle of spring agricultural festivals. The use of dolls or effigies in the Kupala ceremonies is of particular interest to us.

A. Malinka reports from Chernigov Gubernia that on Kupala Day the girls gathered flowers. Afterward they took a stick of one to one-and-a-half arshins in length, forked at the lower end; they attached to it crosswise at the opposite upper end another smaller stick, and wrapped the sticks in garlands of the flowers they had gathered. The result was something like the figure of a man with outspread legs and arms; in order to complete the similarity to a man, a cloth was tied on the head and a necklace of ribbons placed around the neck. This doll was called Ivan. After dinner, Ivan was placed somewhere on a wattle fence or on the gates. To the tune of songs, the girls jumped over nettles, which for this purpose had been tied together in a large bunch and placed in the middle of the street. In the evening Ivan was carried to the river: here one of the girls threw him into the water, and the direction in which Ivan floated indicated where this girl was destined to marry.

Malinka also reports that in some places the doll was torn to pieces. Each girl took a few flowers, and on Saint Peter's Day these flowers were thrown into the water and divination was performed from them (Malinka 1898).

A doll also figured in ceremonies reported in the Ukraine. Snegirev reports that "on St. John's Day they cut down a Marina tree and place it in some place, and afterward each one hangs on it his own garland of various flowers. Previously, they have seated a child or a doll underneath this tree and adorned it with their clothes." The celebration consisted of refreshments, the singing of songs, and round dances around the tree. The end of the festival consisted of the tree being taken from its place and brought to the river with songs. "Having come to the river, all begin to bathe and drown Marina" (Snegirev

1838: 47). What was done with the doll Snegirev does not say, but we can assume that it was also drowned.

Tereshchenko furnishes more detailed information: "In Little Russia, the girls gather on the eve of Ivan Kupala, dressed in festive attire at the Marena tree — a maple or some other tree which has been cut down (it is decorated with grass or flowers). When they come together for the celebration, in which young women also sometimes take part, the girls, after a mutual greeting, join hands, walk around the tree, and sing. Then they separate to different sides, and one of the girls takes a straw effigy, dressed in variegated women's clothes, and places it under the tree; other girls dress its head in a Ukrainian woman's headdress and adorn its neck with a necklace *(namisto)*. This effigy is called Kupalo. In other places, they merely set up a straw effigy with wooden arms, on which they hang wreaths and female adornments. Kupala is surrounded by a pile of straw with nettles and burnt." Those present jump over the fire (Tereshchenko 1848: V, 79). Tereshchenko reports the same thing from Poltava Gubernia. Here "they make, on the eve of St. John's Day, an effigy of straw called a *mara* (ghost), which is also carried at the beginning of spring. They bear it to the water with songs, or else, having laid nettles on its breast, jump over it with bare feet, and afterward lay a fire and jump across it" (Tereshchenko 1848: V, 80-81).

The Kupala ceremonies with a doll or with an effigy are known chiefly in the Ukraine, but were found also in other places. Summarizing the observations of his contemporaries, Sumtsov (1890: 143-144) writes: "In Little Russia on Kupala and in Great Russia at Carnival, the ritual use of a straw effigy or doll is customary; in Little Russia, as the embodiment of the festival, this bears the name Kupala. Girls, and sometimes young men, make an effigy, 'Marena,' of straw, nettles, or maple; they adorn it with wreathes, ribbons, and flowers, dance around it, sing songs, and afterward throw it in the river with pretended lamentations or tear it to pieces, the girls keeping the pieces or taking them to the garden in order that the cucumbers should grow. The boys often take this doll away, and then the girls make a new one."

Not one of the details considered here is typically connected with Kupala. Here, too, we have the destruction and tearing up either of a vegetative object (a tree) or its anthropomorphic equivalent — the doll or effigy. The destruction is carried out to the tune of songs which include motifs of funeral laments. By filling in the gaps in the Great Russian material with data from Belorussia and the Ukraine, we can see the following features of the Kupala ceremony: the tree was burned in the fire; the tree was also drowned; a doll decorated with green branches was placed under the tree; the doll was drowned or torn to pieces, and the pieces were scattered around the garden.

There is, however, one peculiarity which is considered typical of the Kupala festival: people jumped across the lighted fires. This must also be considered in somewhat more detail.

A special power was ascribed to the Kupala fire, just as on the same day a special power was ascribed to plants. The Kupala fire was lighted not by the transfer but by the kindling of new fire by friction. Sakharov reports this from Tula. From Staraia Ladoga, likewise: "In Staraia Ladoga, the St. John's fires are kindled on Pobedishche Mountain, where the creek falls into the Volkhov. There this fire, made by friction from wood, is known by the name of the living forest king of fire, the healer" (Sakharov 1849: 39).

The kindling of new fire, however, was not peculiar to Kupala alone. A large number of such cases were collected and described by Maksimov (1903: 197-225 ["The Fire King"]).

Jumping across a fire is nothing but the act of communion with the power of the fire. A dual force was ascribed to the fire: the power of creating and preserving health and life, and that of curing disease. Both these concepts, while intimately connected, are nevertheless different.

The power which creates life is spread throughout nature. It manifests itself with particular force on this day, the longest day of the year. When people burned a tree or a doll constituting the embodiment of this force, and afterward jumped over the fire alone or in couples, they, as it were, took this power to themselves. Tereshchenko reports: "Girls and men, joining hands, jump in couples through the fire. If the couple does not separate while jumping, this is a clear omen that they will be joined in marriage" (Tereshchenko 1849: V, 83). If the doll was not burned, people jumped across the fire with it, pressing it close to themselves: "In other places, the doll was made not larger than three-quarters of an arshin, and adorned with a wreath of flowers, and people jumped across the fire with it" (Sakharov 1849: 40; cf. Snegirev 1838: 30).

But the fire was also credited with another power: the power of purification. This concept is not connected with the day of Kupala, but on this day, inasmuch as a large fire is kindled, there is an attempt to use this power of the fire. Fresh fires were lit, and people jumped across them during epidemics, without any connection with the celebration of Ivan Kupala. Maksimov reports, on the basis of the data gathered by him, that in outbreaks of typhus all fires were extinguished and a fresh "living" fire was made by friction: "They laid the fire under a large pile of wood and kindled it, and then began to jump through it, goat-fashion, pulling the children and the old men by the hand."

The same thing was done during livestock epidemics. In an epidemic of anthrax, the peasants of Vologda made fire by friction, and through the fire "drove all their livestock, which was how they combatted the anthrax" (Maksimov 1903: 205-209).

On Kupala Day, this custom was particularly widespread. Sakharov reports: "I have often seen old women and mothers burn in these fires the shirts taken from sick children, with complete certainty that by this ceremony the disease would be eliminated." The people also thought that "jumping through the fire frees one from enchantment" — i.e., witchcraft (Sakharov 1849: 39).

These conceptions about the purifying power of fire have led to the theory that the entire Kupala rite of kindling fires and jumping through them is a primeval purification rite and, furthermore, an apotropic ceremony — i.e., one of warding off, protecting people and animals from disease. Our observations show that these conceptions, although they are present, do not explain the entire complex and all the details of the Kupala ceremony. . . . Like the other ceremonies of the calendrical agricultural cycle, it is a fertility ceremony, but this only becomes clear when we summarize our results after considering the subsequent festivals.

VI

The funeral of Kostroma is among the ceremonial funerals.

Unlike the other festivals which have received a more or less fixed calendrical date by being assimilated to the church festivals, the ceremony of the burial of Kostroma was not so assimilated. It was carried out at various dates from Trinity Day to St. Peter's Day (June 29): the burial of Kostroma is not a festival, but was sometimes per· formed in Rusalka Week or on Ivan Kupala. It was severely eroded as early as the 19th century, and in some places was transcribed only as a children's game.

The word "Kostroma" is apparently to be traced to the word *"koster'"("kostra," "kosteria," "kostrika")*, which means "cockle," "broom," "the fluffy tops of certain grasses," and also "the beard of an ear of grain" (Goriaev 1896: s.v. *"kostër," "koster'"*). The local Russian and Ukrainian adjective *"kostrubyi," "kostrubatyi"* is of the same origin. The Ukrainian "Kostrubon'ko" corresponds to the Russian Kostroma. If we disregard the meaning of broom or cockle, since this has no relation to any of the spring ceremonies, in which weeds have never played any part, we can assume that the burial of Kostroma at one time consisted in the lowering of seed grain into the ground.

Kostroma was embodied in a masculine or feminine effigy, which was carried around the village and then submerged in water or buried in the ground somewhere in the fields.

In Saratov Gubernia, a straw doll was made and dressed in a red calico sarafan; a woman's bonnet with flowers was placed on its head and a necklace around its neck — i.e., it was, so to speak, festively adorned. This doll was carried around the village to the tune of songs (Sakharov 1849: 42). Sometimes it was placed in a tub, as in the coffin, and thus carried around the village (Shein 1895: 368). . . . Sakharov reports that in Kostroma Gubernia a masculine effigy, which he calls Iarila, was buried. Iarila's coffin was carried in the arms of an old man, who was dressed in old worn-out clothes. The funeral of Iarila does not differ essentially from that of Kostroma. All kinds of honors were paid to Kostroma. Before him or his bearers one stood "respectfully." The board with the effigy was carried by girls and young men with respected parents (Sakharov 1849: 90). However, all of these marks of honor, the melancholy singing, and the mourning had a feigned and sometimes comic character, which was not at all concealed. On the contrary, the comedy was sometimes emphasized by the introduction of clerical masks into the procession. Shein reports from Muroma Uyezd that "the young men are dressed in sacks." By analogy with the Yuletide funerals, we may conclude that this sack is nothing but a priest's veil — all the more so since "one of them carries a bast shoe, representing a censer" (Shein 1895: 368-369).

"Kostroma" could also be represented by a living being — a little girl. In Penza and Simbirsk Gubernias, on Trinity Day or the Day of the Spirits, the girls, dressed in worn-out clothes, chose one of their number, called Kostroma, laid her on a board, and carried her to the river or to a pond. Here they woke her up and raised her with their arms, and all began to bathe (Snegirev 1838: 134-135). A characteristic feature of these lamentations is that they were frequently accompanied by laughter. The participants in the session, as it were, divided themselves into two parties, one of which lamented (usually the women) while the other laughed (the men, as a rule). "The women during this time, with wailing and lamentations, expressed grief and desperation; the men sang and danced; the children ran back and forth" (Sakharov 1849: 91).

In Muroma Uyezd, Kostroma Gubernia, where the ceremony of the funeral of Kostroma was better preserved than elsewhere, Kostroma was carried to the shore of a lake or river. "Here those who accompanied Kostroma divided into two sides. One guarding the effigy formed into a circle, and the young men and girls bowed down before Kostroma and performed various bodily movements before him. The other side suddenly attacked the first in order to capture Kostroma. Both sides began to wrestle. As soon as the effigy was seized, the clothes, strings, and straw were torn from it; it was trampled underfoot and thrown into the water with laughter." Meanwhile, the others set up a dismal wailing in dispair, and some "covered themselves with their hands, as though mourning the death of Kostroma. After this, both sides joined together, and with merry songs returned to the village" (Sakharov 1849: 90). The funeral took the form of an execution. The doll was first undressed, pulled at, torn to pieces, and then thrown into the water, as was done with dolls at other times. But there were also other forms of burial which we have not yet encountered: the doll was buried in the ground, and not just anywhere, but in the field. Whether this doll was called Kostroma or something else is not a matter of particular importance for us.

Sakharov reports that in Kostroma Gubernia "they dug a grave in the field with sticks and buried Iarila [i.e., Kostroma] in the coffin with weeping and wailing." (Sakharov 1849: 91). Iarila is the same kind of doll as Kostroma, and the ceremony of burying him usually corresponds exactly to the burial of Kostroma.

Iastrebov describes a children's game of burying Kostrubon'ko in Khar'kov Gubernia. The children stand in a circle in the middle of which the boy or girl who represents Kostrubon'ko scratches the earth with a stick to represent plowing; then he scrapes the earth with his fingers, to represent harrowing; then he shows how Kostroma sows, reaps, binds the sheaves, carries the grain, threshes, winnows, and grinds — all to the accompaniment of songs. Then Kostrubon'ko dies, the children weep, and the boy who represents him is taken by the arms and legs and thrown somewhere into a ditch (Iastrebov 1894: 33-36). This connection of the Kostroma ritual with agricultural labor is hardly accidental. Shein reports a song which accompanies the moment of the drowning of Kostroma, in which Kostroma is represented with a scythe:

> *Beyond the creek, beyond the river*
> *Kostroma is mowing hay.*

This is certainly no accident, since haymaking usually begins after St. John's Day. The same song contains the words:

> *The pretty girl*
> *Was carrying water*
> *She asked for rain:*
> *"Make rain, God —*
> *"Sheets of rain,*
> *"To wet the grass,*
> *"To dull Kostroma's sharp scythe"*
>   (Shein 1895: 370)

In this case, the drowning of Kostroma is accompanied by a song containing a prayer for rain.

We have here separated out only those aspects of the ceremony which are directly related to the burial ritual.

In order to explain Kostroma, Afanas'ev, in his "The Poetic Views of the Slavs on Nature," called attention to the similarity of the burial of Kostroma to the Greek spring festival of Adonis, during which the image of the dead Adonis was carried, mourned in song, and then buried or submerged in water (Afanas'ev 1868: 762). Afanas'ev attributes to this, as to other festivals, the character of an invocation of the sun. In agreement with him, Sumtsov writes that all these are various forms in which the spring or summer sun is personified (in some cases) or the hated winter is buried (in other variants of the game) (Sumtsov 1890: 153). This theory does not explain why the hated winter was buried at the height of summer, or why it should have been represented in the image of a tree or an effigy or a union of the two. We will try to find another explanation.

VII

The ceremony of burying the cuckoo corresponds essentially with the burial of Kostroma.

We should not conceive of the matter as though an actual cuckoo were buried. V. E. Kedrina, who made a special study of this ceremony, found only two cases in which a bird was buried. In all other instances, what was buried under the name of "cuckoo" was a branch dressed up in women's clothes, or a plant called "cuckoo's tears." We cannot go into the problem in full: in the present case we are interested in the ritual action (Kedrina 1912 [see Sokolov 1913]; Kharuzina 1912; Eleonskaia 1912).

Maksimov describes the ceremony as follows: "The 'cuckoo' is in some places merely a branch of a tree stuck in the ground, or a plantain, and in others a large doll sewed together from rags of chintz or calico ribbons and lace, paid for with money contributed by all the women of the village on a share basis (one kopek each). The dressed-up doll, with a cross around its neck, is placed in a box put together like a coffin, and some clever woman begins to mourn aloud, as if for a dead person; the others laugh, the children sing and dance, and all are very merry. On the next day the cuckoo is buried somewhere in the garden, and a song befitting the occasion is performed (Maksimov 1903: 429). Maksimov's description agrees with those given of this ceremony by Kedrina and others. "The cuckoo," like Kostroma and Iarilo, was buried in the ground with only this difference, that the place of burial for Kostroma and Iarilo was usually the field, while for the cuckoo it was the garden.

Thus, the form of commitment to the earth is added to cremation, tearing to pieces, or drowning. Iarilo and Kostroma were buried in the field, and the cuckoo in the garden — i.e., in those places where grains or vegetables were planted. Burial in the ground corresponds here to scattering over the earth, at Carnival.

As soon as the doll was destroyed, all mourning came to an end; on the contrary, merrymaking began — games and solo and round dances. After the burial, "having dressed in their festive clothes, the people come out onto the street to perform round dances until the evening" (Snegirev 1838: 134-135). "The festival closed with dances and games" (Sakharov 1849: 91).

VIII

The burial ritual was also applied to *rusalki*. The entire set of beliefs about *rusalki* is very complex, and we will not go into it here. What is important for us is to establish that *rusalki* were buried in the same forms we have already observed. The burials of *rusalki* were carried out during the so-called "Rusalka Week" or at other times. D. K. Zelenin (1916) made a detailed study of the *rusalka*. His theory that the *rusalki* are the unquiet dead (i.e., those who have died a violent death) is not justified. However, his book contains extremely valuable material. According to M. E. Sokolov's observations, cited by Zelenin, in the village of Chubarovka, Serdobsk Uyezd, Saratov Gubernia, the farewells to the *rusalka* take place "on the eve of the fast of St. Peter. It is chiefly old women who take part in the ceremony: they take a sheaf of rye, attach arms to it, dress it up as a woman, and lay it on a litter; they wail and carry the *rusalka* effigy into the rye field, where it is left on the boundary. During the procession with the *rusalka* effigy, the following song is sung several times:

> *Oh, my light, my Kostroma,*
> *You were the lady Kostromushka,*
> *Not Kostromushka but my commere!*[j]
> *You did not leave me in need,*
> *In need or in old age*
> (Sokolov 1908: 24, quoted in Zelenin
> 1916: 242).

The fact that the *rusalka* is here called Kostroma indicates the closeness of the ceremonies dedicated to *rusalki* and to Kostroma. Other materials confirm that the effigy of the *rusalka* was thrown onto the field. Snegirev reports from Riazan Gubernia that here, on the Sunday following Trinity, round dances were held, almost every dance group having a doll called *rusalka*. A struggle is staged for these dolls between attackers and defenders, during which they pour water and throw sand at one another. "Leaving the town, they say that they have bidden farewell to the *rusalki*. Then they tear up the effigies, throw them onto the field, and the girls who accompany them return to the town with lamentation" (Snegirev 1838: 10). An especially detailed description of the farewells (i.e., funeral) of the *rusalki* was given by N. P. Grinkova from the words of the Voronezh story-teller Baryshnikova (Kupriianikha). Concerning the cere-mony of accompanying the *rusalki* it was said here: "The *rusalka* is buried." A doll dressed in white was laid on the bier. One of the girls dressed up as a priest. Rush stalks represented candles; a rug or a sack, the priest's veil; and a worn-out bast shoe, the censer. The procession set out for the rye field where the doll was undressed. The figure of the *rusalka* and the carrying sticks from the bier were thrown into a ravine near the rye field. In regard to this, Baryshnikova explained that if the *rusalka* was thrown into the rye, the grain would brow better. This ritual was performed for the last time in 1936 (Grinkova 1947).

Zelenin showed the numerous connections that unite the figure of the *rusalki* with the rye fields in the folk consciousness.

IX

To what has been said we must add that the burial of a doll or an effigy could also take place at certain other periods. Snegirev reports that in Saratov Gubernia on St. Peter's Day "they carry around the village a dressed up doll of straw with songs, and then throw it in the river" (Snegirev 1838: 65).

On Kuz'minka (i.e., November 1) there took place the burial of Kuz'ma and Dem'ian[k], about which Maksimov reports the following: "Kuz'minka, in certain places (such as, for example in Penza Gubernia), is accompanied by a special custom known by the name 'burial of Kuz'ma Dem'ian': in the salting-shed the girls prepare an effigy — that is, they stuff a man's shirt with straw and make a head for it; then they dress the effigy in a peasant coat and tie a sash around it, lay it on a bier, and carry it into the woods beyond the village, where the effigy is undressed and a merry dance goes forward on the straw"

(Maksimov 1903: 519).

Sakharov reports a ceremony which he interprets as a "farewell to spring," although he gives no time for it. "In the villages of Simbirsk and Kostroma Gubernia, the villagers dressed up in torn old clothes and pretended to be cripples and blind beggars. The girls prepared a straw effigy, and the young men took carts without front wheels onto the street, tying them together with ropes in the manner of a train and harnessing horses to them. Then the train was taken from one end of the village to the other. An old woman sat on the front cart and held the effigy in her lap. After the procession, round dances were held. In the evening, the people set out for the river with songs and threw the effigy in the water" (Sakharov 1849: 93).

X

The quantity of data could be increased considerably, but what has been cited is enough to make some general observations and draw some conclusions. In the first place, for all the differences in detail, we have established the presence of one and the same ceremony in all the festivals considered. The burial, drowning, buring, or tearing up of an effigy or a tree constitutes one of their most import elements and perhaps the basic one.

The study could take two directions. One of the tasks might consist in establishing or explaining the differences found. How are we to explain the variety of names and attributes of the dead man, Carnival, Kupala, Morena, Ivan, Kostroma, Iarila, the *rusalka*, Kuz'ma-Dem'ian, and others? But the question can also be put differently: why, for all the variety of names, attributes, dates, and details, are the ceremonies carried out so uniform — to the point, indeed, where names can sometimes be substituted with no change whatever?

We will not venture to answer the first question. The answer could be given through a wider assembling of material from various peoples, for each element in particular. Here the ancient and modern, the local and borrowed, are mixed together. The second question is easier to answer, and the answer must be given before the details are studied. The similarity of forms presupposes a common ground from which these forms arise.

We have indicated some of the existing theories, which proved unconvincing in the light of the data cited. Relatively recently, the great English scholar James Frazer advanced a different theory. He made a broad study of the Western European carnival, spring festivals, and Whitsuntide, and even knows the Ukrainian Kostrubon'ka. He connected the phenomena which he considered with the religion of the dying and reborn god of vegetation. This religion is widely represented in the ancient Mediterranean East, and in Graeco-Roman antiquity. Among such dying deities Frazer lists the Egyptian Osiris, the Phrygian Attis, the Babylonian Tammuz, who was brought to Greece under the name Adonis, and others (Frazer 1907 —; 1928). These gods died and were buried; their death was mourned; they were reborn, and their resurrection was greeted with rejoicing. What Frazer does not say, and as a member of the Royal British Academy of Sciences cannot say, is that the number of dying and reborn deities also includes Christ. The cult of Osiris strikingly recalls, even in details, the Orthodox ritual for Good Friday and Easter Sunday. With cries of "Osiris is risen," those present rejoiced and kissed each other. But there is also an extremely significant difference. The Christian religion separated itself from the agricultural base on which it was founded, and was transformed into an abstract spiritualized religion, while the religion of the ancient East and of classical antiquity is an applied religion. The killed gods of the East and of antiquity are gods of vegetation. Their death signalizes the death of nature, the extinction of forces of the earth in winter; their resurrection signifies and furthers the new blossoming of the productive forces of the earth. But this religion was by no means passively speculative. The gods died, but they did not die of themselves: they were killed. The corresponding myths, sometimes of high artistic quality, related the history of their sufferings ("passions"). The ceremonial rituals included the killing of these deities — drowning, tearing apart; they were killed to provoke their resurrection, since the resurrection of the deity, it was thought, assured the rebirth of nature after its winter sleep, which without these ceremonies would go on forever. Frazer says: "The tradition of the death of the god — i.e., of the man who embodies him — is necessary in order that the god should be reborn in a new and better form" (Frazer 1928: III, 15). Since these gods were gods of vegetation, their resurrection provokes its growth.

This theory is not widespread in Soviet scholarship, as it applies to Russian ritual festivals. Iu. M. Sokolov recognizes only elements of the cults to which we have referred in the Russian ritual. "The Russian pre-Christian agricultural religion," he says, "was not able or did not have time to develop such complex religious cults as the cults of the ancient Mediterranean peoples which we have just listed; but in the ritual of Carnival and many other peasant rituals we now and then encounter elements of analogous cults" (Sokolov 1938: 148). Chicherov recognizes the presence of this cult only in the ritual of the burial of Kostroma. "The burial of 'Kostroma' is based on the concept of the dying and reborn god of vegetation" (Chicherov 1956: 233).

In specialized monographs, this theory may be encountered more frequently. It is referred to by Kedrina in her study of the christening and burial of the cuckoo, by Grinkova in an article on the ceremony of escorting the *rusalka* in Voronezh Oblast, and by others.

Frazer's theory, although, as we have seen, we cannot accept it entirely, points in the right direction for the study of the ceremonies we are considering. This theory confirms that these ceremonies had the purpose of influencing the fertility of the earth. It also explains why the effigy, the doll or the tree, was killed or buried, beginning at the moment when the first signs of nature's awakening at the winter solstice appeared, and why all festivals came to an end at the moment of highest flowering of the forces of nature at the summer solstice. But this theory is still far from fully explaining the Russian rituals.

In the first place, in the Russian ceremonies we see no deities. Neither "Koliada" nor Kupala nor Kostroma shows any of the features of deities. No worship was paid to them. The Russian ceremony is more archaic in its ideology and in its forms than the Oriental and classical cults. There might be a question about Iarilo. However, there are no data to show that Iarilo was a Russian or a Slavic deity. N. Gal'kovskii is right when he writes that "the ancient sources make no mention whatever of Iarilo. One of the oldest references to Iarilo is contained in the admonitions of Tikhon Zadonskii to the residents of the city of Voronezh [dating from 1763]" (Gal'kovskii 1913: 41).

But if the beings which are destroyed are not classifiable as deities, then who are they? Frazer, in these cases, uses the term "spirits of vegetation." This designation does not correspond to the ideas of the people. The essence of the matter lies not in the "spirit," but in the power. The destroyed beings are the embodiment, the incarnation, the focal point of the vegetative force of the earth. Whence this force comes to them, is a matter to which the people gives little thought. Nevertheless it is clear that this power is of woody or forest origin. At Pentecost a birch tree which has been carried out of the woods is destroyed. We have also seen a tree at Carnival and in the ceremony of Ivan Kupala, although here this is less pronounced. Even the "cuckoo" was made from a branch with twigs which was dressed in a woman's clothes. The *rusalka* doll was likewise made from a dressed-up tree.

We may hypothesize that we have here the most ancient intellectual substrate of these ceremonies. With the development of agriculture, there was an attempt to transmit to the fields the vegetative power of the forest.

Another material from which the destroyed dolls or effigies were made was straw or grain ears. The most characteristic figure in this regard was Kostroma, whose very name indicates its shaggy top. The effigy of Carnival was often made of straw and was called in these cases "the straw muzhik." But wherever the power attributed to these mannikins came from, there was an attempt to use it for the fields. We have seen that the parts of the Carnival effigy were thrown onto the fields, that the Trinity birch was thrown out into the field, that Kostroma is buried in the field, and that the *rusalka* dolls are thrown

401

there.

The only exception to this is the travesty of a funeral at Yuletide. Here the burial of a man, and not of a doll, is represented. This form of fictive funeral may be considered a later development, transferred from the spring into the New Year. All the Yuletide ceremonies, with the partial exception of the caroling, take place in the cottage and not in the open air. The funeral transferred to the New Year was assimilated into the Yuletide games and mumming, and was transformed into a game. One of the masks is that of a dead man, but apparently neither the representation of a funeral nor the performance of the play *Mavrukha* had any *immediate* ritual significance.

There is another reason why Frazer's theory, based essentially on the study of ancient eastern or classical materials, is inapplicable to the Russian materials. The gods were reborn, but Carnival, Kupalo, the Trinity birch, Iarilo, Kostroma, and the *rusalka* are not reborn. How is this to be understood?

It is true that there are some indications that the decorated birch tree was in some fashion associated with a deceased person, and was regarded as his new embodiment. Zernova writes: "In the village, all the cottages [i.e., families] gather birch branches on the previous evening, or adorn with them the front corner of the cottage. According to the belief prevalent in these parts *the souls of deceased relatives settle in these branches* [my emphasis — V. P.]. The branches are not thrown away after the festival, but are inserted above the gates to the courtyard to protect the livestock, or else laid in the corn-bin for protection from mice. For the same purpose they are afterward laid under sheaves of grain, under the hay, or in the potato pits" (Zernova 1932: 29).

If we look closely into these data, it turns out that the deceased takes on a new embodiment ("is resurrected") in the form of a birch tree. If this birch tree is broken and distributed in parts over the byres, potato pits, grain sheaves, etc., this corresponds exactly to what we have repeatedly seen above.

Although this indication is the only one of its kind, it deserves confidence as having been made by a very attentive and thoughtful Soviet ethnographer.

To this we can add one more thing. The ceremonies conducted under a twined birch tree are strikingly reminiscent of the memorial rites conducted at graves. Eggs or egg dishes are brought to the birch tree, as well as pancakes, just as to graveyards on days of remembrance. These offerings are, as it were, sacrifices. They were placed under the birch tree; part was crumbled on the ground, and part was eaten, precisely as at the memorial rites. Why it was precisely eggs or egg dishes that were crumbled and eaten is explained by detailed study of eggs as a ritual dish. The egg was conceived not only as a symbol of immortality and resurrection but as a means of securing them. This is the origin of the concept of Easter eggs. Nevertheless, these vague and somewhat indefinite ideas about the tree as a resurrected being do not give us the right to say that the conception of the resurrection of a being embodying vegetative power is part of the Russian ritual festivals. The farmer does not need literal resurrection of the killed being; he needs the power of these beings given to the fields. If consequently the killed beings whose parts are scattered on the fields are reborn, they are reborn in grain. This conception flows from the entire complex of phenomena which have been considered, and it is also confirmed by certain details. We mentioned earlier the strange riddle about the dead man whom they come to bury, and he is looking out of the window. The answer is "grain." This riddle is explicable from the set of ideas to the effect that the sprouted grain is a resurrected dead man.

The rebirth of gods precisely in vegetation and precisely in grain — this idea can be traced in classical and Egyptian material; but there it was replaced by the concept of the resurrection of the figure of the god, his body, which is completely lacking in the Russian rituals but which corresponds to the theistic religions: according to the doctrine of the church, Christ is resurrected in the flesh.

If this observation is accurate, then the explanation sometimes given of the laughter accompanying the burial falls of its own weight. This explanation resolves to the assertion that mourning accompanies the burial and laughter signifies joy at the resurrection. However, this proposition finds no confirmation either in Russian or European materials. The mourning is deliberate, feigned, ritual mourning. It is transformed into laughter — loud and fierce laughter, also to some degree deliberate — not at the moment of resurrection but at the moment of murder: drowning, tearing up, cremation.

The tearing up, cremation, and drowning represent not burial but a ritual putting to death. This execution is carried out with the accompaniment of laughter. But if this is so, then the being which is put to death is not dead, but lives. In fact, it is a live birch tree and not a withered one which is destroyed, and the same thing happens at Carnival and on Ivan Kupala. It is never said of Carnival that she has died. The dead man who is buried at Yuletide is clearly alive, and this is the origin of the comic force of this ritual. Kostroma constitutes an exception. In the songs accompanying this ritual, it is sometimes said that Kostroma has died. But even this death is, to some degree, relative and semicomic in character:

> *She is killed, not killed,*
> *Covered with taffeta . . .*
> (Shein 1895: 370).

In certain songs, Kostroma is depicted as not dead, but on a spree; or if she died, she died of overindulgence. But if the laughter which accompanies the murder or the burial does not express rejoicing at the resurrection what is its meaning?

The question of ritual laughter in folklore has been treated by us in a special article (Propp 1939).

Death and laughter are incompatible; they are opposites. Laughter is an exclusive accompaniment of life. In primitive folk consciousness, laughter is credited with the ability not only to accompany life but also to create it. There are rather numerous examples. This very ancient conception takes on new forms with the advent of agriculture.

If in fairy tales it is sometimes said that the princess's smile caused the flowers to bloom, this poetic metaphor once had the most literal meaning. We will cite only one example. When Persephone, the Hellenic goddess of fertility and grain, in search of her daughter kidnapped by Hades, throws herself into mourning and anger, all vegetative growth ceases on earth. Then her slave-girl Baubo (or, in some versions, Iamba) amuses her. Demeter laughs — and everything on earth begins to bloom again. This myth reflects a real belief. In the presence of agriculture, there was an effort to use the force of laughter magically, with the aim of influencing the vegetable world by this force.

Thus, laughter at destruction and burial reflects and has the aim of providing the destroyed being with a new life and a new embodiment. Laughter shows that this death is a death into life.

All of this, of course, was long ago forgotten, but there remained the effort during this festival to laugh without interruption; there remained the festive merry-making, in which rituals were transformed into games. The concept of the reproduction of life in nature was connected with rituals of an erotic and phallic character. Thus, Kostroma in his male aspect is sometimes mourned as a husband. The sexual freedom and jokes which were canonized by custom, and which were traditional at this festival, accompanied and reinforced the laughter, and this in turn reinforced its magical influence on the fertility of the earth. This entire aspect of festive rituals cannot be considered here. It could become the subject of a detailed study that would add significantly to the picture of Russian ritual festivals and games.

* * *

EDITORS' NOTES

a. The 50th day after Easter; Whitsunday is the equivalent in Western Europe, but due to the difference in calendars, the Russian Pentecost occurs two weeks earlier.

b. The equivalent of the Western European St. John's Eve, celebrated June 24, Old Style.

c. A festival held in honor of the ancestors, comparable to the Western European All Souls', but celebrated during the week after Easter.

d. A cooperative work group which receives pay as a unit and distributes it among the members in fixed, and originally equal, shares. In this context, the term is being used in a metaphorical and somewhat humorous sense.

e. "Sitting party" — a gathering of young people for singing, dancing, conversation, and sometimes work, part of the traditional Russian peasant courtship pattern.

f. An old Russian measure of length equal to 28 inches.

g. The peasant women's costume in certain parts of Russia, consisting of a long full skirt and a jumper top.

h. Water sprite, mermaid.

i. A collective term for various grains, considered as a single crop.

j. I.e., the godmother of my child, or of the child to whom I am godfather.

k. Saints Kosmas and Damian (Russian form).

NOTES

1. From a manuscript collection of riddles from Vologda by P. A. Dilaktorskii. Archives of the Institute of Russian Literature (Division 15, Section 9, File 4). Communicated by V. V. Mitrofanova.

2. For details on the name and date of this festival, see Zelenin 1916: 221 ff.

3. Reports from Pruzhany and Kobrin Uyezds.

LITERATURE CITED

Afanas'ev, A. N.
1868 *Poeticheskie vozzreniia slavian na prirodu* [The Poetic Views of the Slavs on Nature], Volume 3, Moscow.

Anichkov, E. V.
1903-1905 "Vesenniaia obriadovaia pesnia na Zapade i u slavian" ["The ritual spring song in the West and among the Slavs"] *Sb. ORIaS*, Volumes XXIV, XXVII. St. Petersburg.

Berkov, P. N.
1953 *Russkaia narodnaia drama XVIII-XX vekov* [Russian Folk Drama of the 18th-20th Centuries]. Moscow.

Chicherov, V. I.
1956 "Kalendarnaia poeziia i obriad" ["Calendrical poetry and ritual"], in P. G. Bogatyrev, ed. *Russkoe narodnoe poeticheskoe tvorchestvo. Posobie dlia vuzov* [Russian Poetic Folklore: A Textbook for Higher Educational Institutions] 2nd edition. Moscow.

1957 "Zimnii period russkogo narodnogo zemledel'cheskogo kalendaria XVI-XIX vekov" ["The winter period of the Russian agricultural folk calendar, 16th-19th centuries"] *TIE*, Vol. 40. Moscow.

1959 *Russkoe narodnoe tvorchestvo* [Russian Folklore]. Moscow.

Eleonskaia, E. N.
1912 "Kreshchenie i pokhorony kukushki v Tul'skoi i Kaluzhskoi guberniiakh" ["The christening and burial of the cuckoo in Tula and Kaluga Gubernias"] *EO*, No. 1-2, pp. 146-155.

Frazer, J. G.
1907- *The Golden Bough*. 3rd edition. London.

1928 *Zolotaia vetv'* [Russian translation of *The Golden Bough*, from the abridged French edition]. Moscow.

Gal'kovskii, N.
1913 *Bor'ba khristianstva s ostatkami iazychestva v drevnei Rusi* [The Struggle of Christianity with the Remnants of Paganism in Ancient Rus']. Moscow.

Goriaev, N. V.
1896 *Sravnitel'nyi etimologicheskii slovar' russkogo iazyka* [A Comparative Etymological Dictionary of the Russian Language]. Tiflis.

Grinkova, N. P.
1947 "Obriad vozhdeniia rusalki v sele B. Vereika, Voronezhskoi oblasti" ["The ceremony of bringing in the rusalka in the village of Bol'shaia Vereika, Voronezh Oblast"], SE, No. 1, pp. 178-184.

Iastrebov, V. N.
1894 *Materialy po etnografii Novorossiiskogo kraia* [Materials on the Ethnography of Novorossiisk Krai]. Odessa.

Kalinskii, I. P.
1877 "Tserkovno-narodnyi mesiatseslov na Rusi" ["The ecclesiastical-folk calendar in Rus'"], *Zap. Russk. geograf. obshch. po otdel. etnografii* [Papers of the Russian Geographical Society, Ethnographic Section], Vol. VII. St. Petersburg.

Kedrina, V. E.
1912 "Obriad kreshcheniia i pokhoron kukushki v sviazi s narodnym kumovstvom" ["The ceremony of the christening and funeral of the cuckoo in connection with folk godparenthood"], *EO*, No. 1-2, pp. 101-140.

Kharuzina, V. N.
1912 "Obriad 'Krestit' kukushku' v Orlovskoi gubernii" ["The ceremony of 'christening the cuckoo' in Orel' Gubernia"], *EO*, No. 1-2, pp. 140-146.

Makarenko, A. A.
1913 "Sibirskii narodnyi kalendar' v etnograficheskom otnoshenii. Vostochnaia Sibir', Eniseiskaia guberniia" ["The Siberian folk calendar from the ethnographic point of view: Eastern Siberia, Enisei Gubernia"], *Zap. Russk. geograf. obshch. po otdel. etnogr.*, Vol. XXXVI.

Maksimov, S. V.
1903 *Nechistaia, nevedomaia i krestnaia sila* [The Unclean, Mysterious and Christian Power]. St. Petersburg.

Malinka, A.
1898 "Ivan Kupalo v Chernigovskoi gubernii" ["Ivan Kupalo in Chernigov Gubernia"], *EO*, No. 2, pp. 128-132.

Miller, V. F.
1884 *Russkaia maslenitsa i zapadno-evropeiskii karnival* [Russian Shrovetide and Western European Carnival]. Moscow.

Onchukov, N. E.
1911 *Severnye narodnye dramy* [Northern Folk Plays]. St. Petersburg.

Potebnia, A. A.
  1867 "O kupal'skikh ogniakh i srodnykh s nimi predstav-
  leniiakh" ["On the Kupala bonfires and performances related
  to them"], *Arkheologicheskii vestnik*, No. 3, Moscow.

  1914 *O nekotorykh simvolakh v slavianskoi narodnoi
  poezii* [On Some Symbols in Slavic Folk Poetry]. Khar'kov.

Propp, V. Ia.
  1939 "Ritual'nyi smekh v fol'klore (Po povodu skazki o
  Nesmeiani)" ["Ritual laughter in folklore (On the Tale of the
  King Who Never Laughed)"], *UZLGU*, No. 6, pp. 151-175.

Sakharov, I.
  1849 *Skazanie russkogo naroda* [The Tale of the Russian
  People]. Vol. II, Book VII. St. Petersburg.

Shein, P. V.
  1887 *Materialy dlia izucheniia byta i iazyka russkogo
  naseleniia severo-zapadnogo kraia* [Materials for the Study of
  the Daily Life and Language of the Russian Population of the
  Northwestern District]. Vol. I, Part I. St. Petersburg.

  1895 *Velikoruss v svoikh pesniakh, obriadakh, obychaiakh,
  verovaniiakh, skazkakh, legendakh i t. p.* [The Great Russian
  as Reflected in His Songs, Rituals, Customs, Beliefs, Folktales,
  Legends, Etc.], Vol. 1, No. 1, St. Petersburg.

Snegirev, I. M.
  1838 *Russkie prostonarodnye prazdniki i suevernye
  obriady* [Russian Folk Festivals and Superstitious Rituals].
  No. III. Moscow.

Sokolov, Iu. M.
  1913 Review of KEDRINA 1912, *ZhS*, No. 3-4.

  1938 *Russkii fol'klor* [Russian Folklore]. Moscow.

Sokolov, M. E.
  1908 "Velikorusskie vesennie i khorovodnye pesni,
  zapisannye v Sarat. gub." ["Great Russian spring and round-
  dance songs, transcribed in Saratov Gubernia."], *Trudy III obl.
  istoriko-arkheologich. s"ezda* [Papers of the Third District
  Historical and Archeological Congress]. Vladimir.

Sumtsov, N. F.
  1890 *Kul'turnye perezhivaniia* [Cultural Experiences]. Kiev.

Tereshchenko, A.
  1848 *Byt russkogo naroda* [The Daily Life of the Russian
  People]. Moscow.

Vinogradov, G. S.
1918 "Materialy dlia narodnogo kalendaria Sibiri" ["Materials toward the folk calendar of Siberia"], *Zap. Tulupovskogo otd. obshch. izucheniia Sibiri i ulucheniia ee byta* [Papers of the Tulup Division, Society for the Study of Siberia and Improvement of Its Life]. No. I.

Zavoiko, K.
1917 "V Kostromskikh lesakh po Vetlugo-reke" ["In the forests of Kostroma on the Vetluga River"], *Tr. Kostromskogo nauchn. obshch. po izucheniiu mestnogo kraia* [Papers of the Kostroma Scientific Society for the Study of the Local Area] No. VIII. Kostroma.

Zelenin, D. K.
1914 *Opisanie rukopisei uchenogo arkhiva Russkogo geograficheskogo obshchestva* [Description of Manuscripts in the Scientific Archives of the Russian Geographical Society], No. 1, Petrograd.

1916 *Ocherki russkoi mifologii, vyp. I. Umershie neestestvennoi smert'iu i rusalki* [Outlines of Russian Mythology, Part I. Those Who Died an Unnatural Death and the *Rusalki]*. Petrograd.

Zernova, A. B.
1932 "Materialy po sel'skokhoziaistvennoi magii v Dmitrovskom uyezde" ["Materials on agricultural magic in Dmitrov Uyezd"], *SE*, No. 3.

(Ezhegodnik Muzeia istorii religii i ateizma, Vol. V, 1961)

THE "FEAST OF ATREUS" AND RELATED ETHNOGRAPHIC MOTIFS IN FOLKLORE AND LITERATURE

V. M. Zhirmunskii

I.

The comparative-historical study of literature and folklore has suffered, and in foreign countries still suffers, from a significant methodological fault: it tends to consider any similarity of motifs — real and sometimes also imagined — as the result of so-called "influences" or "borrowings" from outside.

However, the study of international connections and mutual influences in the literary process will become truly scientific and historical only if we distinguish connections between literary phenomena which are due to contact (and which are conditioned by the historical proximity of particular peoples to each other and by the mutual cultural influences) from historical-typological similarities of phenomena which are not genetically related to each other — similarities that are to be explained by similar conditions of social development.

The epos, which depicts the historical past of a people on the scale of heroic idealization — or which, in the words of D. S. Likhachev, embodies in poetic form a people's understanding and evaluation of its past — is least susceptible to external influences. Similarity of epic motifs among different peoples, as we have already had occasion to say, is explained in most cases by convergence at an analogous stage of social development. On the other hand, the forms of narrative literature designed for entertainment, whether aristocratic or popular, which are so characteristic of the literature and folklore of the classical Middle Ages — the chivalric and popular romance, the realistic short story, popular ballads, fairy tales, and folk anecdotes — make wide use of motifs and plot elements of the most various origin, frequently brought from far away; as the catalogues of international folk-tale and ballad motifs and plot elements known to us indicate, these motifs and elements are almost universally current within the historical-geographical limits of Europe, a large part of Asia, and North Africa — of course, in more or less consistent artistic transformations, corresponding to the peculiarities of social and cultural development in the particular ethnic environment (Zhirmunskii 1962: 75 ff.).

The group of motifs to be considered below is interesting methodologically in that it shows, over the course of more than a thousand years of development, unmistakable examples of historical-typological similarity and, later, of international mutual influences. These motifs have their origin in ancient and extremely archaic popular customs and concepts, universally distributed at a particular stage of social development. Accordingly, the group includes a number of classical and well-known works of Graeco-Latin and medieval literature, both oral and written, which have been studied repeatedly but have not yet been fully explained from a historical-ethnographic point of view. This group of motifs may serve at the same time as an example of the profound sociohistorical transformation of these ancient plot elements under new conditions of social and cultural development, in which their original ethnographic foundation is covered over by artistic expression and by fantastic or realistic story-telling for entertainment purposes; thereby, their further dissemination comes to be determined by international cultural contacts and literary influences.

The ancient heroic tales of disputes between blood relatives or affinals, which have developed among various peoples under the historical conditions of the decay of the patriarchal-clan system, have preserved an ethnographic plot element of this type, which may be arbitrarily called "the feast of Atreus," after the best-known classical example of it.

According to the ancient Greek tale, Tantalus, tablemate of the gods and founder of the dynasty of the Mycenaean kings, was cursed by the gods because he offered them at a feast (we would say, as a sacrifice) the flesh of his infant son Pelops. "The curse of the gods" that befell the posterity of Tantalus gives rise to a chain of bloody family disputes.

Atreus and Thyestes, grandsons of Tantalus, quarreled over the throne. Atreus, the victor, expelled his brother, but Thyestes returned to Mycenae and "asked forgiveness at the hearth." Under the pretext of reconciliation with his brother, Atreus set up a feast at which he offered Thyestes the meat of two of his infant sons. Here is how the content of this tale is set forth in the *Oresteia* of Aeschylus *(Agamemnon* 11. 1583-1597), as told by Aegisthus, son of Thyestes:

> ... *But Atreus,* ...
> *With zeal that was not love* ...
> ... *bade my father to his board, and set*
> *Before him flesh that was his children once.*
> *First, sitting at the upper board alone,*
> *He hid the fingers and the feet, but gave*
> *The rest — and readily Thyestes took*
> *What to his ignorance no semblance wore*
> *Of human flesh, and ate: behold what curse*
> *That eating brought upon our race and name!*
> *For when he knew what all unhallowed thing*
> *He thus had wrought, with horror's bitter cry*
> *Back-starting, spewing forth the fragments foul,*
> *On Pelops' house a deadly curse he spake —*
> As darkly as I spurn this damnèd food,
> So perish all the race of Pleisthenes![a]

Aegisthus, younger son of Thyestes, becomes the lover of Clytemnestra, the wife of Atreus' son Agamemnon, who has long been in Troy; Aegisthus subsequently kills his cousin on the day of his triumphant return to the palace. Later, Orestes, son of Agamemnon, kills Aegisthus and his mother in vengeance for his father.

Besides Aeschylus, the plot of the *Oresteia* was treated in succession by Sophocles, Euripides, and Agathon, whose tragedies (except for the *Elektra* of Sophocles) have not come down to us. Greek sources were also used by Seneca in his tragedies *Thyestes* and *Agamemnon*.

Attention was drawn long ago to the similarity between this plot and the bloody denouement of the ancient Germanic epic tale of the Nibelungs in its Scandinavian version, in which Gudrun, wife of Atla (the historical Attila, king of the Huns), takes vengeance on her husband for the murder of her brothers (in contrast to the later German version of the *Lay of the Nibelungs*, where Kriemhild, who corresponds here to Gudrun in the Scandinavian tale, takes vengeance on her brothers for the murder of her first husband Siegfried) (Häusler 1960: 380-402).

King Atla treacherously invites his wife Gudrun's brothers — Gunnar (Gunther) and Hogni (Hagen) — to visit him in order to gain possession of their treasure, the inheritance of Sigurd (Siegfried), Gudrun's first husband whom they had killed. Gudrun takes vengeance for her brothers: during the funeral feast for the murdered men she gives her husband the hearts of two of his infant sons, roasted on the spit to eat, as well as their blood mixed with mead or beer to drink from cups made from their skulls. Afterward (with her son Hogni) she kills Atla and burns him and his retainers in the feasting hall.

Various versions of this story, preserved in cantos of the poetic *Edda* which parallel each other in content (the *Atlakvitha* and *Atlamöl en groenlenzku*), and in the cantos of the prose version of the *Saga of the Volsungs* and the *Edda* of Snörri Sturluson, which are based on these stories (or on similar ones), coincide in all essential points. Snörri relates:

"Shortly after this Gudrun killed both of her sons and ordered that cups set in silver and gold be made of their skulls. When they held the funeral feast for the Niflungs, Gudrun offered Atla mead in these cups mixed with the blood of the boys: their hearts she ordered to be roasted and gave them to the king at the banquet. When he had eaten them, she herself told him in cruel words what she herself had done. Of fermented mead there was plenty, so that most of the warriors were overtaken by sleep where they sat, and on the same night she came to the king when he slept and with her came her son Hogni; they turned their weapons on the king and there his end came. Afterward they burned down the hall and all who were there were burned up . . ."[1]

According to the accepted opinion, the verse tale of the *Edda* and the prose sources based upon it took these details of Gudrun's cruel revenge for her murdered brothers from the ancient Greek tale of Atreus and Thyestes.

Thus, among many others, Hermann Schneider, author of an authoritative history of Germanic heroic tales, declares simply and laconically: "The murder of children *(Kinderschlachtung)* has always been suspect to me as a classical echo" (Schneider 1962: 202). His teacher Andreas Häusler assumed that this borrowing does not date from the Scandinavian period, but goes back to the source of the Scandinavian epic — a Frankish lay of the 6th century. "There have been attempts to trace back to ancient Greek prototypes — Atreus and Thyestes, Tereus and Procne — the feast where the hearts of children were offered on a plate. It is very possible that these tales came to the hearing of some Frankish poet in Gaul, where the ancient literary tradition was never entirely forgotten. Between the book and the illiterate *skop* [ancient Germanic minstrel in a king's retinue] there were a number of possible intermediaries" (Häusler 1960: 86).

Such a point of view, however, seems improbable on the face of it. It assumes that the creator of the epic lay in its Scandinavian (Old Icelandic) or in its original ancient Frankish form, took important details of a traditional heroic tale not from the oral epic tradition but from a literary source — and one, furthermore, which was by no means popular in nature. At the end of the 19th century and at the beginning of the 20th, students of the ancient Icelandic epos, following the Norwegian scholar Sophus Bugge (1889), were inclined, in the spirit of the prevailing "theory of borrowing," to exaggerate excessively the "scholarly" character of Eddic poetry and to see in it "literary," Classical, or Christian influences where the slightest, and often illusory, similarity of motifs, plot elements, or general themes was present. At the present time, this question demands fundamental reconsideration on the basis of more correct conceptions of the nature and character of traditional oral epic poetry; it is difficult to conceive that a storyteller (ancient Frankish or even Icelandic) would wish to "decorate" the ancient Germanic tradition of the vengeance of Kriemhild-Gudrun with literary borrowings from little-known written sources in Latin or Greek. Let us add that with a similarity of themes that would seem to the contemporary reader not only monstrous but "uncommon" or "exotic," the similarity of plot elements in concrete details is by no means such as to indicate beyond dispute the necessity of such a borrowing.

As always, by adducing broader material for a comparison, we are able to show its typological significance.

The theme of heroic courtship is widespread in the south Slavic epic lays. It is attached (with insignificant variations) to the names of various epic heroes, both historical and legendary. The following persons appear in the role of bridegroom: the Serbian emperor Stefan Dušan; Juri Smederevec, i.e., the historical Juri Branković; the Budimian (i.e., Hungarian) king; Ivo Carnojević; in the Croatian lay, Stojan Janković; among the Bulgarians, King Shishman, etc.

The contents of these lays is basically as follows. The hero seeks the hand of the daughter of a foreign king (often a "Latin").[b] The bride's father gives his consent and with treacherous intent invites the future son-in-law to come for the bride, but not to bring with him certain specific famous *junaks* (warriors) of his family, on the pretext that they are drunkards or ruffians. At the same time, the princess secretly warns the bridegroom to bring with him as large a retinue as possible, including the above-named champions. Following her advice, the groom comes with an enormous wedding train (1,000 attendants). Frequently this train includes the most famous Serbian *junaks* whose names are listed in a kind of "catalogue of heroes." On their arrival the guests are not admitted into the gates of the city, but are required to perform a number of herculean feats. These feats are performed not by the groom but by one of the attendants or by several in succession. After this the guests take the bride, and this is followed in some lays by a bloody clash or by pursuit on the part of a military detachment sent in chase, which is destroyed by the groom's warlike retinue (Zhirmunskii 1962: 112-113).

The Marriage of Stefan Jakšić (in two versions) and The Marriage of Dmitri Jakšić, in Petranović's collection (1867: Nos. 54-56), depart from this general pattern, and the same is true, with certain differences, of The Marriage of Hasan-agi, transcribed among the Bosnian Moslems (Hörmann 1888: No. 18).

Stefan Jakšić serves the Emperor of Bech for twelve years and takes no pay from him; he wishes to receive the hand of his daughter but never succeeds even in seeing her. One day when the emperor has gone hunting, Stefan, with the help of an old slave-woman, penetrates the princess's bedchamber and seduces her. The next day he goes home to Belgrade, promising that he will marry her. Upon his return, the emperor discovers what has happened and immediately sends Stefan his consent to marry his daughter. He asks the future son-in-law to come for the bride with the wedding party, but not to bring an armed escort in order to avoid arguments. The bride secretly sends Stefan word to come with his best *junaks*. The groom is accompanied by Marko Kraljević, Relja Miloš, the two young Vojnović brothers, and other eminent champions. The emperor greets the guests affectionately, invites them to a feast, and treats them to wine and meat. Relja is the first to notice the unusual taste of both: *"Braho moja i družina moja! Pivo slatko, a mjaso debelo!"* ["My mates and comrades! The beer is sweet but the meat is strong!"]. Marko guesses what the matter is: "This is not mutton," he says, *"već je ovo od junaka mjeso, će donosi vinon i duvanon."*[c]   He orders that the emperor be bound and hurries to the bride to find out whether two of her brothers-in-law, the young Vojnović brothers, are still alive. The princess relates that they came to her in the evening and she kissed them, but then two fierce executioners appeared with naked sabers and cut down the unreasoning children like stupid lambs, despite her pleas; they carried the dead bodies into another room and there prepared the banquet for the guests.

Then Marko seized the Queen of Bech, took two of her sons from her, slaughtered them and cooked them on spits like lambs, fed the emperor their meat and gave him their blood to drink, cut off the emperor's head and exterminated the entire male population in the castle; but the Jakšiči spared the princess, took her with them to Belgrade, and there celebrated her wedding.[2]

One may, of course, see in the terrible vengeance of the Emperor of Bech on his daughter's seducer the Jakšić a distant reminiscence of the classical "feast of Atreus" plot, or, if one likes, of the vengeance of Gudrun. However, even the most consistent comparativists, such as, for example, Khalanskii (1893: 320-324), were not prepared, in spite of the indubitable similarity of the general theme, to pose this question, in view of the historical improbability of such "influence."

Even in the classical tradition itself, the tale of the "feast of Atreus" is by no means isolated. Analogous plots connected with other legendary or historical names are known, and despite the presence of a general thematic similarity, at least as great as that between the "feast of Atreus" and the vengeance of Gudrun, no attempt has so far been made to establish their derivation from the classical tale of Atreus and Thyestes.

Thus, Häusler, as we have said, mentions, in connection with the vengeance of Gudrun, the similar story of Tereus and Procne (Apollodorus III, 14, 8). Tereus, the husband of Procne, by deceit gained possession of her sister Philomela ("the swallow") and cut out her tongue so that she could not complain to her elder sister. Having discovered her husband's crime, Procne cut the throat of his son Iteus and fed the flesh of the boy to his father.

Closer in certain details to the story of the children of Tantalus is the historical tradition of the Median Emperor Astiagus, which is related by Herodotus (I, 119). This tradition is connection with the miraculous circumstances of the birth of the future Persian Emperor Cyrus, Astiagus's grandson on his mother's side. Frightened by prophetic dreams and by the predictions of soothsayers concerning the future greatness of his grandson, Astiagus orders his high official Harpagus to put the newborn child to death. Harpagus saves and hides the infant. After some years, the deception is revealed. To punish Harpagus for his disobedience, the emperor invites the official to a feast, ordering him beforehand to send to the palace his thirteen-year-old only son. "Meanwhile, Astiagus, when the son of Harpagus had come to him, gave orders that his throat should be cut and his body divided into parts, some of which should be boiled, others roasted, and the whole well prepared and kept in readiness. At the time of the feast, Harpagus and the other guests appeared; tables loaded with mutton were set out for Astiagus and the other persons, but Harpagus was given the flesh of his son — all except the head, fingers, and toes, which were laid apart in a covered basket. When it seemed that Harpagus had eaten enough, Astiagus asked whether he was pleased with the food; Harpagus replied that he was very pleased. Then the servants, who had been ordered to do this, brought Harpagus the covered head of his son, the hands, and the feet, inviting him to open the basket and take from it what he wished. Harpagus accepted the invitation and, upon opening the basket, beheld the remains of his child; but he controlled himself and did not express horror at the sight. To Astiagus's question as to whether he recognized the game he had eaten, Harpagus answered affirmatively, adding that whatever the emperor did was good. After this, he collected the remaining flesh and went home, with the intention, I think, of gathering everything anew and burying the remains. . . ."

Later, Harpagus, conspiring with the young Cyrus for the sake of vengeance, helps the latter to conquer Media and to dethrone the cruel Astiagus (Herodotus [see Mishchenko] 1888: I, 57-71).

Herodotus's story is a historical legend, in which true facts are combined with folkloric traditions. Astiagus and Harpagus, like the Persian Emperor Cyrus, are historical figures of whom we read in other Greek sources (Ctesias) and in the more reliable Babylonian ones (the Nabonid chronicle, and others). I. M. D'iakonov (1956: 412-424) tells us, on the basis of a comparison of these sources, that the war between Astiagus and Cyrus lasted for three years (553-550 B.C.E.) and at first went in Astiagus's favor; the treason of the Median nobility, led by Harpagus, decided the issue in Cyrus's favor. Herodotus, unlike Ctesias, relates traditions hostile to Astiagus, deriving from circles sympathetic to the coup d'état carried out by Cyrus with the help of Harpagus. This tradition is similar to the Greek ones we have mentioned, but it was current, apparently, in Media and Persia — i.e., in an entirely different ethnic environment.

Another historical tradition, concerning Kiaksara, father of Harpagus, and related by Herodotus somewhat earlier (I, 73), shows a certain similarity to this, Kiaksara was patron to the nomadic Scythians, who brought him part of their bag from the hunt as tribute. Once, when they had brought him nothing, Kiaksara addressed them with extreme rudeness. In vengeance, the Scythians decided to cut the throat of one of the boys who was being trained among them in the arts of war, "preparing him as they usually prepared game, and offered him to Kiaksara under the guise of game. . . . Kiaksara, and those who sat with him at table, ate the flesh of the boy," and the Scythians meanwhile left Media and sought the protection of the Median Emperor Atiatta, father of Croesus (Herodotus 1888: I, 37-38).

We may assume that this tradition, which reflects the barbarous custom of vengeance attributed by Herodotus to the Scythians (cf. the story of vengeance of Cyra, Empress of Tomirida, with analogous symbolism; I, 214), also derives not from a Greek but from a local source.

The old Danish and Faroese ballad "Sir Lovmor" or "The Bloody Vengeance," which is not connected, at least by direct content, with the tale of the Nibelungs, has a similar plot (Grundtvig 1853: 29 ff.).[3]

A group of brothers married their sister, the beautiful Signhild, to a foreigner, the knight Lovmor, the murderer of her father. Signhild has not seen her brothers for eight years, and asks her husband to permit her to invite them to visit. The husband is pleased and says with a laugh: "I will treat thy brothers as if they were my own sons." Signhild's seven brothers arrive and she tries in vain to warn them of her husband's evil intentions. At night, when they are sleeping, Sir Lovmor kills them all, and in the morning brings his wife a cup of their blood. Signhild drinks: even if her brothers are dead, she has her husband left, she tells him with pretended humility.

After eight years, Sir Lovmor wishes to invite his seven sons to visit. The beautiful Signhild laughs with gladness. "I will treat thy sons as if they were my own brothers," she says. At night, when the sons of Sir Lovmor have gone to sleep, she kills them all, and in the morning brings her husband a cup of their blood. He answers her in the words: "Although my sons have died, you are left to me." He reaches for his sword, but she binds him hand and foot, kills him in revenge for her father and brothers, and herself goes into a convent.

Wilhelm Grimm, the first translator of the Danish ballad, and, following him, most of those who have written about it, have seen in the story of Sir Lovmor and the beautiful Signhild a reflection of the ancient plot of the vengeance of Gudrun. To the general thematic similarity, there are added some more distinctive features: the treacherous invitation to the brothers and their murder by the heroine's husband; and the vengeance of the wife, who kills his sons and brings him a bloody drink. However, the concrete development of the plot in the ballad is entirely distinctive, and shows little resemblance to its supposed prototype. It has its own internal artistic logic, based (like the south Slavic poems on the courtship of the Jakšiči) on complete symmetry of crime and punishment according to the principle of *par pari* ("like is given for like," or "measure for measure"). The existence of a large number of stories on the same theme, of which some were considered above, frees us from the necessity of seeing in these works a transformation, in ballad form, of an ancient epic motif. It is more probable that we have here an entirely independent artistic development of analogous customs and moral concepts.

We can mention an additional North German

tradition, transcribed by Karl Müllenhoff in the middle of the 19th century in Schleswig and connected with the name of the Danish Queen Margaret (d. 1283), called by the people "Black Margaret" *(Svarte Margret)*, and famed for her treachery and cruelty. It was said that she "sent her son to the city of Oldenburg to collect tribute from the townspeople. But the Oldenburg shoemakers seized him, cut him in pieces, and having salted them, sent them back to his mother." Margaret mounted a campaign against the city, which ended unsuccessfully. "But from that time, the Oldenburg shoemakers were forbidden to go outside the city limits, and to this day they do not have the right to attend fairs" (Müllenhoff 1845: 18).

Despite the obvious modernization of the old historical tradition, in which the chief thing — namely, the purpose for which the Oldenburg shoemakers salted the prince — is left unstated, the similarity of this tradition and the "feast of Atreus" motif is beyond doubt. However, hardly anyone will be prepared to see in this tradition a reflection of either the vengeance of Gudrun or of the classical tales. More probably, the tradition of Queen Margaret is based on a historical incident that was transformed by a widespread folktale motif — the punishment of the witch (see below, Part 2).

The ancient basis, in daily life, of motifs of the "feast of Atreus" type is not connected with so-called "ritual cannibalism" or anthropophagy, as some ethnographers, oversimplifying the matter, believe (Pauly-Wissowa 1936: 664, s.v. "Thyestes"; MacCulloch 1905: 228; cf. also Voevodskii 1874: 352-361). Ritual anthropophagy presupposes human sacrifices, which are pleasing to the deity and which are accompanied by the eating of the sacrificial flesh by the whole tribe. Such eating is a means of sympathetic magic, in order to partake ("take communion") of the strength of a killed enemy; certain parts of the body — heart, liver, etc. — are of particular significance in this regard, in that they are the seat of the soul of the killed person. Correspondingly, the eating of the meat, or especially the heart, of a killed beast of prey (tiger, leopard, etc.) can give the person the courage of these beasts. For the same purpose, the blood of an enemy conquered in battle is drunk (for example, repeatedly in the Kirgiz epic *Manas).*

The ancient Greek myth of Tantalus reflects the phenomenon of ritual anthropophagy or, more precisely, the abolition of human sacrifice, which has ceased to be pleasing to the deity (just as, doubtless, does the Biblical story of the sacrifice of Abraham, in a different form).

But entirely different concepts lie at the basis of tales of the "feast of Atreus" type, which we have considered above. Here cannibalism constitutes not a normal ritual establishment, but an act of individual vengeance in a clan or family feud, condemned by men and gods as a repulsive misdeed, whose meaning consists in compelling one's rival or enemy to commit unknowingly the greatest sin and sacrilege: eating the flesh or drinking the blood of his closest relative.

What is essential in this regard is that even under conditions of cannibalism — both the everyday variety and the ritual one connected with it — the eating of the flesh of blood relations is considered by many tribes as a very serious breach of a religious prohibition ("taboo"). Citing instances of such "exophagy," MacCulloch notes that "tribes of cannibals which consider it quite permissible to eat people of other tribes, in most cases decisively condemn similar treatment of one's fellow-tribesmen, on the same principle according to which they consider it unlawful to eat the flesh of the totem animal of their own clan" (MacCulloch 1905: 299; cf. Frazer 1935: I, 73) — i.e., an eagle, swan, tortoise, kangaroo, etc., which are considered as ancestors or, in other words, as blood relatives of the particular tribe. . . .

Of course, in the later development of the motif, this ethnographic background of ancient customs and beliefs falls away. There remains only the over-all somber artistic coloration of the ancient tale, and the feeling of dread that is common to every human feeling in the face of unheard-of misdeeds, and repulsive and cruel forms of vengeance, which constitute an outrage against this feeling.

II

Clear testimony to the extremely wide distribution of the concepts discussed above, which lie at the basis of the "feast of Atreus" motif, is provided by the group of international folktale motifs in which a cannibal (demon or witch) suffers the fate prepared for his victim. However, here, in accordance with the moral canon of the folktale, punishment of the malefactor and vengeance by his victim are perceived as just retribution, according to the already mentioned principle of *par pari*.

To this category belongs, first of all, the group of folktales designated as No. 327 in Aarne's international catalogue; of these, the first two subgroups — No. 327a ("Tom Thumb") and No. 327b ("Hänsel and Gretel") — are constructed on the same principle of folk ethics, but do not contain in the denouement the motif which interests us, while the last subgroup, No. 327c, reveals in the majority of its variants a certain closeness with the "feast of Atreus" and related motifs.

The Aarne-Thompson international catalogue gives the content of this folktale as follows: "A demon (or witch) brings the hero in a sack into his dwelling. The wife or daughter of the demon is supposed to cook him, but is herself thrown into the oven" (Aarne and Thompson 1961: 120). The Aarne-Andreev catalogue gives a somewhat different scheme for this motif, oriented toward the Russian material, but not covering all the links and variants of the motif: "A witch (fox) entices a boy to come by imitating his mother's voice; her daughter, and afterward she herself, ends up in the oven" (Andreev 1929: 30). In all variants, Russian or international, the victim saves himself by craft: the witch (or her daughter) prepares to cook the captured boy (or little girl) in the oven (or to boil him or her in a pot), in order to eat him; the boy, feigning stupidity, asks the mistress (or her daughter) to show him an example, and pushes her into the oven on a shovel (or into the boiling pot). Both versions lack indication of the denouement of most variants, which is essential to our theme: the cannibal or witch eats the meat of his own children, boiled in a pot or roasted in the oven, in the belief that he is devouring the captured victim.

Variants of this folktale are represented in most Russian folktale collections — in that of Afanas'ev under the title "Baba-Yaga and the Peasant") (No. 106-107) and in "Ivashka and the Witch" (No. 108-109). Usually the rescue of the victim is followed by retribution of the type described above. See No. 108:

"Now Alenka fired up the stove very hot, and said to Ivashka, 'Go ahead: sit on the shovel!' — 'I'm still little and stupid,' answers Ivashka, 'I still don't know how to do anything and don't understand; teach me how you sit on a shovel.' 'Good,' says Alenka, 'it doesn't take long to teach that' — and she sat down on the shovel. So Ivashka shoved her into the oven and closed the cover, and himself went out of the hut, closed the door, and climbed into a tall, tall oak tree.

"The witch comes with the guests and knocks on the door of the hut; no one opens it to her. 'Ah, that damned Alenka! Probably she went out somewhere to play.' The witch climbed in through the window, opened the door, and let in the guests; they all sat down at the table, and the witch opened the cover and brought out the roasted Alenka and put her on the table: they ate and ate and drank and drank, and then went out in the yard and began to roll around in the grass [cf. variant No. 107: "They gathered all the bones, laid them in a row on the ground, and began to walk on them."][4] 'I am walking, I am rolling, having eaten Ivashka's flesh!' And Ivashka says to her from the top of the oak tree: 'You are walking, you are rolling, having eaten Alenka's flesh!'" This is followed by the revelation of what has occurred and by a rather complex denouement (the witch pursues the boy, who saves himself by magic).

In some Russian tales, the central motif is tripled, in accordance with the esthetic canon of folk narration: the hero avenges himself in the same way on the three daughters of the witch in succession — the oldest, the middle one, and youngest (cf., for esample, Onchukov 1908: 191-192 [No. 73]).

According to Andreev's note, this tale is "one of the

most popular." In "various versions," it is known through-
out Europe, in the Caucasus, in Siberia, in Asia Minor, in
India, in Indonesia, on the Philippine Islands, in Japan, in
Africa, among the American Indians, and on Samoa
(Azadovskii et al, eds. 1936: I, commentary, 581).[5]
Cosquin traced its distribution from India, which he considers its place of origin, through Asia and North Africa,
over the whole African continent and to the most distant
boundaries of Western Europe (Norway and Iceland)
(Cosquin 1922). However, his hypothesis seems doubtful,
since the ancient Indian tales (about Emperor
Vikramadittya, etc.), from which Cosquin proceeds (1922:
351-361), lack the motif which from our point of view is
fundamental: the punishment of the cannibal by "like for
like." The great similarity of the basic group of European
tales to each other, which confirms their dissemination
from one people to another, does not exclude the possibility that they originated independently beyond the bounds
of the Eurasian area (for example, among the peoples of
Black Africa) (see, for example, Snegirev, tr. 1937: 41-43,
from Callaway 1867: 18), in view of the great simplicity
of the basic story line of the tale, which is determined by
two fundamental motifs: the feigned clumsiness of the
victim ("La feinte maladresse," as Cosquin has it) and
retribution by "like for like."

An analogous denouement is found in certain tales of
another type, with the widespread basic motif of the
"substitute wife" — for example, in "Cinderella" (Aarne,
No. 510a) and other tales. This denouement was produced
by the same idea of just retribution, and the figures of the
cannibal witch and her daughter (the "false wife"), of
whom the beautiful and virtuous heroine becomes the
victim.

The stepmother, with the aid of sorcery, substitutes
her own daughter, evil and hideous, for the beautiful wife
of the prince, the beautiful one being her unloved step-
daughter. When the deception is revealed and the prince
again finds his beloved, he orders the deceiver to be killed
(variant: she throws herself into a tub of boiling water,
wishing to become as beautiful as her rival). The prince
orders that her flesh be salted, and sends it as a present to

the evil witch, who eats it all up until she sees her daughter's head at the bottom of the tub.

Tales with this denouement have been transcribed in Sicily, among the Arabs and Berbers of North Africa, in Spain, and at the same time at the other end of the world — in Vietnam. Without doubt, they spread from a single source, as is shown by the similarity of certain specific details (a crow or, in other variants, a tomcat, proves more perspicacious than the witch: he asks that he be given some of the daughter's flesh in return for helping the witch to mourn her loss). Probably this tale was distributed in the past over the whole territory, on the periphery or which it has survived, but in this form it was forgotten or lost the denouement, which was too cruel for a children's tale."

Let us cite as an example the conclusion of the Vietnamese tale "Tam and Kam" (a variant of "Cinderella"), recently published in Russian translation (Karpov, comp. 1958: 14-27; cf. Cosquin 1922: 387; Anon. n.d. a: II, 359-360; Lande 1884: No. 22). "The death of Kam" (who was boiled in a pot) "did not grieve the king in the least, but, on the contrary, made him rejoice. Having resolved to play a trick on her evil mother, he ordered that the boiled flesh of Kam be sent to her, saying that this was a gift from her daughter. Having received the present, the stepmother rejoiced and began to boast to her neighbors about what good care her daughter took of her. And she did not share even a piece with anyone, because she was very greedy, so she ate almost all the flesh herself. But at that time a crow came flying and cried out: Karr, Karr! The mother eats her daughter's flesh and doesn't even let me try it! Karr, Karr! The stepmother waved at him and chased him away. And then she looked at the bottom of the pot and saw her daughter's head. In horror, she threw the pot away, cried out in a voice not her own, and went out of her mind on the spot. And soon she died altogether."

We can mention still a third type of tale, arbitrarily entitled "The Juniper Tree" (Aarne No. 720; Grimm No. 47 "Van den Machandelboom"), in which the motif of the "feast of Atreus" is present, but it lacks the retribution according to the principle of "like for like." In Andreev's rendering: "A stepmother kills her stepson and gives him to the father to eat; the remains of the boy are transformed into a bird, which brings grains and kills the stepmother; the boy returns to life" (Andreev 1929: 51). In most variants the resurrection of the killed boy is accomplished in this manner: his little sister gathers his bones and buries them under a juniper tree (or some other tree). The gathering of the scattered parts of a killed person, and his resurrection by the aid of one or another magical means ("living water," etc.), constitute an ethnographic motif based on ancient beliefs and known in the folklore of many peoples (Bolte and Polivka 1913: I, 422-423; Thompson 1933-1934: II, 342-343).[6] This tale is distributed over all of Europe and in some places beyond its boundaries.

Let us mention one more African tale — "The Lion and the Man" — which is not included in Aarne's catalogue, but which in its isolation is all the more indicative of the ethnographic concepts which lie at the foundation of the others.

A lion and a man build a hut together and get into an argument over who is to live in it. In order to chase the man away, the lion kills the father of the latter and orders the man to prepare his meat for the table. The man, having recognized the body, fulfills the order but refuses his share. Then the man, for revenge, kills the mother of his rival and brings him the meat. The lion recognizes his mother, gives the man his share, but also refuses his part. The lion now kills the man's mother, and the man kills the lion's father. The same thing is repeated, but the frightened lion decides to leave the hut to the man (Ol'derogge, ed. 1959: 50-52).[7]

Here the prohibition ("taboo") against the meat of kinsmen is shown in its purest form, resulting in an original plot, constructed on the same principle of "like for like."

The enumerated fairy tales, of course, while not genetically connected with the ancient Greek, Germanic, or South Slavic epic tales, have a remarkable typological similarity to them. By their wide international distribution, they testify to the existence of a common basis of ethno-graphic conceptions and the artistic images connected with them, in the tradition of which these plots developed.

III.

The principle of just retribution, *par pari*, which is at the base of all the tales examined, is widely distributed in the customary law of pre-class slaveholding and early feudal society, and in the legal code based on it among all peoples of the world; it is retained in a number of cases in later times as ethnographic and folkloric survivals, and has received the designation, borrowed from Roman law, of *lex talionis* (Shargorodskii 1957: Pt. 1, 21-23). Its classical formulation is known from the laws of Moses in the Bible: "A soul for a soul [that is, a life for a life], an eye for an eye, a tooth for a tooth, an arm for an arm, a leg for a leg." The vengeance of Marko Kraljevič against the King of Več in the South Slavic songs about the courting of the Jakšiči is constructed according to the principle of the *talion*. This principle appears clearly in the Danish ballad "Sir Lovmor," in which just retribution is the foundation of the artistic parallelism characteristic of the ballad's style, which is carried out in strikingly consistent fashion in the two symmetrically developed parts of the story. Finally, the same principle also comes to light in the tale of the vengeance of Gudrun: Atli orders the heart cut from the breast of Gudrun's brother Hogni; Gudrun brings him the hearts of his infant sons to eat, roasted on a spit.

"The talion," writes M. D. Shargorodskii, a student of the history of criminal law, "was applied both in a material sense (eye for eye, tooth for tooth) and in a symbolic one. According to the code of Hammurabi, the tongue of an insolent foster son, the fingers of an unskillful surgeon, the breast of a bad wet-nurse — all are torn out" (Shargorodskii 1957: Pt. 1, 23). We encounter this kind of symbolic punishment in the tale — widespread among the peoples of the Near and Middle East, and semi-historical in origin — of the noble robber Kĕr-oglu, "the son of the blind man" *(kĕr* = "blind"). His father, an old groom of

the evil khan Hassan, was blinded by his master for having chosen, as the two best horses of his herd, two skinny
and sickly colts, in which he was able to foresee pro-
phetically their future marvelous qualities (the motif of
the fairy tale "Humpbacked Horse") (Zhirmunskii and
Zarifov 1957: 357). The khan's sentence runs: "Let the
price of each of these colts be one of his own eyes"
(Takhmasib 1959: 3). We find an analogous form of punishment in the Uzbek epic "Alpamysh": Here the Kalmyk
batyr Kokaldash orders the blinding of his *sinchi* (groom),
who recognizes in a horse the former's rival, the Uzbek
champion Alpamysh, the winged *"tulpar,"* and predicts
his victory in the forthcoming contest of suitors
(Pen'kovskii and Zhirmunskii, tr. and ed. 1958: 123-125).

The injury done to Abelard by the relatives of his
beloved Heloïse is a form of the talion (Sidorova, ed. and
tr. 1959: 199). Testimony of the barbarous form of
punishment for a seducer or rapist is preserved in the
customary law of many peoples.[8]

The tale of the "eaten heart," which occupies a
prominent place in the poetic literature of the High
Middle Ages and which received wide distribution in
Western Europe in the form of novellas and popular
ballads, is a softened and romantically sublimated variant
of the punishment for an amorous crime.

In the poetry of the Provençal, troubadours, the
German Minnesingers, and the Italian poets of the *dolce
stil nuovo*, the heart of the lover is considered as the
"abode of love" and as the "culprit in amorous passion"
(Ecker 1934: 55-61). Hence the poetic metaphor of the
lover's heart as the "food" of his beloved.

In the first sonnet of Dante's *La Vita Nuova*, Love
appears to the poet in an allegorical vision, and humbly
allows his beloved "to bite his flaming heart": *"e d'esto
core ardendo lei paventosa umilmente pascea" (Vita
Nuova*, 3).

Therefore the heart becomes the material object
upon which the retribution by the principle of the talion
is exercised in symbolic form.

Two versions of this widely popular medieval plot
are represented, in the *Decameron* of Boccaccio, in stories

of the same day — the fourth, which is devoted to stories "of those whose love had an unhappy issue." In the first of these novellas (II, 1), Tancred, Prince of Salerno, orders the killing of Guiscardo, the lover of his daughter Ghismonda ("a man of very low origin, but more noble than others"), and sends her his heart in a golden goblet with the words: "Your father sends you this so as to please you with that which you love most, as you have pleased him with that which he loves most." Ghismonda, having poured poisoned water over the heart, drinks it and dies, "placing the heart of her dead lover upon her own heart" (Veselovskii, tr. 1928: 387-400; see Landau 1884: 111-116; Lee 1909).

The heroes of the second story (II, 9) are two noble Provençals, Guglielmo Rossiglione and his friend Guglielmo Guardastagno. Messer Rossiglione, learning of his wife's infidelity, kills Messer Guardastagno, her lover, having found him unarmed in the forest. Cutting out the heart with his own hands, he orders it to be roasted and given to his wife on a silver dish. "When the knight saw that his wife had eaten everything, he said: 'Madonna, how did you like this dish?' She answered: 'My lord, verily, I liked it very much.' 'I swear before God,' said the knight, 'I believe you and am not surprised that that pleased you in death which in life you loved above all else. . . . That which you have eaten was verily the heart of Messer Guglielmo Guardastagno, whom, like a wicked woman, you so loved. . . .' To this the lady answers: 'God forbid that any other food should pass my lips after the heart of such a noble, valorous, and worthy knight as was Messer Guglielmo Guardastagno.' And rising, without thinking, she threw herself backward out of the window which was behind her. . . ." (Veselovskii, tr. 1928: 462-466).

Of the two stories by Boccaccio, the role of avenger is played in the first by the heroine's father and in the second by her husband. The first lacks the motif of the eating of the heart that has been cut out in punishment. However, this may be a later softening. In the opinion of John Meier (1934: 56), the first variant (with the father as murderer) is a late transformation of the second (with the husband as murderer); in any case, in all earlier versions, the culprit is the husband.

Boccaccio refers to the Provençals as the source of the second novella ("as the Provençals relate"). The course of Boccaccio's story was a legendary biography of the well-known Provençal troubadour, Guilhems de Cabestaing, which has come down to us in two versions (mss. of the 13th and 14th centuries) (Chabaneau 1885: 99-103). Boccaccio gives the name of Cabestaing the form "Guardastagno." The name of his murderer in the biography is Raimond de Rossillion, and the name of the lady is Seremonda or Margarita. The story coincides in all essentials with the novella by Boccaccio, except for one detail: Raimond attacks his wife with a naked sword; she flees from him and throws herself out of a window (or from a balcony).

Gaston Paris (1879; cf. also Academie Française [date lacking]: 352-390) assumed that the basis of this biography was the lost Provençal romance which also served as the immediate source for Boccaccio's novella. In accordance with his general theory of the derivation of the plots of French chivalric romances, he expressed the opinion that in this case, too, a romance plot going back to Celtic oral tradition ("vieilles traditions celtiques") had become attached to the name of a Provençal troubadour. "The criminal love and the cruel vengeance which make up its content are characteristic of this poetry — melancholy, amorous, and at the same time barbaric — which found its most beautiful expression in the wonderful tale of Tristan" (Paris 1879: 362). In Paris's opinion, the existence of such a Celtic source is indicated by the romance of Tristan Thomas (ca. 1160), where Iseult, separated from her beloved, sings a lai while accompanying herself on the harp — the song-tale of Guirun and how he was killed for the love of his lady and how the earl, her husband, gave his wife Guirun's heart to eat ("Et comment li cuns puis dona Le coeur Guirun à sa moiller Par enjin un jor a mangier . . .") (Michel, ed. [date lacking]: III, 39).

The lai of Guirun has not survived, although it is mentioned in two Old French epic poems (chansons de geste) (Paris 1879: 362). Another lai, however, has survived, in which the same plot appears in metamorphosed form. Its hero, Ignaurès, was the favorite of twelve ladies whose love he enjoyed simultaneously. The knights who were the ladies' husbands, having killed him, roasted his heart and gave it to their wives to eat at a common banquet. The plot of this verse tale might be considered a grotesque multiplication, were it not for the presence in the story of one apparently archaic feature: the twelve knights possess in common a castle in which they live with their twelve wives (Paris 1879: 367-368).

This third version of the tale of the "eaten heart" enjoyed a certain popularity. It existed in Provençal and German treatments. It penetrated from French into Italian literature: in the anthology *Cento novelle antiche* (ca. 1300), the heroines are a noble lady and her ladies-in-waiting. The lady's husband gives the culprits the heart of their murdered lover to eat, repeating the same words which in different variants contain the concept of merited retribution according to the principle of the talion: "You liked him living and now you have liked him dead" *("Vi piacesse viva ed ora vi è placiuto morto")* (Landau 1884: 114).

One more (the fourth) version of the same plot exists; it is embodied in the well-known Old French verse tale "Le Châtelain de Couci et la Dame de Faiel" (late 13th-early 14th centuries) and in the Middle High German "Tale of the Heart" *(Herzmeere)* by Conrad of Würzburg (d. 1287), which is earlier in time and considerably shorter. Both of these works, according to Gaston Paris's supposition, go back to a common Old French source (Paris 1879: 366).

The hero of the French tale, having learned that his beloved's husband, Seigneur de Faiel, knows of their love, sets off for the crusades; wounded by a poisoned arrow, before dying he orders his faithful squire to embalm his heart and take it to his beloved in a precious box. Seigneur de Faiel, attacking the squire, takes the box from him and, using the heart, prepares a dish for his wife. Having learned that she has eaten her lover's heart, Madame de Faiel says to her husband: "I swear to you that I will never eat anything else after such precious food" — and dies of grief.

The heroine's last words indicate the connection, either direct or more distant, with the legendary biography of the troubadour Guilhems de Cabestaing, although a new motif (the crusade) has been introduced, and the violent denouement — the heroine's suicide — is lacking. Like the Provençal troubadour, the hero to whose name the plot has been attached in the French tale is a real historical person: this was also a poet-knight, the author of love songs in the troubadour manner, which are included within the verse tale; a contemporary of Richard Lion-Heart, he actually was a participant in the Second Crusade (end of the 12th century), in accordance with the biographical legend.

The tendency to depict the relations between the lovers as a pure exalted platonic love is characteristic especially in the later renditions of this plot (in Konrad of Würzburg, he is a *tugenthafter man*, and she a *reinez wîp*).

The Old French tale is known in an English verse adaptation: "The Knight of Curtesy and the Fair Lady of Faguell" (preserved in a printed source of the mid-16th century [Ritson 1803: 193 ff.; 353 ff.]). The name of the English knight apparently represents a reinterpretation of the French, which was not understood: Couci → Curtesy. Of the heroine it is said that she was "as chaste as a dove at the top of a tree."

The English verse tale, in turn, served as the source for a much-modernized chap-book in prose of the early 18th century — "The Constant but Unhappy Lovers," London, 1707. The heroes are a certain Madam Butler, a wealthy heiress; her husband, Mr. Harvey, the son of a rich merchant; and a young English officer, mortally wounded in the Spanish wars, who sends his beloved a letter written with his own blood, and his heart in a precious box (with the usual denouement) (Clouston 1887: 191).

The numerous ballad adaptations of this plot in Italian, English, German, Dutch, Swedish, and Danish versions may serve as proof of the wide popularity of the tale of the eaten heart.

The folk ballads transcribed in Northern Italy —

"The Cruel Father" *(Il padre crudele)* and others — go back directly to Boccaccio's tale of Ghismonda and Guiscardo (IV, 1), as is shown by the names of the heroes *(Risguardo bello e Rismonda bella* and others). Independently of them, the English (more precisely, the Scottish) folk ballad "Lady Diamond" (or "Daisy," etc.) is derived from the same source: Boccaccio's story was translated into English in 1566 and became the source for a whole series of poems and plays. In the Italian version, the lover is a servant; in the English, a kitchen boy; he is killed by the heroine's father, a king; the motif of the eaten heart is lacking, as in Boccaccio's first story; having received the fatal gift, the heroine dies of grief (in the English version) or takes poison (in the Italian) (Child 1894: 29-38; No. 269).[9]

In Germany, a folk ballad entitled "Der Bremberger" (Anon. n.d. b: 161-170; No. 16; Uhland n.d.: No. 75; Kopp 1908; Rostock 1925: 16) was attached to the personality of yet another poet-knight — the German Minnesinger Reinmar von Brennenberg, who was killed in 1276 by the burghers of Regensburg for unknown reasons. Somewhat earlier, in 1256, the Bavarian Duke Ludwig the Strict ordered the beheading of his wife, suspected of adultery; one of her ladies-in-waiting, who was killed at the same time, bore the name Brennberg — a circumstance which as a whole, in Meyer's opinion (Anon. n.d. a: 168), may explain why this plot was attached to the name of the poet-knight. The ballad uses the strophic form of Brennenberg's genuine songs, and the beginning of one of the poems attributed to him. The traditional plot has received an independent denouement in the German ballad, as well as some new details (the hero is thrown into a dungeon, where he remains for many years, and only then is his heart cut out). The culprit of the murder is the king, who was informed by slanderers that Brennenberg had seduced his wife. The plot source of the ballad was probably the verse tale of Konrad of Würzburg; both the ballad and the tale emphasize the innocence of the lovers. Only printed texts of the 16th century (nine in number) have come down to us, but the ballad is considerably older, since it has retained the name of a forgotten

Minnesinger and a stanza of his song; Meyer attributes its origin to the end of the 13th century (Anon. n.d. a: 168-169). It served as the source for a poem on the same theme, written in the scholastic manner of the Meistersingers (the printed text of the Meistersingerleid dates from 1500) (Anon. n.d. c: No. 505).

From North Germany the ballad about Brennenberg penetrated, on the one hand, into the Netherlands and, on the other, into Sweden and Denmark.[10] The hero's name in the Scandinavian folk ballads (Swedish, Fröydenborg, Danish, Frydenborg) constitutes a distortion (folk etymology) of the German Brennenberg. The Scandinavian variants are, in part, translations of the German original, and in part show independent features; they have been contaminated with another version of the same plot, in which the heroine's father is the avenger (Boccaccio II, 1), but the motif of the eaten heart, and the heroine's statement that she will never take any other food, are always present.

The wide popularity of this plot is shown by its "reversed" form, in which the place of the offended husband is taken by a jealous wife, but most of the traditional elements of the story are preserved.

In the tale by the French writer Madame d'Aulnoy, allegedly based on a real occurrence in Spain during the 17th century, the Marquesa d'Astorga kills her husband's mistress, tears out her heart, and orders it to be roasted and brought to the unfaithful husband. There follows the usual question as to how he liked the food, and the usual explanation: it is not surprising that it seemed good to you, since it is the heart of her whom you loved so much. In conclusion, the Marquesa shows her husband the severed head of his beloved (d'Aulnoy 1691: 108; see Child 1894: 34).

The German ballad "The Horrible Feast" ("Grausiges Mal") is of another and more independent character (Anon. n.d. b: 171-173 [No. 17]). Here the wife brings her husband a dish containing the chopped-off arms and legs of his sweetheart, but he swears to her innocence and kills the evil wife in the marriage bed. The text of the ballad which has come down to us is corrupt, and the circle of its distribution is extraordinarily narrow (only three transcriptions of the mid-19th century, all of them from Silesia).

The Danish ballad "Living Water" *("Livsbandet")* is set off from the others (Grundtvig 1856: 504-507, No. 94). [11] A king overhears a conversation between the queen and an earl, her lover, to whom she promises her hand and throne when her husband dies. When put to the question, both deny their guilt. The king orders that the earl be killed, and his body chopped into little pieces and given to the queen to eat, but the queen guesses that what is in the dish is not merely game. She refuses the food, collects the chopped-up body piece by piece, and takes the pieces to a well of living water, where she resurrects her beloved; afterward they both leave the country. The happy ending, unusual for this plot, was suggested by the popular folk tale "The Juniper Tree" (see above).

The numerous versions and variants of the same plot which developed over the course of five centuries (12th through 17th) testify to its wide popularity among the peoples of Western Europe and to its vigor as a poetic expression of the tragedy of love and jealousy. They are genetically connected by a common source from which they developed in different directions, in part sequentially and in part in parallel, on the basis of the traditional concepts of chivalric literature, as a product of individual literary creativity, but in close interaction with the anonymous folklore tradition.

After the appearance of Gaston Paris's study of the sources of the tale "Châtelain de Couci" (1879), these ordinary European limits, geographical and chronological, were unexpectedly widened by the discovery of new material indicating the oriental origin of this classic medieval plot. In 1883, the journal of the British Folklore Society published for the first time a translation of an Indian (Punjabi) popular romance on the adventures of Raja Rasálu. At the present time this old popular romance, which shows a certain similarity to the Western European chivalric romances of later times, has been recorded in a number of rather similar variants from popular storytellers of the Punjab, and has been translated into English (Swinnerton 1883; Temple n.d.: 1-65; Clouston 1887: 192-195). The time when Raja Rasálu and his wife's lover Raja Hodi, or rather their supposed historical prototypes, lived is considered to be the first and second centuries C.E., although the recorded texts show signs of recent Islamization.

Of the many adventures of this popular hero of the Punjab, the one directly related to our theme concerns his marriage to the beautiful Rani Koklan, the daughter of Raja Sirikala, defeated by Rasálu in a chess game, whom Rasálu then brought up from infancy. One day, when Rasálu was out hunting, at which he spent all his time, the neighboring Raja Hodi, following the trail of a magical deer, reached the mountain fastness where Rasálu's young wife lived; enchanted by her beauty, he climbed up to her by a rope ladder, which she let down for him from the window of her prison. A faithful parrot, keeping watch over the beautiful woman, informed its master of his wife's unfaithfulness. Rasálu and his rival fought a duel in the forest, and Rasálu pierced his wife's lover with an arrow, chopped off his head, and cut out his heart. After a conversation with his wife, who confirmed her guilt, he brought her the lover's heart roasted on a spit (in other variants, his flesh or liver), as game taken in a hunt. Ah, cried the Rani, "what is this food that you have brought me, my beloved? I think that no game was ever so pleasant to my taste!" To this Rasálu replies: "When he was alive, he brought you pleasure, Rani, and now that he is dead you have eaten his flesh. How can you not take pleasure in the flesh of him who brought you joy?" Then Koklan, jumping up from her place in horror, throws herself from the walls of the prison into the chasm (or through the railing of the balcony). Shortly after this, the brothers of Raja Hodi took vengeance on the murderer, and Rasálu perished in battle with them.

The closeness of this to the European version, and in particular to Boccaccio's second tale (II, 9) and its immediate source, the legendary biography of the troubadour Cabestaing, is so striking as to exclude the possibility of chance coincidence or typological similarity. This applies particularly to the denouements — the conversation between husband and wife, the formula of retribution according to the talion, and the culminating catastrophe of the heroine's suicide. The basic difference lies in the moral evaluation of this tragedy of love: the Indian tale is entirely on the side of the offended husband, and his vengeance according to the formula *par pari* is considered fully justified and legitimate. In the Western European variant, the evaluation is the reverse: the spirit of the chivalric ideology of the troubadours and the knightly love-romances, individual love as the highest value is here placed above formal familial ties. "Among all historically active, that is, among all ruling classes," Engels wrote in an analogous connection, "marriage remained what it had been from the time of paired marriage — a business arrangement for the convenience of the parents. And the first form of sexual love to appear in history as a passion, and, furthermore, one which was accessible to any person (at least of the ruling classes), a passion as the highest form of sexual attraction (which is what constitutes its specific nature) — this first form of sexual love, the courtly love of the Middle Ages, was by no mean conjugal love. On the contrary. In its classical form, among the Provençals, courtly love races at full speed toward the destruction of conjugal fidelity, and its poets praised this" (Marx and Engels 1955-1964: XXI, 72).

It is no accident that the tale of the eaten heart furnished material for the legendary biographies of three poets, knights of love — the Provençal troubadour Guilhem de Cabestaing, the French *trouvère* Châtelain de Couci, and the German Minnesinger Reinmar von Brennenberg.

As a result of this reinterpretation, there remained of the old concept of legitimate retribution only a formula based on the principle of the talion, which, under the new conditions of social life and ideology, lost its immediate literal sense.

We are faced with yet another clear case of oriental influences in Western literatures, which cannot be waved aside by denying the so-called "migration of plots" or by criticizing the dogmatic theories of the so-called

"Indianists," like Benfey or Cosquin. After the publication of the Indian material, Gaston Paris had to return once more to the question of the sources of the plot he had studied (Paris 1883). He of course recognized the priority of the Indian version as the source of the Western European one. However, holding to his previous Celtic theory, he was obliged to advance the farfetched hypothesis that the oriental plot had reached the southern romance chivalric poetry by way of the Celts. This artificial construction, however, is not supported by any real facts. The Indian plot probably reached Europe by the ordinary route — through Persian and Arabic literature during the period of the Crusades — although the intermediate links of this chain have not come down to us. Brought by the Crusaders into Provence, the tale became, by virtue of its romantic character, a model embodiment of the new concept of individual love in its tragic collision with patriarchal family relationships.

★ ★ ★

We have thus traced the development of a group of plots which are essentially very different, but which we arbitrarily designated, on the basis of their thematic similarity, as "feast of Atreus." In the heroic tales of the ancient Greeks, the Scandinavian peoples, and the southern Slavs, they are connected with traditions of clan and family feuds, and their typological similarity among various peoples is conditioned by ancient customs and concepts. The folk tale plots, of probably still more ancient origin, passed from people to people, under conditions where the general prerequisites in daily life and world view were present, and appeared in generalized form as the just retribution of "like for like. . . ."

EDITORS' NOTES

a. Translation by E. D. A. Morehead from *The Complete Greek Drama*, edited by W. J. Oates and E. G. O'Neill, Jr. N.Y., 1938.

b. That is, someone of Romance speech and Roman Catholic religion, as opposed to Slavic speech and Eastern Orthodox religion.

c. Unfortunately, we are not able to supply a literal translation of this passage, but the sense — a warning that human flesh is being eaten — is clear enough from the context.

NOTES

1. See Häusler 1960; "Iz 'Eddy' Snorri Sturlesona," translated by N. A. Sigal, pp. 400-401; cf. "Saga o Volsungakh," translated by V. I. Iarkho, "Academia" 1934, Chapt. XI, pp. 232-234.

2. In the version of "Ženidba Jakšiča Mitra" in the collection of Vuk Karadjić, the motif of anthropophagy is absent (see Karadjić 1958: Book II, 597-600, No. 95). However, this variant gives the impression of an uncompleted fragment (perhaps abridged by Vuk?).

3. German translations: Grimm 1811: 253 ff.; Raszmann 1863: 303-306 (the Faroese version). English translation: Prior 1860: 26-37.

4. "Rolling" on the bones of another also represents a method in sympathetic magic, with the aim of acquiring the "strength" of the dead person. See Zelenin 1927: 9.

5. G. 61: "Relatives' flesh eaten unwillingly."

6. E. 30: "Resuscitation by arrangement of members. Parts of a dismembered person are brought together and resuscitation follows."

7. Tales of the Lamba tribe, translated by N. V. Okhotina.

8. The rudiments of this more ancient form of vengeance have been retained in some variants of the "tale of the eaten heart." See Académie Française 1881: 245-246, 383.

9. Five texts recorded in Scotland.

10. Swedish: "Hertig Fröydenborg och Fröken Adelin" (Gejer and Afzelius 1880: 18, 81-84); Danish: "Hertug Frydenborg" (Olrik and Grundtvig 1890: 216-247, No. 305.

11. English translation: Prior 1860: 390-394, No. XXXIX "Maribo well."

LITERATURE CITED

Aarne, A. and Thompson, S.
1961   *The Types of Folktale: Second Revision.* Helsinki.

Académie Française
1881   *Histoire littéraire de la France,* Vol. XXVII. Paris.

Andreev, N. P.
1929   *Ukazatel' skazochnykh siuzhetov po sisteme Aarne*
[Index of Folktale Plots According to the Aarne System].
Leningrad.

Anon.
n.d. a   *Contes populaires de Lorraine,* Vol. II, Paris.

n.d. b   *Deutsche Volkslieder mit ihren Melodien, Bd. I:
Balladen.* Berlin.

n.d. c   *Deutsche Sagen, herausgegeben von den Brüdern
Grimm,* Vol. 22 [place of publication not given].

Azadovskii, M. K., Andreev, N. P. and Sokolov, Iu. M., Eds.
1936   *"Narodnye russkie skazki" A. N. Afanas'eva* [A. N.
Afanas'ev's Russian Popular Tales]. Academia Series [place of
publication not given].

Bolte, J. and Polivka, G.
1913   *Anmerkungen zu den Kinder- und Hausmärchen der
Brüder Grimm,* Vol. I, Leipzig.

Bugge, S.
1889   *Studien über die Entstehung der nordischen Götter-
und Heldensagen.* Munich.

Callaway, H.
1867   *Nursery Tales, Traditions and Histories of the Zoulous.*
Natal.

Chabaneau, C.
1885   *Les biographies des troubadours en langue provençale.*
Toulouse.

Child, F. J.
1894   *The English and Scottish Popular Ballads,* Part IX.
Boston.

Clouston, W. A.
1887   *Popular Tales and Fictions, Their Migrations and
Transformations,* Vol. IX. Edinburgh and London.

Cosquin, E.
1922 "'Le conte de la chaudière bouillante et la feinte maladresse' dan l'Inde et hors de l'Inde," in *Etudes folcloriques*, Paris, 349-399.

d'Aulnoy, M-me
1691 *Mémoires de la Cour d'Espagne*. The Hague.

D'iakonov, I. M.
1956 *Istoriia Midii ot drevneishikh vremen do kontsa IV v. do n. e.* [History of Media from the Most Ancient Times to the End of the Fourth Century B. C. E.]. Moscow-Leningrad.

Ecker, L.
1934 *Arabischer, provenzalischer und deutscher Minnesang.* Bonn and Leipzig.

Frazer, J. G.
1935 *Totemism and Exogamy.* London.

Gejer, E. G. and Afzelius, A. A.
1880 *Svenska Folkvisor,* Bd. I. Stockholm.

Grimm, W.
1811 *Altdänische Heldenlieder.* Heidelberg.

Grundtvig, S.
1853-1856 *Danmarks Gamle Folkeviser,* 3 vols. Copenhagen.

Häusler, A.
1960 *Germanskii geroicheskii epos i skazanie o Nibelungakh. Vstupitel'naia stat'ia i primechaniia V. Zhirmunskogo* [The Germanic Heroic Epos and the Tale of the Nibelungs. Introductory Essay and Notes by V. Zhirmunskii]. Moscow.

Hörmann, K.
1888 *Narodne pjesne muhamedovaca u Bosni i Hercegovini,* Vol. 1. Sarajevo.

Karadjić, V. S.
1958 *Srpske narodne pjesme,* Vol. 2. Belgrade.

Karpov. V., ed.
1958 *Skazki i legendy V'etnama* [Folktales and Legends of Vietnam]. Moscow.

Khalanskii, M.
1893 *Iuzhnoslavianskie skazaniia o kraleviche Marke* [South-Slavic Tales About Marko Kraljević], Part I. Warsaw.

Kopp, A.
1908 *Brembarger-Gedichte.* Vienna.

Landau, M.
1884 *Die Quellen des Dekameron. Zweite Auflage.* Stuttgart.

Lande, A.
1884 *Contes et légendes annamites.* Saigon.

Lee, A. C.
1909 *The Decameron, Its Sources and Analogues.* London.

Mac Cullough, J. A.
1905 *The Childhood of Fiction. A Study of Folktale and Primitive Thought.* London.

Marx, K. and Engels, F.
1955-1964 *Sochineniia, izdanie 2-e* [Works, Second Edition], Moscow.

Michel, [first name lacking, ed.]
n.d. *Tristan (Thomas),* Vol. III [place of publication not given].

Mishchenko, F. G., tr.
1888 *Gerodot, "Istoriia" v desiati knigakh* [Herodotus, *The History,* in Ten Books].

Müllenhoff, K.
1845 *Sagen und Märchen aus Schleswig-Holstein.* Kiel.

Meier, J.
1934 "Drei alte deutsche Balladen," *Jahrbuch für Volksliedforschung,* Vol. IV.

Ol'derogge, D. A. ed. and intro.
1959 *Skazki narodov Afriki* [Folktales of the Peoples of Africa]. Moscow-Leningrad.

Olrik, A., and Gruntvig, S.
1890 *Danmarks Gamle Folksviser,* Vol. V. Copenhagen.

Onchukov, N. E.
1908 *Severnye skazki* [Northern Folktales]. St. Petersburg.

Paris, G.
1879 "Le roman du Châtelain de Couci," *Romania,* Vol. VIII, 343-373.

1883 "La légende du Châtelain de Couci dans l'Inde," *Romania,* Vol. XII, 359-363.

Pauly-Wissowa
1936 *Realenzyklopedie der klassischen Altertumswissenschaft,* 2 Reihe 11. Halbband. Stuttgart.

Pen'kovskii, L., and Zhirmunskii, V. M., trs. and eds.
1958   *Alpamysh. Uzbekskii narodnyi epos* [Alpamysh. An Uzbek Folk Epic]. Moscow.

Petranović, B.
1867   *Srpske narodne pjesme iz Bosne i Khertsegovine.* Belgrade.

Prior, R. C. A., tr.
1860   *Ancient Danish Ballads,* Vol. I. London.

Raszmann, A.
1863   *Die deutsche Heldensage und ihre Heimat,* Vol. I, Part 2. Hanover.

Ritson, J.
1803   *Ancient English Metrical Romances,* Vol. III. London.

Rostock, F.
1925   *Mittelhochdeutsche Dichterheldensagen.* Halle.

Schneider, H.
1962   *Germanische Heldensage,* Vol. I, 2nd ed. Berlin and Leipzig.

Shargorodskii, M. D.
1957   *Nakazanie po ugolovnomu pravu* [Punishment According to Criminal Law]. Moscow.

Sidorova, N. A., ed. and tr.
1959   *Petr Abeliar, Istoriia moikh bedstvii* [Peter Abelard, "The History of My Calamities"]. Moscow.

Snegirev, I. L., tr. and intro.
1937   *Skazki Zulu* [Folktales of the Zulus]. Moscow-Leningrad.

Swinnerton, C.
1883   "Four legends of King Rasálu of Sialkot," *The Folklore Journal,* Vol. I, 129-185 (published separately as *The Adventures of the Punjab Hero Raja Rasálu.* Calcutta, 1884).

Takhmasib, M. G.
1959   *Këroglu.* Baku.

Temple, R. C.
n.d.   *The Legends of Punjab,* Vol. I. Bombay and London.

Thompson, S.
1933-1934   *Motif Index of Folk Literature.* Helsinki.

445

Uhland, L.
    n.d.   *Alte hoch- und niederdeutsche Volkslieder.* [Place of
    publication not given.]

Veselovskii, A.
    1928   *Dzhovanni Bokkach'o, Dekameron, so vstupitel'noi
    stat'ei V. F. Shishmareva* [Giovanni Boccaccio, Decameron,
    With an Introductory Article by V. F. Shishmarev].
    "Academia" Series [place of publication not given].

Voevodskii, L.
    1874   *Kannibalizm v grecheskikh mifakh* [Cannibalism in the
    Greek Myths]. St. Petersburg.

Zelenin, D. K.
    1927   "Skidno-slov'ians'ki khliborobs'ki obriadi kachaniia i
    perekidaniia po zemli," *Etnografichnii visnik,* Vol. 5.

Zhirmunskii, V. M.
    1962   *Narodnyi geroicheskii epos* [The Heroic Folk Epic].
    Moscow-Leningrad.

_____, and Zarifov, Kh.
    1957   *Uzbekskii narodnyi geroicheskii epos* [The Uzbek
    Heroic Folk Epic] Moscow.

PART V

PROBLEMS OF HISTORY AND THEORY

PART V. PROBLEMS OF HISTORY AND THEORY

Introductory Note

This section differs from the others in a number of important respects. The selections in it are intended not to elucidate particular empirical issues, but to illustrate theoretical problems and, in particular, the strengths and limitations of the Marxist model as currently understood in the Soviet Union, and as applied to the problems of primitive religion (Tokarev) and to the succession of social orders (D'iakonov, Semenov, and Melikishvili).

Of the four authors represented, Tokarev is the only real ethnographer. D'iakonov and Melikishvili are philologists and historians specializing in the languages and civilizations of the ancient Near East. The primary source base for their work consists of transcriptions and translations of ancient texts, made in many cases by German, French, and British scholars. The issues between the Soviet authors in this field and their Western counterparts are therefore issues not of fact but of interpretation. Accordingly, work in the field of ancient Near Eastern history — particularly the structure of the state and the economic and social organization of the population — provides a test of the intellectual efficacy of the Marxist model which is hardly available in any other field.

Semenov, despite his prominence in the recent ethnographic literature, is a philosopher by training and current specialty, and in the ethnographic and historical fields works mainly from secondary sources.

The central issue addressed by D'iakonov, Semenov, and Melikishvili is that of the criteria by which social

449

orders are to be distinguished from each other and by which particular societies are to be assigned to this or that type. As we pointed out in the general introduction, the basic criterion for distinguishing social orders and assigning concrete societies to them is the "relationships of production" — those relationships which arise between human beings in the process of producing the material means of existence — taken as a whole. The specific question with which the authors are concerned has to do with whether the ancient Near Eastern societies should be assigned to the slaveholding or the feudal social order, or to yet a third type, designated by certain Marxist scholars as the "Asiatic mode of production" and by others with other names, which usually imply its hybrid nature: "patriarchal-slaveholding," "early-slaveholding," "protofeudal," and the like. The controversy relating to the Asiatic mode of production has a long and involved history in Marxist thought. Purely scholarly issues are closely intertwined in it with important political questions that arose during the early 1930s in connection with the character and tendencies of the Chinese revolution. Obviously, the proper strategy for a revolutionary movement in a given country at any particular time depends upon the precise nature of the relationships prevailing there and the corresponding disposition of the class forces. Athough D'iakonov, Semenov, and Melikishvili do not mention the Asiatic mode of production or allude to it only in passing (the original publication of their articles, with the exception of Melikishvili's, predates the most recent phase of the controversy), it must always be remembered that the issue is in the back of their minds.

Under the slaveholding social order, the ruling class consisted of slave-owners who extracted the surplus product and part of the necessary product as well — that is, that part of the product which is needed to maintain life — from their slaves by sheer physical force. Under the feudal social order, the ruling class consisted of feudal lords who extracted the surplus product from the serfs by means of a combination of physical (military) force and the power of custom. The Asiatic mode of production was characterized, according to its proponents, by the fact that the ruling class was coextensive with the state and that, accordingly, extraction of the surplus product took the form of taxation. The specific empirical questions dealt with in three of the four articles in this section are: What was the relationship of the immediate producers in the ancient Near Eastern societies to the means of production (primarily land)? Were they slaves comparable in status and in their role in production to those of ancient Greece and Rome?[1] Were they, rather, serfs enjoying the use of plots of land in return for specified services? Or did they belong to a third category not identifiable with either of these? Specifically, were they free commune members exploited through taxation by the state as a corporate entity? This last possibility, of course, would correspond to the Asiatic mode of production as a specific social order.

This last question — in other words, whether the ancient Near Eastern societies were in fact characterized by the Asiatic mode of production — accounts for the heavy emphasis placed by D'iakonov and other Soviet scholars on the position and internal structure of the commune in the ancient East. Although D'iakonov avoids taking an explicit "pro-Asiatic" position, it is clear that in his view it was the communes as such, rather than individuals, which were the objects of exploitation in the ancient Near Eastern empires. Other Soviet authors, of whom Semenov is a good example, feel themselves compelled by the obvious differences in status between the slaves of classical antiquity and the immediate producers of the ancient East to seek some kind of middle ground, without admitting the Asiatic mode of production as such into the sequence of social orders.[2]

The article by S. A. Tokarev illustrates another key problem of Marxist methodology, although one not attended by the wide swings of opinion and stormy debates which have marked the development of ideas on the Asiatic mode of production. Tokarev is essentially discussing the derivation and social role of primitive religion. From the Marxist point of view, the particular relevance of this problem lies in the fact that, in a primitive setting not marked by the presence of antagonistic classes,

religion cannot be considered (as it normally is by Marxists) as an ideological mechanism of class domination. The
reader will notice that Tokarev ends by, in principle, removing the whole cult of the dead from the sphere of
religion (see Tokarev, page 509 in this collection). However
in his discussion with S. Dunn (Tokarev 1969*), he qualified this stand and indicated that the same reasoning
might well apply to other aspects of primitive religion.
Another solution to the problem, one that is favored by
some Soviet scholars, particularly B. F. Porshnev (1969*),
is to reserve the term "religion" for the belief systems
current in class societies and to designate the religions of
the primitive world in some other way.

We have stated in the general introduction our views
concerning Soviet religious policy and its relation to the
genuine Marxist tradition. It is rather sad to see Tokarev,
for all his erudition and breadth of grasp as a scholar —
and Porshnev, too, in a different way — fall victim to this
stultifying set of ideas. It is worth noting that Snesarev
(1971-1973, XI: 250-251), in his discussion of the cult of
the dead among the Khorezm Uzbeks, shows his usual
forthrightness and takes issue with Tokarev on this point:

"Neither theoretically nor practically is Tokarev's
conclusion in this connection acceptable. . . . [There
follows a quotation from the passage from Tokarev just
cited.] From the standpoint of theory, this concept
receives absolutely no support from the factual material,
part of which we have presented. Moreover, the author
somehow leaves out of consideration the fact that 'we'
(the word is taken from his formulation) do not consist
solely of the intelligentsia of the capital city, among
whom, in this situation, it is true that only a feeling of
respect for the dead has remained, but also the peoples
of the country, among whom — it must be stated with
regret — it is precisely funerary and memorial ritual that
continues to be marked by a certain archaicism and stagnation and to derive from very primitive notions of the
soul, the spirit, and life beyond the grave. The atheist
public of the entire country is bending efforts to free
people's minds of these primitivisms and, in certain cases,
to emancipate them further from the unbearable material

costs of memorial feasts."

Sergei Aleksandrovich Tokarev was born in Siberia on December 29, 1899. After graduating in 1925 from Moscow State University, he took up graduate studies in the Institute of History of RANIION (Russian Association of Scientific Research Institutes in the Social Sciences, which operated from 1923 to 1930) in the ethnological section. In 1935, he was awarded a degree of Candidate of Historical Sciences without defending a dissertation, and in 1940 he defended his doctoral dissertation. He worked for many years in the Museum of the Peoples of the USSR and in the Museum of the History of Religion, and was professor in the Departments of Ethnography of the Faculties of History of Moscow State University and the Moscow Institute of Philosophy, Literature, and History. Since 1943 he has worked at the Institute of Ethnography, Academy of Sciences, USSR, heading first the section of Peoples of Australia, Oceania, and America, and, since 1957, that of Peoples of Non-Soviet Europe. He is concurrently professor at the Department of Ethnography, Faculty of History, Moscow State University. His major areas of specialization are Australia and Oceania, Western Europe, and Siberia. However, his work has been largely historical in tendency. A major specialist in comparative religion and in the history of Soviet ethnography, Tokarev is one of the few Soviet scholars who serve on the editorial boards of Western journals, for example, *Ethnologia Europaea (Sovetskaia etnografiia* 1969).

* * *

NOTES

1.   Slaves, of course, have existed in other social orders besides the slaveholding one. In particular, they were found in immature capitalist societies (such as the ante-bellum American South and the 19th-century West Indies) as the labor force of a particular kind of plantation economy. They are also found at many times and places in the role of personal or household servants. This last kind of slavery, however, is not significant from the Marxist point of view in characterizing a social order, since, in it, the slave does not produce goods or an income

for the slave-owner.

2. We will list here, with a few brief critical remarks, the materials available in English on the Asiatic mode of production and related questions in Marxist historiography. The best-known treatment of the question is probably that by Karl Wittfogel in his *Oriental Despotism* (1957: 378 ff.), but this treatment is seriously misleading in several respects, and in any case does not cover the recent revival of interest in this and related questions, either in the Soviet Union or among Marxist scholars in Eastern and Western Europe. The early phase of this revival can be documented from the Spring 1966 issue of *Soviet Studies in History*, which contains translations of articles by the specialist in ancient history, V. V. Struve (originally one of the fiercest opponents of the Asiatic mode of production, who just before his death in 1965, seemed to be changing his views), L. V. Danilova, Ia. A. Lentsman, and other scholars. In addition, the article by Vasil'ev and Stuchevskii (1966-67) deserves mention as one of the many attempts to find a compromise solution to the problem by positing a number of coequal alternative paths of development. The discussion on D'iakonov's paper (VDI 1964) should be carefully studied by all those interested in problems of historical method and Marxist model-making. An exchange of views between French and Soviet scholars on the Asiatic mode of production was translated in the Fall 1965 issue of *Soviet Anthropology and Archeology*. This exchange gives the setting and some of the precipitating factors for the current revival of interest in the question. Detailed articles by Iankovskaia (1964-65) and D'iakonov (1968-69) shedding light on the social structure of ancient Mesopotamia, and indirectly on the question of the Asiatic mode of production, have also been translated.

Finally, the article by the Czech scholar Jan Pečirka (1964) is important as revealing the emotional factors and political considerations underlying the discussion at various stages of its development. Scholars in the West tend to forget that, under Soviet (and Eastern European) conditions, the issues with which they deal can become literally matters of life and death and can involve complex cross-currents of personal loyalty or emnity and political commitment of which the outside observer, under normal conditions, knows nothing.

REFERENCES CITED

D'iakonov, I. M.
1968-1969 "Problems of Property: On the Structure of Society in the Near East Before the Middle of the Second Millennium B.C.E.," SS, Vol. VII, No. 3, 9-32.

Iankovskaia, N. B.
1964-1965 "Communal Self-Government in Ugarit (Guarantees and Structure)," SA&A, Vol. III, No. 3, 46-65.

Pečirka, Jan
1964 "Die sowjetischen Diskussionen über die asiatische Produktionsweise und über die Sklavenhalterformation," *Eirene*, No. III, 147 ff.

Sovetskaia etnografiia
1969 "Sergei Aleksandrovich Tokarev (K 70-letiiu so dnia rozhdeniia)," [Sergei Aleksandrovich Tokarev (For his 70th birthday)], SE, No. 6, 145-146.

Vasil'ev, L. S., and Stuchevskii, I. A.
1966-1967 "Three models for the origin and evolution of precapitalist societies," *Soviet Studies in History*, Vol. V, No. 3, 24-37.

VDI
1964 "Discussion on the Problem of the Clan and Rural Communes in the Ancient East," SA&A, Vol. II, No. 4, 61-65; Vol. III, No. 1, 37-53.

Wittfogel, Karl A.
1957 *Oriental Despotism: A Comparative Study of Total Power.* New Haven and London.

THE FUNERARY CULT
AS A FORM OF RELIGION

S. A. Tokarev

The term "funerary cult" usually denotes the set of religious ceremonials relating to the dead, and the beliefs associated with these ceremonials. The broad distribution of funerary rites is well known. Ceremonials and beliefs associated with the deceased are more or less prominent in all religions, from the most primitive to the most complex.

Many capitalist-oriented and Marxist researchers recognize the major role of the funerary cult in the history of religion. Some of them view the funerary cult not only as an independent but also as the most ancient form of religion, regarding all, including the most complex religious concepts and ceremonials, as the further development of beliefs associated with the dead. We find this point of view even among the 18th-century materialists. John Toland (1927: 53) wrote (1704): "From the most ancient historical evidence it can be concluded that all superstitions (Toland included religious beliefs in general in this category — S. T.) were initially associated with the cult of the dead, which has its main source in funerary ceremonials." Joseph Priestley (1934: 56-59) (1777) agreed with this, although he avoided Toland's one-sidedness, recognizing other sources for the origin of religious concepts besides funerary ceremonials.

This idea of the exceptional significance of the funerary cult in the history of religion found wide acceptance after 1870 in the works of adherents of the "animist" theory of the genesis of religion, notably a few of them.

Herbert Spencer (1876: 277-281, 292-300, 270-274, etc.) assumed that the most ancient religious concept was belief in the soul and its existence after death, and that the elementary form of worship was the cult of the dead; temples arose from tombs, sacrifices from the "feeding" of the dead, prayer from petitions made to the deceased, and all kinds of religious ceremonials from funerary ceremonials. One of the most extreme advocates of this point of view, Julius Lippert (1881: 3, 5, 9-13, etc.), was convinced that the "cult of souls" (which he identified with the "cult of ancestors") lay at the basis of the entire history of religion and that its root was the unaccountable fear in the presence of the dead or its soul. Similar views were held by Nikolai Kharuzin, who also recognized the "cult of the dead" (or the "cult of souls") as the earliest form of worship. True, Kharuzin, unlike Lippert, did not confuse it with cult of ancestors, dating the latter — quite correctly — from a considerably later stage of historical development; however, the cult of ancestors "developed," in Kharuzin's view, from the same "cult of the dead in general" (1903: 247, 252, 254, and 255). Approximately the same view was held by Heinrich Cunow (1925: 146, 159, etc.), though he did attempt, as we know, to give the animist theory a Marxist basis. The German psychologist Wilhelm Wundt (n. d.: 169), while largely departing from "classical" animist theory, remained firmly attached to its premises in regard to this question: "Unquestionably," he wrote, "the cult of the dead is the earliest form of worship in general, and remained its sole form for a very long time."

All the authors cited, as well as their many supporters, in one way or another derived the funerary cult and everything connected with it, and also the entire development of religious beliefs in general, from belief in the soul and its existence in the other world. Some recent researchers have viewed this question somewhat differently. For example, Max Ebert (1921-1922: 2, 4, 5, 11), an eminent German archeologist, suggested a different explanation for the origin of the "cult of the dead." In his view, this cult was initially wholly unrelated to belief in the soul and its existence after death, since the very distinction between soul and body did not exist among primitive man, just as fear in the presence of the dead did not exist — otherwise people would not have interred their corpses close to or actually in their dwellings. Ebert saw the root of the cult of the dead in the fact that primitive man in general did not distinguish the moment of onset of death, and continued to regard the dead person as still alive, and therefore felt concern for him. The ties of the deceased with his family and with his home were not broken: "The roof of the cave or hut still protects him, the fire of the hearth warms him, he drinks and eats as before." This is the idea of the "living corpse." Thus, "the primeval cult of the dead is nothing but a continuation of social obligations beyond the limits of death." There is much truth in this view of Max Ebert, as we will see below.

In contemporary Soviet science, we have to a large extent overcome the lopsided view of the funerary cult as the most ancient, and primevally the only, form of religion — as the elementary form of worship, from which all other forms supposedly derive.[1] Hardly any Marxist researcher would attempt to derive from the cult of the dead, for example, totemism, hunting, and agricultural ceremonials, erotic cults, shamanism, witchcraft, etc. But even now everyone recognizes that the funerary cult is very prominent in the history of religion, and that its rudiments trace back to the remotest antiquity.

In fact there is no doubt that the funerary cult is among the most ancient forms of religion. It is enough to recall that it is directly attested to by very early archeological sites; even if the question of the Neanderthal burials remains debatable, it is in any case beyond dispute that Upper Paleolithic burials were already associated with some religious concepts.

The Neanderthal Burials

At the very outset it is necessary to establish an essential distinction which unfortunately is not usually made in science. It is necessary to distinguish: (1) the funerary cult (cult of the dead) — that is, the complex of religio-magical ceremonials and ideas associated with burial of the dead or with the dead per se, and (2) burial *customs* per se — that is, various traditional methods of treating the body of the deceased and other related acts which may or may not be religious in content.

That these categories are not one and the same thing, and that burial customs may have no relationship to religion, is known to everyone. An example is our present-day customs associated with funerals; these may be very solemn, magnificent, and involved, but at the same time not associated with any religio-magical ideas — that is, superstitions. But where we are concerned with the past, and especially with the most ancient burial sites (the Paleolithic), it is commonly believed that these relics were inseparably linked to religious beliefs. Moreover, it is usually considered axiomatic that even the earliest burials could have appeared solely *as the result* of such beliefs. It is regarded as common knowledge, and not requiring proof, that our remotest ancestors buried their corpses exclusively by virtue of superstitious convictions.

Therefore, the very presence of remnants of burials in the epoch of the Lower Paleolithic (Mousterian burials) is taken by most scientists as indisputable evidence that at that time there already existed some kind of religio-magical ideas. As to those investigators who do not admit the possibility that our Mousterian ancestors (Neanderthal men) already possessed religious ideas, they attempt to deny the very fact that deliberate burials existed in this epoch.

Since the question of the proper interpretation of Neanderthal burials is of key importance for our problem, it is necessary to consider the burials in somewhat more detail.

Few skeletons and bones of Neanderthal men have been preserved. Still fewer of them can be viewed as remnants of deliberate burials. One of the best qualified experts on the subject, the archeologist A. P. Okladnikov (1952), has listed 18 discoveries thus far known to science. Here is a concise list of them.

In 1886, remains of two Neanderthal skeletons were discovered in Spie (Belgium); of these, one plainly lay on its right side, with legs and arms flexed under it.

In 1908, a male skeleton lying on its back in a

special pit was found in the grotto of Buffia near La-Chapelle-aux-Saints (France).

That same year, the skeleton of an adolescent in an unclear but evidently bent pose was discovered in the cave of Moustier (France).

From 1909 to 1921, six skeletons were found at different times in La Ferrassie (France), some of which lay in man-made depressions.

In the period 1929-1939 five skeletons with flexed arms and legs were found in the caverns of Mugaret-es-Tabun and Mugaret-es-Skhul (Palestine).

In 1924, two skeletons (adult and child) lying on the right and left sides were found in the cavern of Kiik-Koba (Crimea); the adult lay in a niche specially gouged out of the cliff.

In 1938, a child's skull surrounded by several pairs of goat horns was found in the grotto of Teshik-Tash (Uzbekistan).

To this list we must add an additional find made in 1939 in the Guattari (Circea Mountain near Rome): the skull of a Neanderthal man with a crushed occiput — perhaps evidence of a cannibalistic rite.

These few remnants of Neanderthal skulls and skeletons are the focus of an extended scientific controversy. Prior to 1908, before the discoveries in Le Moustier and La-Chapelle-aux-Saints, no one had expressed the idea that ceremonial burial existed among Neanderthal men. The French archeologists Abbe Buisoni and Bardon, and after them Hugo Obermayer (1913: 486), Osborn (1923: 179), and others, were the first to advance this point of view. Among most archeologists the conviction gradually became established that Neanderthal man interred his dead, and did this for superstitious reasons: either belief in the continuation of the soul's life after the body's death, or ascription of supernatural properties to the body itself.

Soviet researchers for the most part approach such proposals cautiously, but do not reject them. Thus, in the view of V. I. Ravdonikas (1939: 184), "It is entirely possible that they (Neanderthal burials — S. T.) are proof of the *inception* even in the Mousterian period of those primitive religious beliefs which were unquestionably attested in the Upper Paleolithic sites." A. V. Artsikhovskii (1954: 35) writes: "It is not known what was responsible for the burials found in the Mousterian campsites of various countries — fear of the dead, concern for the dead, or simply the desire to safeguard the deceased from wild animals." P. P. Efimenko (1953: 252) noted: "Regardless of the interpretation of the motives that led man to bury his dear ones at the sites of cave settlements where their remains have now been found, in any case they bear witness to the fact that the primeval consciousness of Neanderthal man already contained the beginnings of concern for the dead."

The most cautious and also the most correct view of the ancient burials was expressed, it appears to me, by I. I. Skvortsov-Stepanov (1959: 245), who took a very skeptical attitude toward attempts to explain these burials on the basis of "belief in the soul," "the cult of the dead," etc. "It is erroneous to think" he wrote, "that when a burial-ground is discovered, the methods of burial necessarily bespeak the existence of a 'cult of the dead.' And it is still more erroneous to assume that they bear witness to a 'cult of the soul.'"

In recent years the debate over the Neanderthal burials was revived, and even took on sharper forms. M. S. Plisetskii (now deceased) attempted to reexamine the question of the Neanderthal burials: critically analyzing all the data on the remains of Neanderthal skulls and skeletons, he concluded that in no case were there adequate grounds for considering them relics of deliberate interment. Therefore he held that there is also no evidence that religious ideas and ceremonials in general existed in the Neanderthal period. Those who hold the opposite view, in the opinion of M. S. Plisetskii (1952: 151-152, 156, etc.), knowingly or unknowingly defend the reactionary theory of the "primordiality of religion." In opposing him, A. P. Okladnikov (1952: 179, etc.) attempted, in contrast, to defend the traditional point of view on Neanderthal burials: in his opinion, the facts unquestionably testify to the existence of deliberate interments in this period, and therefore to the existence of already formed religious ideas. "The Mousterian burials," wrote Okladnikov, "show

the primeval emergence of the rudiments of religious
beliefs as a complex of false fantastic ideas of himself
and of nature held by man . . ."; and "this is still not at
all a genuine or in any way full-fledged religion, even a
primitive one" (Okladnikov 1952: 179, etc.).[2]

Which of the debating sides is correct, and which in
error? To make this clear, it is necessary to analyze more
clearly the essence of the debate. It is not difficult to see
that the debate revolves specifically around two questions
which, however, have not been distinguished with sufficient clarity by the opposing sides themselves. These questions can be formulated as follows:

    1. Did Neanderthal men bury their dead?

    2. From what motives did they bury them?

On the first question, it appears that Okladnikov is
more correct; he has an excellent grasp of the factual data
of archeological finds. The fact that the burials of Neanderthal skeletons were premeditated is hard to doubt.
Plisetskii and his supporters vainly try to refute this fact.

But the situation is different for the second question.
Both opposing sides agree that primitive man could inter
his dead only from superstitious, religious motives. "As
we know," wrote Plisetskii, "any premeditated cultic interment presupposes continuation of life beyond death"
(Plisetskii 1952: 151). He consequently did not doubt that
any "premeditated interment" must necessarily be a
"cultic interment"! The same position is taken by
Okladnikov, who, although referring to the views of
scholars who admit other, nonreligious motives for primeval burials, still personally holds to the opinion that the
"concern for a fellow member of the Mousterian collective," manifested in the custom of burying the deceased,
"was expressed here in *special* forms springing from false,
incorrect ideas on man"; furthermore the author already
assumes here "rudiments of animism" (Okladnikov 1952:
159, 177). Therefore, much of Okladnikov's argument is
directed toward a theoretical demonstration of the
possibility of the genesis of religious ideas among Neanderthal men, which he believes can alone explain the
existence of burials.[3]

In this second question, it seems to me, Okladnikov's

position is considerably weaker and his arguments are less convincing.

Is it true that primitive man could bury his dead only from superstitious, religio-magical motives? Is it true that these ancient burials bespeak the existence of "false, incorrect ideas on man" — that is, belief in the life of the soul beyond the grave, in supernatural properties of the corpse, and so on, or an incapacity to distinguish the quick from the dead? Is it actually necessary to assume the existence, among Neanderthal men, of such religio-magical ideas in order to explain Mousterian burials? Cannot these burials be explained otherwise and more simply?

Instinctual Motives for Interment of the Dead

There is no reason to assume that at this stage of man's development, when his consciousness was only the consciousness of "the conditions of individual practical useful results" (Engels 1952: 14), he had any abstract concepts at all, including religio-magical. All we know about Neanderthal men compels us to think, rather, that they were governed in their acts not by conscious ideas, but by instincts, in large measure inherited from their animal forebears. Cannot the interments of the dead in the Neanderthal period be explained by the action of some elementary biological instincts?

Such a point of view has been advanced in the literature. It has been proposed (Spencer 1878: 269-270, Lippert 1881: 5, 10-13, etc.) that the most ancient basis for the funerary cult was an instinctive dread in the presence of the dead, supposedly characteristic of all living creatures. In the Soviet literature, A. V. Lunacharskii (1924: 9, 16-18) defended a similar view. Furthermore, several authors (including M. N. Pokrovskii) attempted to further generalize this idea of "dread in the presence of the dead" by elevating it to a general biological instinct of dread of death, and on its basis explaining not only funerary rites but all religion in general.

But this viewpoint is plainly untenable. Dread in the presence of dead individuals of one's own species is not characteristic of the entire animal world in general. What is called "fear of death" is in reality the instinct of self-preservation, and makes itself evident in quite other forms. In addition, it is known (in what follows we will see examples of this) that in the funerary customs of the most diverse peoples it is very often not fear of the dead one, but just the opposite motive which is manifested. In other words, dread in the presence of the corpse (where it actually exists) not only cannot serve as a universal explanation of the funerary cult, but, on the contrary, itself needs explanation. We will turn to this question later.

Yet does this mean that any attempts to search out roots of funerary customs in biological instincts are foredoomed to failure? Do there not still exist in the animal world some kinds of instinctive actions with respect to the dead specimens of one's own species?

Such instinctive actions undoubtedly do exist. We find in animals two opposing instincts in this respect. One of these is inherent to many, even lower, animals — for example, insects — and consists of the effort to remove the dead body; thus, bees and ants toss aside or cover the dead bodies of their fellows. Evidently, this is the very same instinct of cleanliness that compels, for example, dogs and cats to throw dirt over their excrement.

Another instinct is shown by higher animals, among whom there exists a mutual attachment of individuals within the group or herd: dogs, monkeys, and some other animals sometimes show displeasure at the death of their fellows, and part with their bodies reluctantly. Most interesting in this respect are the observations on simians collected in a book by Zuckermann (1932: 298-305). I present several examples.

A certain plantation owner, who one day caught a troop of baboons in his maize field eating maize, killed one of them; the other baboons, instead of running, surrounded the carcass of their fellow and did not give way to the man, who succeeded in driving them away and seizing the killed baboon only when he called some servants to his side. In the London Zoological Gardens, female baboons never voluntarily surrender their deceased young, always continuing to nurse them. One female macaque, of whom systematic observations were made, and her mate did not leave the pair's dead infant for two weeks, until its body had completely disappeared from constant licking, hugging, and pinching.

In a book by Yerkes (1929: 299) on apes, the following case is presented: when Moses, a young chimp, died, his friend Aaron looked most disconsolate: later it was found that Moses' body had been covered with a piece of canvas that had been in the cage; evidently this was done by Aaron.

Also of interest are the observations of Prof. Karl Max Schneider (1956: 90-91), director of the Leipzig Zoological Gardens. He writes: "The moment a lion cub dies, its mother covers it with dirt in the den, even though it may not have stopped breathing. It no longer interests her. This is known to be the case also with birds. But this is not true for all animals. Simians — for example, baboons — drag their dead offspring after them for weeks at a time, even when the little carcass is already half decomposed and completely wrinkled. I have also been told about one bitch dog that carried its dead puppy around for two days."

There are also reports — not especially trustworthy, it is true — that apes in the wild sometimes cover the bodies of their dead fellows with leaves (Bouyssonnie 1927: 55).

Based on such observations, which are quite numerous, Zuckermann, like other students of monkeys, deems it possible to conclude that these animals do not differentiate the living from the dead (Zuckermann 1932: 305, etc.; Schneider: 1956: 91). But this conclusion is hardly correct. It would be more accurate to say that in all the instances cited there is evidence of an instinct of mutual attachment between individuals of the same group, especially of mother to offspring — an instinct which does not disappear even after the death of a member of the group. This instinct manifests itself in the effort to cling to the body of the dead, and to shield it against encroachment by outsiders.[4]

These two opposing instincts — the effort to get rid of the dead and the effort to keep it close to oneself —

which are characteristic of many animals, must have existed also at the dawn of human history. And actually, study of archeological and ethnographic material relating to funerary customs plainly shows that for all the diversity of these customs, they are underlain, in a more or less modified form, by either one or the other of these opposing motives or, more commonly, by a combination of both.

Naturally, however, both of these motives constitute only the *primary* bedrock of the funerary customs practiced by various peoples. The amazing diversity of these customs is determined by highly varied historical and even simply geographical causes. These causes call for attentive and detailed study, if we wish to understand in each specific instance the features of funerary customs of a given people.

Variety of Forms of Burial

The forms of burial among various peoples are so diverse that it is not easy to structure them into a definite system. Archeological material cannot give even a remote notion of this diversity. Though archeologists usually pay great attention to funerary ritual, as a rule they are concerned only with two of the numerous ways of dealing with the body of the deceased: cremation and "inhumation" (that is, interment in the earth) — with modifications, of course, within each of these basic methods. On the other hand, the ethnographic literature abounds in descriptions of the most multifarious procedures in dealing with the deceased.

The French ethnographer Georges Montandon made an attempt at classifying these ways (1934: 651). He divided methods of dealing with the deceased into eight basic types: (1) abandonment or expulsion *(abandon);* (2) water burial *(immersion);* (3) air burial *(surélévation);* (4) interment *(ensevelissement),* with two modifications: (a) interment in earth *(enterrement)* and (b) cave burial *(inhumation);* (5) cremation *(ignition);* (6) mummification *(momification);* (7) dismemberment *(décharnement);* and (8) cannibalism. But this is only the crudest breakdown, which fails to take into account various mixed and more complex forms of burial.

Methods of dealing with the dead not only differ from people to people; there are also often several, for each individual people, depending on the age, sex, and social standing of the deceased, on how he or she died, and on various other circumstances. Social differences are especially distinctly manifest in the funerary ceremonial. Even among peoples still at the stage of the clan-communal order and not cognizant of class differences, incipient social differentiation — separation of elders, chiefs, sorcerers, shamans, etc. — is reflected in the methods of burial.

It suffices to cite two or three examples of the staggering diversity of burial methods. Among the Australian aborigines, for all the simplicity and the primitiveness of their culture, almost all possible ways of dealing with the body of the deceased have been noted: simple abandonment to the whims of fate, air burial, interment in the ground (with various complications of this ceremonial), cremation, mummification, corpse eating, secondary and partial interment, etc. In some cases the same tribe practices various modes of burial, depending on the sex, age, and other characteristics of the deceased.[5]

Widespread in Melanesia is water burial in various forms (simple sinking of the body, placement of it in a boat on the water, etc.), air burial, with mummification in certain places, cave burial, interment in the earth in various postures, interment in the living hut, cremation, etc. Different forms of burial have often been noted on one and the same island: for example, on the small island of San Cristobal (southern Solomon Islands), the researcher Fox (1924: 217) noted six different ways of handling the dead: (1) the corpse, in a flexed position, was placed in a narrow pit so that the head remained above the surface, after which it was separated from the body and taken away; (2) the corpse, wrapped in a shroud, was placed in an extended posture in a cave; (3) it was set out on the rocks or in a tree; (4) the corpse was mummified, impregnated with a special juice, after which it was interred in a hut, which was then placed under taboo (this is how the bodies of chiefs were dealt with); (5) the body was placed in a standing position in the hollow of a tree; (6) the corpse was placed in a boat (this was used only for chiefs) (Glaumont, 1888: 126-129). Other researchers have also described other methods of burial among the New Caledonians (de Rochas, 1862: 270-271).

This diversity of burial methods has led researchers into a blind alley more than once. Efforts aimed at explaining the diversity failed. Adherents of the diffusionist school (Graebner, W. Schmidt, Rivers, and Montandon) tried to connect various forms of burial in the same country with different "cultural circles" or with successive waves of settlement of the country. Such a relationship probably does exist in many cases, but, in the first place, this is by no means always true, and secondly, even if a relationship between some specific form of burial and a given ethnic group or "culture" can finally be established, it by no means explains the origin of the given form of burial.

The American ethnographer Kroeber, who devoted a small article to the question of the variability of burial methods, whose distribution does not coincide with any cultural boundaries, refused to give a firm explanation of this fact: he merely advanced the suggestion that since burial practice is not associated with economics or other key aspects of the life of people, but is instead linked with strong emotions, it more readily lends itself to the sway of fashion, etiquette, etc. (Kroeber 1927: 314).[6]

It is evident that customs of various peoples involving methods of dealing with the body of the deceased were shaped under the influence of diverse historical and simply geographic conditions, all of which can by no means be dealt with in the present state of our knowledge. At present we can scarcely hope to provide a satisfactory explanation of the predominance, in each case, of particular forms of burial among a given people.

For all this, however, it is possible to discover, in the most widespread methods, the manifestation, albeit in highly complex forms, of those very primary motives which, in the form of obscure instinctive actions, existed among our prehuman ancestors. These motives include the striving to rid oneself of the body of the deceased and the striving to keep it close to oneself. Though complicated by different historical accretions, these basic motives confront us in the burial practices of various people, either separately, or combined with each other in various ways.

These primary motives can be traced most easily among the most backward peoples — the Australian aborigines and some others; but they can be recognized, though greatly modified, in the funerary ritual of more highly advanced peoples. Unfortunately, it is not possible to give a detailed survey of them here.

Their genetic relationship is shown (very approximately, of course) on the diagram in Figure 1.

Funerary Customs: Sacrifices, Wake, Mourning, Etc.

Let us now look briefly at those complexes of customs and ceremonials which generally accompany the burial of the dead and which are commonly called "funerary rites" or the "cult of the dead." Let us examine them for the purpose of revealing their true roots.

These customs and ceremonials can be broken down arbitrarily into several groups: (a) funerary gifts and sacrifices; (b) fires built on the grave; (c) funeral wakes, banquets, and games; (d) post-mortem mourning and prohibitions.

In the scholarly literature it is customary to derive all these funerary customs and rituals from magico-religious ideas, from belief in the soul and its afterlife.

Thus, the custom of offering gifts and sacrifices to the deceased is explained by the belief that the deceased (or his soul) needs food, clothing, weapons, etc., and that therefore these things must be supplied, whether out of respect for him or from fear that otherwise he will be incensed and will harm those who remain alive (Spencer 1876: 279-280). This is how Spencer, Tylor, Kharuzin, and others have looked at this question. Such an interpretation of the origin of funerary gifts and sacrifices is very vividly formulated by L. Ia. Shternberg as follows: "Since the afterlife is a continuation of earthly life, the idea naturally arose that the deceased had to be supplied with

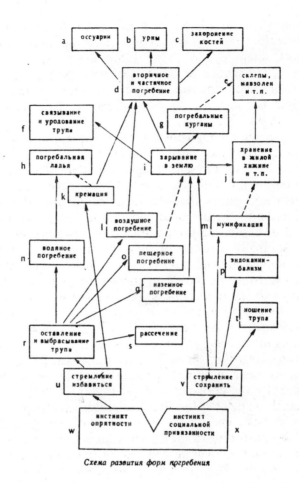

Схема развития форм погребения

FIGURE 1: Scheme of development of burial forms.[7]

LEGEND TO SCHEME: (a) ossuaries; (b) urns; (c) interment of bones; (d) secondary and partial burial; (e) crypts, mausoleums, etc.; (f) binding and disfigurement of the corpse; (g) burial mounds; (h) funerary boat; (i) interment in the earth; (j) preservation in an occupied hut, etc.; (k) cremation; (l) air burial; (m) mummification; (n) water burial; (o) cave burial; (p) endocannibalism; (q) surface burial; (r) abandonment and expulsion of the corpse; (s) dismemberment; (t) carrying of the corpse; (u) effort to rid oneself; (v) effort to preserve; (w) instinct for cleanliness; (x) instinct for social cohesion.

everything he needed for existence in the present world. Therefore the deceased is given clothing, means of transport, weapons, tools, etc." (Shternberg 1936: 330).

The lighting of a fire at or near the grave also derives, usually, from the superstitious idea that the deceased needs fire just like the living (Spencer 1876: 174-175; Kharuzin 1903: 258).

Some ethnographers tend to explain funerary banquets, often accompanied by military or other games, contests, etc., by the same religious motives. Thus, L. Ia. Shternberg (1936: 331 and 209) suggested that these banquets and games "had the fundamental aim of giving pleasure to the deceased, who continued to see and hear, and of expressing sympathy and devotion to him."

Finally, customs of funerary mourning — that is, the ceremonial manifestation of grief in the most diverse forms, from the most barbaric self-tortures during funerals down to the innocuous custom of wearing mourning dress — are explained by many on the basis of religious motives. In Kharuzin's view (1903: 201) all or almost all kinds of mourning "can be subsumed under the following main categories: the striving by those still living (1) to change their outward appearance in order not to be recognized by the deceased, and (2) to express to the deceased actual, or more often fictitious, regret at the parting which has come. In the first case, the dead is deprived of the opportunity to inflict harm on his fellow tribesmen; in the second, he will be pacified by the profound sorrow over his departure shown by members of his group or tribe." In other words, according to Kharuzin, the basis of all mourning customs is found in superstitious ideas about the dead.

This prevailing effort among most scientists to derive all funerary customs from purely superstitious — that is, religious — motives is engendered by an idealistic tendency familiar to us, the tendency to reduce everything to religion that can be so reduced and to stand the real facts on their heads. If, however, one looks without idealistic spectacles at the vast number of descriptions of funerary ceremonials among various peoples available to us, it is not difficult to see that they are basically not at all engen-

dered by superstitious ideas, but, rather, like the actual
burial procedures, by more profound, instinctive-emotional
impulses manifestly inherited from the epoch of man's
beginnings.

First of all, the breakdown of funerary customs into
the categories given above — funerary sacrifices, games,
mourning, etc. — is highly arbitrary and can be clearly
applied only at late stages of historical development, when
these customs actually lend themselves to delimitation and
are obviously permeated with religious motives. But this is
not the case for backward peoples: among them the various acts associated with death and with burial are still
highly undifferentiated. It proves very difficult to say,
upon reading descriptions of burial scenes in ethnographic
literature, what is mourning, what is a funerary gift or
sacrifice, what is a funeral feast, and what a war game. In
addition, those magico-religious ideas which, in the view of
many ethnographers, gave rise to funerary ceremonials
often recede into the background or are even wholly invisible, and the direct manifestation of emotions produced
by death of a member of the group, a fellow tribesman, or
a relative comes to the fore. However, even more commonly, this manifestation of emotions occurs not directly,
but in a plainly ritualized manner, strictly regulated by
custom. In obedience to custom, the executor of the
ceremonial performs the prescribed acts; but for the most
part it cannot be seen that he is inspired by any abstract
ideas, religious or otherwise.

I cite two examples out of a great many.

N. N. Miklukho-Maklai (1950-54: II, 348-352)
describes how, in the village of Bongu (Astrolabe Bay),
the wife of the Papuan Mote was buried: "Near the hut of
Mote I saw Mote himself: he was alternately strutting
about, squatting at each step, and next running, as if he
wanted to catch up with or attack someone; in his hands
he held a hatchet with which he hacked (only for show),
at the roof of the hut, the coconut palms, etc." In the
hut itself Maklai saw that the "deceased lay on a plank-
bed and pressing in around her were women wailing and
moaning." After an hour or two the bound corpse was
placed on a special chair. "Meanwhile, onto the platform

in front of the hut thronged natives arriving from Korendu and Kumbu, all armed, with warlike cries and gestures. And speeches were given, but so rapidly that it was hard for me to understand what was being said. Mote continued his pantomime of grief and despair, only now he was dressed in a new *mal'*, and on his head he had an enormous *katazan* (a crest with a feather fan . . .) . . . the hatchet was over his shoulder. He strutted, squatting as before — that is, this was a kind of dance which he performed in time with his whining speech and the howling of the women. That all this was a comedy which the people present deemed it necessary to perform was clear, and manifested itself at a time when Mote, in the midst of his monologues, . . . becoming excited, began to furiously hack at a coconut palm; then one of the women, apparently his sister, who was also wailing, suddenly interrupted her despairing howls, went up to Mote, and remarked to him in the most businesslike tone of voice that he must not harm the tree; after this, Mote, striking two more blows, but already less fiercely, went off and began to pour out his grief, breaking down an old and useless fence. Also, when it began to drizzle, Mote chose a place under a tree where the rain could not spoil his new *mal'* and the feathers on his head." Friends of the widower gave him presents as a sign of sympathy. The burial laments continued all day. On the following day, Maklai observed the continuation of the ceremonial. The corpse was placed in a wicker basket, a *gambor,* but here all the adornments previously put on it were removed, and none were placed in the *gambor.* During the weaving of the basket, the "women, not ceasing to wail, began to whirl about and dance in a circle"; "some scraped and rubbed the *gambor* with their hands, as if petting it, while they lamented in different tones of voice." On the next morning Maklai found all the village inhabitants with face, chest, and hands bedaubed with a special paint. On that day none of the natives went to work.

Several things strike us in this description (presented here in abridged form). First of all, the basic meaning of all the acts performed at the funeral — from the wailing and lamenting to the conspicuous destruction of property and from the dances to the bedaubing of the face or body — is the expression of grief, anguish, excitement, and various other emotions caused by death. Secondly, this is the expression of emotions that are by no means immediate, and may not even be entirely heartfelt, but are strictly prescribed by custom. Thirdly, all these actions are unified. The dances, warlike gestures, destruction of property, and the painting of the body for mourning — all serve to express emotions; a well-defined custom of funeral sacrifices, games, feasts, and mourning is not yet visible here. Fourthly, there is not the slightest hint of any religious or magical ideas associated with funerary ceremoniality; in all probability, these ideas were present among the Papuans described by Miklukho-Maklai, but it is equally probable that at the moment of performance of the ritual the ideas were the last thing thought of, and in any case did not give rise to the ritual itself; in particular, the notorious concern over the well-being of the soul of the deceased in the afterlife and the striving to provide him with all he needs — all this is completely lacking here. Finally, in the fifth place, it is highly important that the funerary ceremonials by no means involve only the closest relatives of the deceased, but that the community as a whole, and even other friendly communities, all participate in the ceremonials to some extent.

Here is another example: a description of the cremation of an influential chief of a California Indian tribe (the Senel) set forth by Powers (1877: 169-170) from the words of the eyewitness Willard. On the burial bonfire were placed, along with the body of the deceased, all his valuable possessions: feather cloaks, shell money, weapons, American gold coins, etc. "When the bonfire was lit with a torch, the graveside howling, singing, and dancing around the corpse began, and the people gradually brought themselves to a wild, ecstatic frenzy, almost to the point of demonic possession, leaping, wailing, torturing their bodies. Many, it would appear, lost all self-control. . . . Women, being even more frenzied, wildly threw into the fire all that they had, the most costly items of their adornment, their most resplendent dress, and strings of shining shells. Screaming, sobbing, tearing out their hair,

beating their breast, as if insane, some of them were
ready to throw themselves on the flaring heap of logs and
perish together with their chief, if friends had not re-
strained them. . . ."

For all the difference in certain details, the general
picture is almost the same as that given in the preceding
example. Here again we see the prevalence of pure affect,
not mediated by any clear, let alone abstract, ideas, but
nonetheless regulated and legitimized by custom. In the
furious show of emotions, there is a merger of crying,
ritual self-torture, graveside dances, and the merciless destruction of property; it is interesting, incidentally, to note
that here the property of both the deceased and his
fellow tribesmen was destroyed. In this example we can
see the rudiments of funerary sacrifices and gifts and —
most important — we can see the roots of this custom.
There is no trace here of those logical considerations
which, in the view of Tylor, Spencer, and their supporters,
gave rise to the custom of funerary sacrifices; people here
think and speculate least of all about the needs of the deceased in the afterlife: they act in a purely affective
manner.[8] It seems that precisely in this reckless, impulsive
striving to express grief by inflicting wounds on oneself,
by destroying valuable possessions, and by frenzied dancing, one can find the authentic roots of mourning and
funerary games as well as of sacrifices for the deceased.

In the later course of history, however, with the
general growth of culture, with the increasing complexity
of social relationships, and with the development of
social consciousness arising from both, these customs are
transformed, and each develops in its own special way. We
cannot trace in detail here the development, on the one
hand, of the custom of funerary sacrifices and, on the
other, of the lighting of fires on the grave and, further, of
funerary mourning, prohibitions, and funeral games. Each
of these customs requires separate investigation; we shall
here limit ourselves only to the most general observations
and remarks.

Sacrifices represent, as we know, an important part
of all religious practice in general, and especially of its
developed forms. Various theories on the origin of the

actual custom of sacrifices have been advanced. One of them, usually associated with the name of Herbert Spencer, consists in the attempt to reduce any and all sacrifices to gifts for the deceased, and ultimately to the feeding of the deceased (Spencer 1876: 277-281). The one-sidedness and erroneousness of this viewpoint would not be hard to demonstrate, for it is quite obvious that there are not a few kinds of sacrifices (for example, the sacrifice of the firstborn as a ceremonial for the removal of a taboo, the totemic banquet, the purification sacrifice, etc.), which do not have, and never have had, any relationship to the feeding of the deceased or to funerary rites in general. But we cannot deny that some kinds of sacrifices actually sprang from customs associated with the burial of the dead, and completely retain this connection.

Among Australian aborigines, only in a very small number of cases has the custom of placing something with the deceased in the grave been observed; the existing accounts refer only to some eastern and southeastern tribes (Howitt 1845: 450, 451, 453, 458, 461-462, 464, 468-469, and 474). We have direct contrary testimony on this matter for tribes of South and Central Australia.[9]

In Melanesia, too, few examples of the custom of placing any objects, food, etc. with the deceased have been noted. But the custom of destroying the property of the deceased is widespread (Moss 1925: 182-184). And even in those relatively few cases, where there is evidence of the practice of laying something in or on the grave, this practice is hardly connected in the consciousness of the natives with the belief that the dead needs food, weapons, etc. More likely it is associated with a vague feeling that things belonging to the dead person are his property and must not be touched (Moss 1925: 182-184). The latter idea is still more pronounced among the Polynesians, with their well-developed system of taboos embracing various aspects of life: the property of the deceased, especially of a chief, must be buried with him, for it is taboo for everyone else (Moss 1925: 184-185).

Of course, it is wholly possible that from this practice there may have sprung and developed the idea that the dead person is in need of precisely those articles which the living man needs: food and drink, clothing and weapons. And this idea is actually very widespread among peoples of well-nigh all parts of the world: America, Africa, Asia, and Europe. The numerous instances that are usually cited by investigators of the history of religion need not be mentioned here. This is one of the very common examples of how a practice, formed in remote antiquity and originally associated with the semi-instinctive actions of man, was later preserved, but underwent reinterpretation, and various ideas, including magico-religious ones, were accreted on it.

At first, not at all guided by any clear, even if superstitious ideas, people threw onto the corpse of the deceased or onto the funeral bonfire the articles belonging to him simply in a fit of passion caused by the death of a kinsman; later such actions, reinforced by custom, began to be performed by tradition, according to an obligatory ritual (which may exclude the display of sincere emotion); ultimately people began gradually to interpret their own actions in the spirit of developing religious ideas: the dead person needs his things, he is in need, just like the living, of food and drink, of weapons and utensils.

Such ideas doubtless already existed in the Bronze Age (if not earlier), when archeological sites revealed large differences in the inventory of "rich" and "poor" burials: the diverse valuable articles found in "rich" graves obviously were placed there specially for the deceased, to provide him with everything needed in the afterlife.

Where the funerary cult fused with the cult of the chiefs and kings, especially in the native states of Africa and Asia, the custom of sacrifices for the dead was developed in unrestrained and at times monstrously fanatical fashion. At funerals of African chieftains — in Dahomey, Benin, Ashanti, and other regions — into the grave of the deceased were thrown not only many articles, implements, decorations, stocks of food, etc., but animals and people were slain: slaves or condemned criminals were slain; the deceased's concubines and wives were slain. In several African states, human sacrifices at the funerals of chieftains took on massive proportions: to wit, several hundreds of people — chiefly the condemned, who had

purposely been held in prison for such an eventuality —
were slain and thrown into the graves of Benin chiefs
with the deceased.

Similar cruel customs are well known outside Africa
— from the ancient states of Central America and Mexico,
in the states of the classical East — Assyria, etc., and in
Homeric Greece; traces of such customs have been found
in Scythian and ancient Slavic mounds. In a famous description of the "burial of a noble Russ," Ibn-Fadlan tells
of the abundant sacrificial gifts that were burned on the
funeral bonfire, and included among these victims was one
of the favorite wives of the deceased.

In more modest and peaceful forms, the tradition of
sacrifices for the deceased has been preserved to our days
in the customs of very many highly cultured people. For
example, among all Slavic peoples even today there is a
custom of bringing to the graves of relatives on certain
days of the year all kinds of food, eating some of it, and
leaving some at the tomb (the "parental Sabbath"
among the Russians, *"zadushnitsa"* among the southern
Slavs, etc.).

Thus, both comparison of the facts and purely theoretical considerations lead to the conclusion that the
custom of funeral gifts and sacrifices was engendered not
at all by superstitious motives, and not be belief in the
afterlife existence of the soul. Initially it was associated
with the display of passion and was expressed in the heed-
less destruction of the deceased's property. Only subsequently did this destruction of property, already hallowed
by tradition, begin to be thought of as a sacrifice to the
dead, as a method of providing him with necessary food
and articles. But this idea, once it had arisen and developed, subsequently influenced, especially in relation to the
cult of leaders, the development and formation of the
custom of funerary sacrifices.

It appears to me therefore that I. I. Skvortsov-
Stepanov was very close to the truth when, in arguing
with M. N. Pokrovskii, he wrote the following on the
relationship between funerary customs, ceremonials, and
beliefs:

"'In the beginning was the deed.' First there were,

for instance, funerary customs (in the sense of mere funerary practice), then they became consolidated into funerary ceremonials (this is the cult), and then on this soil sprang up the 'kingdom of the dead,' 'the afterlife' (this is already, if you please, 'dogma'). Or yet another example: the deceased was left with certain supplies: this is the starting point for the development of sacrifices (the cult); as time passed, a vocation took form, one of whose functions became the presenting of sacrifices (a religious organization — the 'church'), and then the practice of sacrifices was interpreted in a 'dogma'" (Skvortsov-Stepanov 1959: 387). [10]

Still more obvious is the similar conclusion on funerary revelries and games; in origin they are not at all associated, as some suppose, with any superstitious ideas. It is clear from the concrete facts above that here, too, we are dealing initially with a purely affective display of accumulated emotions, with a particular way of venting them. This venting was manifested in frenzied dancing, in screams, in the flourishing of weapons, sometimes also in mock skirmishes; here the participants are divided into two parties (by phratries or otherwise — this does not concern us here). Later the forms of the "venting" of accumulated emotions were also consolidated by tradition and became obligatory. The development proceeds along different paths, depending on the concrete conditions, and various ideas of more or less superstitious content became attached to the traditional customs.

It can be supposed that feasting in the true sense was added to the funerary rituals later: no mention is made of them in descriptions of funerals among backward peoples. Possibly, the custom of funeral feasting developed together with the tradition of offering sacrifices for the deceased; initially the property of the deceased, including victuals, was simply destroyed, but then, apparently the idea gradually arose that these victuals were eaten by the deceased himself; however, the greater part began to be eaten by his relatives, the participants in the funerary ritual.

Graveside games similar to war competitions were known among the Greeks as early as the Homeric period, and also among the ancient Romans; among the latter, the games were later transferred to the circus, changing into the bloody "games" of the gladiators.

Among some peoples, graveside revelries and games were instituted together for a very long time. Such were, for example, the ancient Slav *strava* and *trizna;* by both concepts most researchers simultaneously denote the funerary revelries and the war games — competitions in the presence of the deceased. Later, the second element of the ritual faded out among many peoples; for example, of all the Slavic peoples, funerary games are now preserved, it appears, only among the western Ukrainians.

Funeral feasting, however ("funeral banquets" *[pominki]*, etc.), is now preserved among almost all peoples. Among some, it is intimately associated with the idea of feeding the dead. Thus, among the Ossetes the funerary *khist* — an extravagant banquet, for which the host sometimes had to slaughter all his cattle and go into debt — is viewed at the same time as a necessary feeding of the deceased. Among the Chuvashi, Mari, Udmurts, and Mordvins, deceased persons were invited to the banquet table, their entrance being staged: one of the dead person's relatives put on his clothes and played his role. The Belorussian custom of *"dzyadov"* is also a funeral banquet in which, according to popular belief, the deceased themselves participate.

Finally, the custom of mourning — initially only an immediate display of emotions, at times in the coarsest and most barbaric form: tearing out of hair, slashing of the skin, self-mutilation, etc. — was later introduced in more regulated and composed forms. To the traditional customs were again added superstitious ideas to the effect that the expression of grief is agreeable to the deceased and appeases him, that the mourning abstention from certain kinds of food has the purpose of making this food reach the deceased in the other world, etc.

But it must be said that mourning customs evidently contain a much smaller admixture of superstitious motives than do other forms of funerary ritual. The wearing of mourning dress, compliance with certain prohibitions, and abstention from certain kinds of food, from participation in social life, amusements, etc. — all these signs of mourning still retain their original meaning as immediate expressions of grief, of despair. Religious ideas are often associated with them only artificially — perhaps only in the mind of the idealist researcher ready to see religion in everything.

Therefore, one can scarcely agree with Shternberg (1936: 206-207) that "contemporary customs, such as the placement of monuments, mourning music in burial corteges, and funeral banquets . . . represent the survival of the corresponding primitive customs of the savage and the barbarian" and that all these customs were engendered by belief in the afterlife of the soul. It is true that their inception dates back to the period of "savagery," but they are by no means based in religious ideas and can in no way be regarded as "survivals" — that is, as vestiges. If one throws away one's idealist spectacles, it becomes clear to anyone that the funeral-mourning customs referred to by Shternberg, to which we also adhere, derive not from gross superstition, but from simple respect for the memory of the deceased.

Superstitious Ideas Associated with the Funerary Cult: Belief in the "Living Corpse"

In the preceding account, we were predominantly concerned with customs and ceremonials associated with the deceased and their burial, and not with the attendant popular beliefs. As we have seen, these customs and ceremonials were not initially formed under the influence of any abstract — even less, superstitious — ideas, though such ideas did, in the later course of development, influence the change and complication of customs and ceremonials.

Let us now attempt to analyze the question of the origin of those magico-religious ideas — those beliefs which are associated, among various peoples, with the deceased and with burial customs, and which constitute, so to speak, the conceptual content of funerary rites and customs.

To introduce any clear system into these ideas is of

course even more difficult than to classify the ceremonials and customs themselves. But in a grossly approximate way we can attempt to analyze all magico-religious beliefs associated with the deceased and with funerary ritual into several main groups: (1) the attribution of supernatural properties to the corpse itself — belief in the "living corpse"; (2) belief in the soul of the deceased and the idea of its fate after death; (3) the image of a spirit or a deity — a patron of the dead, the ruler of the next world.

We will first try to delve into the origin and further development of the idea of the "living corpse." This idea is essentially nothing but a personification of the vague sense of dread that gave rise to superstitious ideas of the deceased. It is precisely this dread and these superstitious ideas that caused people to resort to such, so to speak, force majeur means of rendering the deceased harmless, as binding him, breaking his bones, etc. But whence came this dread itself?

Various explanations have been advanced. According to the classical Spencer-Tylor theory, the root of dread in the presence of the deceased consists in the belief in the soul, which, supposedly, abandoning the body after the person's death, can harm those remaining alive. But this explanation, besides its idealist nature (of which enough has been said above), is unsuccessful if for no other reason than that the above-cited ways of rendering the deceased harmless pertained chiefly to the body of the dead person, and not at all to the spirit separated from the body. Another explanation, supported, for example, by M. N. Pokrovskii, is that dread in the presence of the dead is a general-biological instinct. But this explanation, as was shown, is still less successful, for neither biological nor ethnographic data confirm the universality of this proposed "instinct." [11]

Finally, a third explanation has been put forth: superstitious fear in the presence of the deceased is a reflection of elementary dread of contamination. "The cause of fear of the corpse," writes Iu. I. Semenov (1962: 438), "is a genuine danger emanating from the putrefying, decomposing corpse." This view unquestionably is more rational: spontaneous efforts to escape the danger of contagion probably had an effect. But this explanation falls short: if fear of the actual danger of contamination were the whole story, we would not see such a diversity of ways of dealing with the body of the dead in the customs of various peoples, including also methods where the fear of contamination is the last thing we should look for: endocannibalism, the smearing of one's body with cadaver fluid, the carrying of the corpse, etc. The question obviously calls for special examination.

Dread in the presence of the dead is not an inborn emotion of man, so it must have developed historically. What gave rise to this dread? Two conditions, it appears to me.

First of all, the very custom of burial of the dead, of whose origin we have spoken above, as well as the custom of leaving the dead to the whims of fate, must have produced a certain psychological inclination. Emotions, like ideas, are produced by tradition. The custom of interring the deceased in the earth could not help, with the passage of time, but give birth to feelings (in the beginning, precisely feelings and not ideas) that close proximity with the corpse was dangerous. Various echoes of this dim emotion show up in the burial rituals of almost all peoples: among some it is the fear that the corpse will come back from the grave which makes itself felt; among others, the feeling that the corpse was impure, the fear of defiling oneself by contact with it; and among still others, the belief in an evil demon into which the deceased is transformed. All these are merely various forms of the manifestation of that unaccountable feeling of alienation of the dead person from the living, which to a certain extent was produced by the tradition of disposing of the dead whether by interment in the earth, by expulsion, or otherwise.

But this is only one aspect of the issue, which in itself probably could not have led to those extreme forms of fear of the dead, and to those exaggerated measures of rendering him innocuous, of which we have learned. Still another and more important condition was active here.

Researchers of Australia and other countries have

noted more than once that funeral ceremonials differ widely in nature and complexity, depending on just who is being buried. The higher the deceased's standing in the community, the more complex the ceremonies usually were. Children, adolescents, and sometimes even women and little-known persons, were buried without special ceremonies. On the contrary, burial of chiefs, influential elders, and valiant warriors was conducted with especially involved ceremonials. What interests us most here is the fact that ceremonials for rendering the deceased harmless, ceremonials in which fear of the dead is manifested, occurred for the most part precisely in the burial of such influential persons. "The closer the relative and the more influential in life," Curr (1886:87) wrote in his summary work on Australian aborigines, "the greater the fear generated by the deceased." "Since women and children are deemed to be vastly lower in status than men in life," he continues, "and since their spirits also are little feared after death, they are buried without special ceremonies" (Curr 1886: 89). The same thing has been noted by other observers (Howitt 1904: 451-452, 455-459, 464-465, 471; Parker 1925: 89; Basedow 1925: 203-204).

What does this mean? This means that dread in the presence of the dead is a socially conditioned phenomenon. The dead is not feared because he is dead, but above all because he was feared in life. Posthumous honor goes to a person who even when living occupied an influential position.[12]

Fear of the dead is not a biological "dread of death," but to a certain extent a reflection of incipient social stratification. This to a large degree explains the ceremonials directed toward rendering the corpse innocuous: binding, breaking of limbs, etc.

Similar phenomena have often been noted among many peoples at higher stages of historical development. Although, in most cases, more or less spiritualized ideas of the dead are already formed, and superstitious fear of the corpse itself had yielded to the equally superstitious fear of the spirit of the deceased — which will be discussed later — in many cases more archaic ideas about the deceased were preserved: the attribution of supernatural qualities to the corpse itself. And it is often found that these ideas are associated, once again, not with all dead persons, but only with those who were feared even in life, or those whose manner of death has placed them in a special situation: these included various kinds of sorcerers, or suicides, and persons suffering violent death.

As an example, we can cite the East Slavic beliefs excellently studied by D. K. Zelenin (1916), who convincingly demonstrated that two categories of the deceased were sharply distinguished in the folk mind: the dead by, so to speak, normal or natural death (among the people these are called "parents"), and the dead by premature or violent death — the slain, suicides, victims of drowning or alcoholic poisoning, children who die unbaptized, and also dead sorcerers and sorceresses. This second category of the deceased, called by different names — *"mertviaki,"* *"zalozhnye,"* etc. — are an object of superstitious dread among the folk. Terrible tales are told about how they leave their graves by night, how they can harm the living, produce natural disasters such as drought, etc. In order to avoid these dangers, the corpse of such a dead one was not buried in the common burial ground; efforts were sometimes made to render it harmless; it was pierced through with an aspen stake, drenched with water, thrown into the swamp, etc. Such actions were always directed at the corpse itself, and it is precisely with the corpse, and not with the soul of the deceased, that superstitious ideas and superstitious fears are associated. Similar beliefs are known also among the southern and western Slavs.

Thus, the idea of the "living corpse" was by no means a product of the purely rational activity of primeval man. The idea has considerably more emotional than rational features. This was an indeterminate complex of emotion of dread, unreasoning repugnance, mixed with respect and attachment.

Centuries and millennia of historical development, and new conditions pushing the thought of man ever ahead, were still required for the further growth of this idea of the "living corpse." The idea of the "living corpse" proved to be one of the most vital magico-religious ideas preserved in the beliefs of the most diverse peoples. The popular beliefs of European peoples about vampires, *upyri* [Russian for vampires], ghosts, and apparitions essentially differ but little from similar religious ideas among the Botokudo or the Australian aborigines.

Remote echoes of belief in the living or revivified corpse can be found even in such complex religions as Christianity and Islam. Christian ideas of the afterlife, as we known, are double-faced and contradictory; on the one hand, they supposedly center on the doctrine of the soul of man and its existence after, and on concern for its "salvation." On the other hand, one of the important dogmas of orthodox Christianity is belief in the "resurrection of the dead," which is taken to mean literally the reviving of the dead who are in graves, though they have long since putrefied; the bodies of these resurrected will become, according to the church concept, "incorruptible," and the bodies themselves will go — some into paradise and others into hell.

The Concept of the Spirit of the Dead

The question of the origin of another mythological-religious idea associated with the funerary cult — the concept of the soul or spirit of the deceased — is more complex.

The Tylor-Spencer school, as we know, regarded the idea of the spirit of the dead as a logical development from the elementary idea of the human soul. This view continues to prevail in the literature up to now. It is, however, based not on facts, but only on a priori deductive reasoning.

True, among many peoples the idea that the human soul after death leaves the body and is transformed into a spirit or into a demon does actually exist. But this idea in itself by no means shows that belief in the spirit of the deceased arose from belief in the soul. On the contrary, this idea of the transformation of the soul into a spirit is only an attempt to link the two ideas together. By origin, in fact, they are completely heterogeneous. [13] This heterogeneity is immediately obvious in some cases, and in others it is confirmed by the difference in the names for the soul and the spirit of the deceased.

Among the Aranda Australian aborigines, the soul of a living man is called *kuruna (guruna)*, but the soul or the spirit of the deceased is called *ltana (ultana)* (Spencer and Gillen 1927: 423; Strehlow 1907: 15-16). This same difference in names exists among the tribes of the Loritja (Strehlow 1907: 6-7), the Kurnai (Howitt 1904: 436-438), the Mara (B. Spencer 1914: 248-249, 254), and among several other tribes.

Among most Melanesian tribes the idea of the spirit of the deceased is not associated with belief in the soul of man, except for a feeble attempt to connect these concepts through the idea of the transformation of one into the other. On the island of Florida the human soul is called *tarunga* (hogs also have a *tarunga*), and the spirit of a deceased person is called *tindalo;* the same difference prevails on the islands of Isabel and San Cristobal.

On the Banks Islands the soul is designated by the words *talegi* and *atai,* and the spirit of the deceased by *tamate* and *natmat.* On the island of Motu the idea is held that the *atai*, soul, upon death is transformed into the *tamate*, spirit; but on the other hand, the aborigines of this island attempt to connect these two ideas in another way: in their words, the spirits of the deceased in the underworld have their *atai* (souls), like those of living persons (Codrington 1891: 248-250, 254, 256-257, 266, 276). The Papuans of Marind-Anim designate by the word *vikh* the soul of the living person, and by the words *gova* and *khais* — the spirits of the deceased (Wirz 1925: I, 2 - 2-4, and II, 3-120). A very curious belief is held in the region of Massim: the aborigines believe that the soul upon death is not transformed into a spirit but, on the contrary, perishes soon after the death of the person, while his spirit flies off into the afterworld, located on a far-off island (Malinowski 1922: 42).

In Africa, among most peoples a clear distinction has been observed between two ideas: the idea of the soul of the living person and the spirit of the deceased person. The first disappears at the moment of death, the second appears precisely at this moment. This difference was noted, for example, by Ankerman, one of the best experts on African ethnography (Ebert 1924-25: 404).

Among many examples we can cite the following: among the Kikuyu, an Eastern African people investigated by the missionary MacGregor and the Routledges, the belief is held that the spirit of the deceased, *ngoma*, appears just at the moment a person dies, but that during his lifetime the *ngoma* does not exist (the soul of a living person is called *ngoro)* (Routledge and Routledge 1910: 240).

Rattray (1927: 152-155), a student of the religion of the West African Ashanti, had noted that among this people the idea of the soul — *okra (kra)* or *sunsum* — is wholly unassociated with the idea of the spirit, apparition — *saman* (plural — spirits of ancestors: *samanfo).* Among the Kaonde tribe (Central Africa) the soul of a living person is called *chimvule* (researchers relate it to the "shadow"), but the spirit of a deceased person is called *mukishi* (plural *vakishi)* (Melland 1923: 132-133).

According to the religious ideas of the Crow Indians (typical of the beliefs of many North American tribes), the spirit of the deceased person is not at all the soul which remains after his death (Lowie 1924: 23).

In ancient Roman religion, the soul — the double of the living person — is called the *genius.* The genius of a person perishes at the moment of his death. But the spirits of the deceased were called *"manes."*

One of the essential differences than can be observed almost everywhere between the ideas of soul and spirit is that the soul (of a living person) is usually a weak, passive, fearful creature, while the spirit is a strong, vigorous, and aggressive one. This characteristic difference is in fact very noticeable in Melanesia. It was underscored by V. G. Bogoraz in speaking of the beliefs of the Chukchi; according to these beliefs, the soul "is small, fragile, helpless, and subject to danger from antagonistic spirits. . . . The dead, in contrast, are depicted as invisible spirits, great and powerful, vastly stronger than man" (Bogoraz 1939: 3).

Even if it is assumed that the idea of the spirit developed from belief in the soul, as traditional theory asserts, this assumption in no way helps us to understand this characteristic difference between these two ideas. How can the powerful and menacing spirit be derived from the powerless and passive soul? This transformation cannot be explained from the traditional standpoint of the logical development of ideas.

In reality, the idea of the spirit of the deceased is connected by origin not with belief in the soul of a living person, but with the complex of ceremonials constituting the funerary ritual; in the most general form, it can be said that the development and complexity of funerary ceremonial (especially in those of its forms in which rapid destruction of the corpse is achieved — cremation, for example) led to the gradual distillation and spiritualization of the concept of the deceased, which initially was quite material. [14]

Of course, it would be erroneous to see in the forms of funerary ceremonial the sole, or even the principal, factor responsible for the process of spiritualization of the concept of the dead. This process, one of the most interesting in the history of religion, took place under the influence of a whole series of conditions. But one of these conditions may have been funerary practice. Vastly more important here, however, is the fact that the image of the spirit of the deceased has in the course of historical development been contaminated with animistic images of a different origin.

We must dwell on this aspect of somewhat greater detail. As we know, the question of historical (genetic, conceptual) associations between belief in spirits of the dead and belief in spirits of nature has often been posed in the scientific literature, and it has been resolved in different ways. The old mythological (naturistic) school was little interested in images of spirits of the dead (and the funerary cult associated with them) and was inclined to view them as the personification of those same elemental forces of nature (Afanas'ev 1865-1869: I, 578, II, 74, II, 563, etc.). In contrast, adherents of the animistic theory saw in the concept of the soul of the deceased precisely the primeval religious idea, and were convinced that all supernatural creatures in general — spirits, demons, genii, the deity — arose essentially from those same souls of the deceased.

Some authors attempted to reconcile these contradictory views. Thus, according to the view of Vladimir Solov'ev, primitive man in general did not clearly distinguish the soul of the deceased from the elemental spirit, and for him all religious ideas merged into the idea of "dim pandemonism": the deceased and the spirit of the wind, of the thunderstorm, etc. — all this was one and the same (Solov'ev n.d.: 163-166, 213).

Solov'ev was correct in stressing the one-sidedness of both the then-disputant sides in the study of primitive religion — the naturistic and the animistic. But he was scarcely right in attempting to derive all primitive religious concepts from an undifferentiated "dim pandemonism." Deeper investigation of the concrete data shows, on the contrary, that the different categories of spirits — spirits personifying diseases, shamanistic spirits, the spirits of the forces of nature, spirits of the dead, etc. — have in each case their own roots, their origin, associated with a definite kind of human activity. But we cannot deny — and in confirmation of this we can cite a multitude of facts — that the obscure images of religious fantasy continually reveal a tendency to diffuse and merge together. Therefore, it is by no means always possible to draw a clear boundary between animist images of different origins, between the spirits of the dead, the spirits of nature, the spirits of diseases, etc.

The Yuin tribe in southeastern Australia believed in spirits, which were called *tulugal*, literally meaning "grave" [adjectival form] (from *tulu* — grave, and *gal* — adjectival suffix). The *tulugal*, as can be seen even from the name, is associated above all with the deceased; it was believed to respond to the voice of the sorcerer during the funerary ceremonial; but this same word also denoted in general spirits living in the woods, in the mountains; they were feared since it was believed that they ate children (A. Howitt 1904: 462-463). According to the report of Eylmann (1908: 190), among tribes of Central Australia in general there is no clear distinction drawn among spirits of the dead and the various evil creatures, the spirit-demons. However, according to information presented by Spencer and Gillan, the Aranda quite clearly differentiate categories of spirits: *ultana* — spirits of the dead; *uruntarinia* — spirits associated with totemic "ancestors" and at the same time benefactors of the sorcerers; *oruncha* — evil spirits (Spencer and Gillen 1899: 512-517, 523-526).

In Melanesian beliefs, according to the observations of Codrington (1891: 121), a clear distinction is drawn between spirits of the dead and other spirits, which never were people; they in fact are called by different names. And in Northern Melanesia, where more features of the archaic social order — the matriarchate, etc. — have been preserved, the spirits of the dead have greater significance in religious worship; but in Southern Melanesia — spirits not associated with the dead (Codrington 1891: 122). The latter is called into question, however, by F. Speiser (1932: 322), according to whose information, in Southern Melanesia as well, the spirits of the dead ranked first as an object of worship. Based on his same data, by the way, there was in practice no clear-cut distinction between the two categories of spirits.

In many beliefs of backward peoples we can note that ideas about the dead merge with images of evil spirits, which by their origin are associated with belief in black magic. Thus, for example, among the Kurnai the spirits of dead kinsmen were held to be friendly, but the spirits of deceased enemies were held to be evil (Fison and Howitt 1880: 246). Among the tribes of the Tyolli River (Queensland), the belief was held that if one saw a spirit of a dead enemy *(picharu)*, one might die (Roth 1903: 17). It is quite clear that such beliefs represent a contamination of various motives: on the one hand, ideas of the dead and, on the other, the personification of the dim fear of a hostile tribe, the fear which constitutes the psychological basis of belief in black magic. The interweaving of these different motives favored the spiritualization of the concept of the dead.

Very instructive in this regard is the following fact, noted by Paul Wirz (1924: 53-54, 59, 77) among the Papuans of the Mamberamo River region. These Papuans have the idea of the *kugi*. This idea is fairly complicated.

The word *kugi* denotes, above all, the body of the deceased, and after its cremation — the special remaining force or substance. Papuans do not believe that *kugi* is the soul of man: the soul is not preserved after death, while *kugi* begins to exist only after death and the cremation of the corpse. These *kugi* live in mountains and rivers, fly about in the form of flying dogs, and bring disease to people. According to the words of Wirz, the term *kugi* in general is taken by aborigines to designate evil and crafty forces, about whose origin they do not inquire.

From this example we can clearly see one of the psychological routes along which the ideas of the spirits of the dead have developed. At the basis of this example lies only the personification of the vague feeling of dread. The closest object of this feeling is the deceased, the attitude to which is interwoven from dual motives of fear and attachment. Annihilation of the corpse, especially rapidly and radically in such forms of burial as cremation, emancipates the concept of it from connections with material remains and facilitates its spiritualization.

The image of the nonmaterial spirit emerging in this way becomes the center of crystallization for all kinds of unreasoning feelings of dread and uncertainty, which flood the savage, powerless both before nature and before the secret onslaughts of enemies. The image of the spirit of the dead associated with the funerary ritual is here only the core, around which are accreted ideas and emotions of a quite different origin. This example is highly typical.

The development of ideas of the spirits of the dead is very strongly influenced by motives of a social kind. We have already said that both funerary practice and the attitude to the dead are determined to a very large extent by the social standing of the deceased in his lifetime — that is, that both factors reflect the element of social differentiation. This is still better seen in the development of animistic ideas associated with the deceased. Beliefs of the Melanesians are especially typical in this respect.

Codrington, who studied these beliefs most profoundly, emphasizes that on all the Solomon Islands a sharp

distinction is drawn between two classes of the spirits of
the dead; one class consists of the spirits of those persons
who during their life were noted for their valor, influence,
and material successes; the spirits of these persons are the
object of fear and veneration on the part of those remaining alive; the second, more numerous class consists of
spirits of rank-and-file community members, in no way
distinguished during their lifetime; the spirits of these
persons "are a nonentity upon death, as they were in life,"
they "do not receive worship and soon begin to be
thought of simply as a crowd of the nameless population
of the netherworld" (Codrington 1891: 253-254). On the
island of Malaita even the names of these two categories
of spirits are different: the spirits of the chiefs, valiant
warriors, and the wealthy are called *lio-a;* to them, special
magical force *saka* is ascribed and veneration is given; the
souls of simple folk, however, remain after death what
they were in life — *akalo* (soul) — and enjoy no honor
whatever; they are soon transformed into nests of white
ants and serve as food for the strong spirits, *lio-a.* On the
island of San Cristobal the spirits of eminent people serve
as an object of fear, veneration, and propitiation; the
spirits of simple folk, however, live passive and colorless
lives; they not only do not inspire the living with fear, but
they themselves fear the living and disappear when a
person approaches (Codrington 1891: 257, 258, 260).

   With further growth of social differentiation to the
middle and higher degrees of barbarity, this difference of
concepts on the spirits of people of different social categories becomes stronger still. This is especially sharply
seen among Polynesians. According to old beliefs among
Tongans, for example, only the souls of the higher
estates — *egi, matabule,* and *mua* — live after death and
occupy in the pantheon of the gods and spirits ranks com-
mensurate with their earthly standing; the souls of the
simple folk, however — *tua* — perish upon death (Martin
1818: 103-104, 109-110, 128-129). Tahitians believe that
only the souls of priests and members of the *areoi* secret
society continue to live after death, and the souls of the
rest of the people are eaten up by the gods (Moss 1925:
118, etc.). On other islands of Polynesia the belief is held

that acceptance of the soul of the deceased into the after-life depends on the wealth and fame of the person in his lifetime (Moss 1925: 118 ff.).

Also in Oceania, in particular among Melanesians, one can observe the contamination of the images of spirits of the deceased with animistic images engendered by the system of male secret societies. Such an association, of course, lends greater social and ideological import to the belief in the spirits of the dead.

Among peoples where shamanism is strongly developed, images of spirits of the deceased have often been contaminated with shamanistic spirits and with the spirits of diseases, the images of which have their own special roots. Thus, in the ancient beliefs of the peoples of Siberia, although shamanistic spirits were in most cases clearly differentiated, still at times they were identified with the spirits of the dead — not, indeed, all of the dead, but only of deceased shamans. Such beliefs are noted among the Altais, Tuvans, Buryats, Yakuts, and Yukagirs.

A special and complicated problem is presented by the genetic relationship of the image of the spirit of the dead with the image of the venerated ancestor. Adherents of the traditional animistic theory, though they sometimes distinguish the cult of the dead from the cult of ancestors, are nevertheless inclined to derive the latter from the former by way of a unilinear and purely immanent evolution. Actually, the relationship of these two categories of supernatural beings — the spirit of the dead and the venerated ancestor — is vastly more complex. I will attempt to show later (cf. Chapter 9) that the idea of the spirit of the dead actually is one of the important conceptual components of the image of the venerated ancestor, but only one of them, for the image of the venerated ancestor is vastly more complex.

So, while the origin of animistic ideas associated with the dead is rooted in funerary ritual, various conditions influence their further development. Of these conditions, only a few have been referred to above. The practice of sorcery brings the idea of the spirits of the dead closer to the belief in evil spirits. Social differentiation, and the cult of chiefs and eminent persons growing out of it, make the image of the spirit of the dead an object of veneration. In the later course of history, several other conditions also influenced the evolution of these ideas: the system of secret societies, shamanism with its innumerable multitude of spirits, and especially the cult of ancestors, which took shape on the basis of the breakdown of the tribal order.

Superstitious Concepts Associated With Funerary Rituals: The Idea of the Afterlife

Within the framework of this general essay, it is not possible to examine in detail a very important facet of funerary rites and customs: the development of the ideas about the afterlife. This question has been given much attention by many writers, though for the most part only as it pertains to individual peoples and epochs, to individual religions. There is no doubt that ideas about what happens to the soul of the deceased began to take shape incomparably later than given traditions of funerary ceremonials; when they did appear, these ideas were initially extremely vague.

Evidently, no definite views as to where the souls of the dead dwell and what happens to them are found among those same Australian tribes. The available information on this point is confused and contradictory. Evidently, the idea prevails that the souls of the dead dwell somewhere near the place of burial and can appear to the living, in sleep or during waking; they can be heard or even seen. As a rule, no special world of souls or "afterworld" exists. Such conceptions are obviously very typical of the most primitive peoples in general.

Another idea concerning the souls of the dead, found among some backward tribes, is more characteristic of civilized peoples: this is the idea of reincarnation — i.e., the belief that the soul of the dead person is embodied anew in an animal, in a plant, or, what is more interesting, in a human body.

This belief, in addition to other ideas about the dead, was noted in those same Australian aborigines; among thém the belief was prevalent that the soul of the deceased could be reborn, being embodied in a person with light skin. It was repeatedly noted in this regard that the aborigines of Australia regarded the white colonists as their fellow tribesmen, returned from the beyond. But a doubt comes to mind: did such an idea actually exist before the whites came? And even if it did exist, perhaps it was associated with the extremely rare fact of the birth of albino individuals, and was not a widespread belief. There is reason to believe that it was precisely the arrival of the white colonists that gave the impetus to the new superstitious idea; this is not surprising, for the sight of human beings of a kind so unusual to the aborigines may quite possibly have provoked in them an attempt to relate this fact with the previously existing vague ideas of the fate of the dead. It seems that the first white man to be taken for a resurrected deceased person was William Bakely, a runaway exile, who lived for many years among the aborigines: the latter had found in him some similarity to one of their recently deceased fellow-tribesmen, and decided that Bakely was this person; then this idea was extended also to other whites. [15]

There is a report that central Australian tribes (especially the Aranda) believe in totemic reincarnation: the "totemic embryo" entering in the body of a woman produces pregnancy and the birth of a child, and when this infant grows up and later dies, his soul returns to the initial place as this very same "totemic embryo," in order to be embodied anew by the very same method. Spencer and Gillen (1899: 124-127) have reported this idea of "perpetual rebirth." But this report is debatable: the missionary Strehlow (1907: I, 56; Vatter 1925: 83-84, 130-132), who studied the Aranda beliefs more deeply, denied the existence of such a belief.

The belief that the dead are transformed into animals (less often, into plants) is fairly widespread among backward peoples. It is indisputably associated with totemism and is even a key element in totemism. This has often been written about. This belief has been noted in Australia among the Milya-Uppa tribe; in America among the Bororo, the Hopi, and the Zuni (Curr 1886: 179; Tylor

1939: 304-3-5; Frazer 1910: 34-35; in Oceania it is
known on the island of Lifu (Frazer 1910: 80-81); in
Africa among the Pygmies of the Ituri River
(Schebesta 1941-50: 442-443).

The belief that the soul of a dead person is born
again in human form, usually embodied in an infant form
in the same family, or tribe, is also quite prevalent. This
has been noted among the Eskimos, the Algonkian
tribes, the Takulli, and the Nootka (they have an idea of
the embodiment of the soul of a dead person in a member of an alien tribe), etc. In Africa it is known in Old
Kalabar, among the Yoruba, etc. (Tylor 1939: 302-304).

Among several peoples an unusual version of the idea
of reincarnation has been noted: the dead person's soul
settles in a newborn infant, but only temporarily, until
the infant's own soul has grown strong; then it leaves the
infant. This idea is held by the Aranda (Strehlow 1907: I,
15-16) and by the Eskimos (Stefansson 1925: 244-247).

The idea of the "transmigration of souls" (metem-
psychosis) became, as we know, part of several complex
religio-philosophical systems, especially in India, where it
was one of the main dogmas of Brahmanic Hinduism and
underlay Buddhist teachings; here this idea was colored by
a pronounced moral ideology: the doctrine of ethical responsibility for one's acts *(karma)*, according to which one
incurred a worse or better rebirth — a doctrine born of
the caste system. This same idea was assimilated in the
classical world by the Pythagoreans, and later by the
Manicheans, and has been preserved in several Islamic
sects, especially among the Ismaili.

The third and most widespread idea on the fate of
the souls of deceased persons is the belief in a separate
world of souls ("the next world") to which they will
be sent after the person's corporeal death.
This belief is found among almost all peoples of the
world, though with large differences. It is very difficult to
systematize the diverse ideas on this subject in the beliefs
of various peoples — all the more so since the ideas of
each individual people on the other world of souls are
usually far from clear. This question can be the subject of
a special large study, and here we must limit ourselves to

the most general observations.

Concepts regarding the location of the world of souls are most varied. Among the most backward peoples, ideas about this subject are extremely vague: the world of souls is somewhere far away, and sometimes a specific direction is given — northward (Aranda) (Strehlow 1907: 15-16), westward (Narrinyeri) (Curr 1886: 249), eastward (Marind-anim) (Wirz 1925: 24). There is reason to believe that this direction is not given randomly: it evidently corresponds to the direction whence in the past came the settlement of the tribe or some cultural influence.

Among maritime peoples and islanders, particularly in Oceania, the idea of an afterworld located somewhere beyond the sea, on an island, is widespread. Among the peoples of Oceania and eastern Indonesia, we can observe variations on the idea of an island world of souls; among some this is one of the neighboring islands, among others — a mythical island somewhere far to the west (Moss 1925: 4-14). The roots of these ideas are easily visible; they are twofold. On the one hand, they undoubtedly reflect past ocean voyages, which left in the mind of the people a vague memory of the land of their ancestors, lying beyond the sea (and furthermore, to the west — the direction whence came the main stream of resettlement); and since the islanders of Oceania do not know any other form of land except the island, this land of their ancestors is depicted by them as an island; there is where the souls of the dead go. This is unquestionably the case with Polynesian beliefs. On the other hand, the influence of the practice of water burial, particularly in its more complex form — the sending of the corpse in a boat onto the open sea — may be at work here: the dead person is supposedly being directed to the world of souls beyond the ocean. Such, perhaps, is the origin of this belief in Melanesia, where memories of voyages are not preserved, and where the island of the souls is not a mythical far-off island, but one of the nearby islets. [16]

Also in Oceania, a belief about an underwater world of souls, similar to the foregoing, is known: it has been noted on New Caledonia, on the Bismarck Archipelago (the souls of the dead are in a submarine river), on the

Marquesan Islands, on Samoa, etc. (Glaumont 1888: 119; Parkinson 1907: 692-697, 706-707; Moss 1925: 37, 41, 212, 227, 228). Most probably this idea originated directly from the practice of water burial; but the facts do not show any precise correspondence between the two, which, by the way, is not surprising in view of the complex ethnic and cultural history of the population of Oceania.

The notion of a subterranean world of souls is very widely current among peoples of all countries. The assumption of several authors that this idea was influenced by the custom of interring the deceased in the earth, or burying them in caves, is quite plausible. [17] But there were other roots of this belief. In particular, its connection with volcanic activity is indicated: where active volcanoes are located, we often find the belief that the souls of the dead descend into the netherworld through the volcano's crater. This is the situation, for example, in Southern Melanesia (Codrington 1891: 286; Rivers 1914: 261, 263; Moss 1925: 42).

Finally, many peoples locate the world of souls in heaven. This idea is found also among several Australian tribes — in Kurnai, the Wakelburra (A. Howitt 1904: 463) — and in places among peoples of Oceania (Moss 1925: 78-84). Sometimes the abode of the souls of the dead is located more precisely: the stars, the Milky Way, and the sun. The association of the dead with the stars has been noted in the beliefs of the most diverse peoples, from these same Australian aborigines (Palmer 1844: 294) to the peoples of Europe. The association with the sun is a notion that some researchers have attempted to restrict to a specific cultural-ethnic group,[18] and others to a definite stage of historical development: the age of ancient advanced civilizations. Some authors point to the association of the idea of a celestial world of souls with the practice of cremation. It is possible that such a relationship does hold in some cases (though others deny it) (Frobenius 1904: 16); but of course we cannot agree with Rivers, who turns the situation upside down in suggesting that the belief in a celestial world of souls gave rise to the custom of cremation (Rivers 1914: II, 550-580). [19]

Among the vast majority of peoples, however, and

even among the relatively backward, the idea of the abode of the souls of the dead is differentiated and the same place is not indicated for all the dead (much as the same funeral ritual is not followed for all). The reasons why, for some of the dead, one place is prepared in the other world, and for others another, are varied. Sometimes moral motives are indicated: let us say, the good will go to some bright place, and the evil to a dark one (Fison and Howitt 1880: 278); but such reports are doubtful, since the influence of missionary teaching is highly probable here. Another motive apparently is more genuine: to the happier place go the souls of those who observed tribal customs — for example, those relating to tattooing, piercing of the nasal septum, etc. (Krieger 1899: 295). A different fate in the afterlife is also associated, among many peoples, with the mode of death, and with the execution of funeral ritual by relatives — with their observance of established customs and restrictions (Moss 1925: 118-131, 144, etc.; Cunow 1925: 107).

Among peoples celebrated for their bellicosity, the belief in the possibility of going to a happier place after death serves as a religious reflection and sanctification of the war ethic: such a place awaits brave warriors who fall in battle. Such a belief is especially widespread in North America (Dorsey 1894: 422, 485, 518). [20] It is also known among peoples of other parts of the world (Bromilow 1929: 88-90); the best-known example is that of the ancient Germans, with their belief in a shining Valhalla, the abode of the souls of fallen warriors.

Where property-based stratification is far advanced, a similar belief is connected precisely with this: only the rich and influential can count on their souls entering the bright other world. This idea is particularly pronounced among the peoples of Oceania, and most of all in Polynesia; in almost all the archipelagos there, two afterworlds are sharply defined in the minds of the islanders — one for the chiefs and nobility, the other for the common folk, the former of course being provided with all the advantages. Usually it is believed that the souls of the chiefs go to heaven; the souls of the common folk — to the subterranean or underwater world (Hawaii, the Marquesan

Islands, Tahiti, etc.). On Samoa and on Futuna the souls of chiefs enter the underwater world Pulotu, but the souls of the simple folk go under the earth, to some "bad place" (Moss 1925: 227-228).

All these ideas about the difference in the fate of the dead in relation to his earthly status, to social rank, and in part to his personal qualities boil down to one main idea: the other world is a continuation of the terrestrial one. This means that, first of all, in the other world social distinctions between people are preserved: the rich and the elite remain rich and elite, and the poor stay poor. Secondly, the living conditions in the other world and the way of life of the souls are reminiscent of earthly conditions and the earthly mode of life: among souls the same needs and habits exist as among living people — there they eat, drink, hunt, etc. Only the details vary. According to some beliefs, life in the next world is better than in this: food and drink are plentiful, etc.; according to others, everything there is scarcer, more dreary. The beliefs of some people have it that in the other world everything is reversed: it is day there when it is night for us, etc.

The concept of the next world as a continuation of earthly life is essentially nothing but a religious sanctification of the existing social order; in fact, religion always and everywhere plays this role. But this same concept has an element of morality: among many peoples the belief has been noted to the effect that the best lot beyond the grave awaits the "good" people (the content of the concept of "good" varies, of course, depending on the social conditions and the cultural level). In this sense, belief in the next world does to some extent contain the germ of the idea of *retribution.* [21]

The idea of retribution reached its fullest development only in the religions of class society, in religions reflecting sharp class antagonisms. We find it in ancient Egypt — not in an earlier epoch, but only in the period of the New Kingdom *(Book of the Dead)* — and especially in Christianity and Islam. Here the dogma of reward and punishment in the next serves a quite obvious function: to console the deprived, the oppressed, to paralyze their protest, to pacify them with the hope of a heavenly reward: he who suffers and submissively endures suffering here, on earth, will be rewarded with eternal bliss in the life to come; in contrast, sinners and rebels will burn in eternal fire.

Beliefs About the Judge of the Otherworld

Obviously associated with funerary rites and customs is the image of the judge of souls, the king or god of the world beyond. This image, known in many religions, is very unstable and variable; it takes on the most various forms and is often contaminated with other images — with the mythological figure of the "first man," with chthonic deities of fertility, etc.

This image is generally not found in the beliefs of the most backward peoples, just as there is no well-defined idea about a special world of souls. Among peoples with a decaying clan order, where incipient social differentiation has given rise to differentiation in ideas about the life beyond, special mythological images appear, which play some role in the destiny of souls, in their admission into one of those worlds where souls abide. This is either a guide of souls, or a monster who frightens them away or devours them, or a gatekeeper who admits into the kingdom of the dead only those who satisfy certain conditions, or a judge who decides the fate of souls (Moss 1925: 110, 112, etc.). Here are a few examples.

According to the belief of the inhabitants of the island of Vao (New Hebrides), entrance into the otherworld is guarded by a monster in the form of an enormous crab who pounces on souls if they do not bring pigs with them, and devours them; if, however, the soul brings pigs (slaughtered at the funeral), the monster eats these up, but allows the soul to pass through (Speiser 1923: 322-323). In the southern part of Malekula Island there is the belief that a gatekeeper spirit is present at the entrance to the otherworld and admits only those who have been tattooed (Speiser 1923: 323). On the island of Aurora it is believed that there is an enormous pig who devours the souls of those who have not planted a pandanus tree in their lifetime; but the person who has planted such a tree can climb it and thus save himself from the monster (Codrington 1891: 280). In many parts of Melanesia there is the belief that the gatekeeper — a monster or a spirit — allows into the otherworld only those who have joined the men's society. In other cases, the passage requires payment to the gatekeeper for which funerary sacrifices are prescribed (Moss 1925: 114-115).

Among the Sakay-Jakun there is a belief in the old woman Arud ruling over the netherworld (Moss 1925: 116).

On several Polynesian islands — Rarotonga, Tahiti — the image of the deity of the netherworld is merged with the image of Tiki, the first man and the common ancestor or creator of man (Moss 1925: 114; Craighill-Handy 1927: 106-107).

The fusing of these two images — the first man and the king of the netherworld — is known also among several other peoples. Such a figure is Gaech' among the Itel'mens (Krasheninnikov 1949: 410), and Yama in ancient India (Hillebrandt 1929: 335, etc.).

Several gods of death and the netherworld kingdom figure in the extensive pantheon of the ancient Aztecs: Mictlantekutli, "ruler of the realm of death"; his spouse Mictlansiuatl; Teoyaomiki, the "god of dead warriors," etc.; one of them, Tlantekutli, was also the personification of the earth (Vaillant 1949: 209). The Mayas also had several gods associated with death and the otherworld: Akh Puch ("destroyer"), depicted as a skeleton; Khun Akhau ("first ruler"), king of the netherworld; Ish Tab — goddess of the heavenly kingdom of souls; etc. (de Landa 1955: 50-53).

According to Chinese beliefs, Ti Chiang-wang is the "supreme ruler of the nether regions"; all ten "princes of the nether regions" come to worship him. In line with the tendency of the Chinese to historicize mythological images, this Ti Chiang-wang is depicted as a certain Buddhist monk who lived in China under one of the T'ang emperors (Popov 1907: 24-25).

The images of underworld gods — rulers of the world of the dead — are highly varied among the religions of the classical East. Among the Babylonians, the world of the dead, located under the earth, was governed by the underworld gods, the Anunaks; the myths make mention of the fearsome queen of hell, Ereshkigal; in some myths Nergal emerges as the god of the dead (Turaev 1935: 120-121, 123). Ancient Egyptian religion reveals a complex evolution of images of underworld gods. Evidently, it was believed at first that the souls of the dead were devoured by an underworld god, the jackal. At the time of the first dynasties, the art of embalming and preserving corpses was developed, and there arose the idea of a patron god of this art — the god of the dead, Anubis. But Anubis was at first a nomic (local) deity — it is not quite clear of what nome (Siuta?) — and by origin evidently a totem-dog (or jackal, as some believe) (Vandier 1944: 78); perhaps it was precisely this similarity to the jackal — the devourer of corpses — that helped Anubis to occupy the honored place of the god of the dead. But he did not occupy this place alone. In other parts of Egypt the gods of the dead were the dog god Kentimentiu (Abydos), the wolf god Upuaut (Assiut), and the god Sokaris (Memphis) (Vandier 1944: 125). This was the situation up to the close of the fifth dynasty, when all these gods — protectors of the dead — were pushed to the background or absorbed by Osiris, initially the local god of Busiris, and then transformed into the national god of fertility and plant life, a chthonic deity; Osiris was also associated with the dead in folk beliefs (Vandier 1944: 78; Breasted 1915: 62-69).

Ancient Germanic mythology — reflected, even though in a modified form, in the Icelandic *Edda* — knew of several personifications of the afterworld; in addition to the terrible goddess of death and the netherworld, Hel, there was Odin, the guide of souls and king of the bright realm of Valhalla, where the souls of warriors went. The latter was transformed in the course of time into the main god of the North Germanic pantheon.

The history of the images of gods of the netherworld in Greek religion is highly complex, and its analysis is difficult, for different ethnic elements participated in the formation of the ancient Greek pantheon, but the sources reflected different stages of development of mythological ideas, complicated, in addition, by poetic fantasy. The Greeks personified the somber underworld kingdom of souls in the figure of Hades, according to Homeric mythology the brother of the Olympian Zeus and the sea god Poseidon. But the word Hades also means the underground kingdom, and the figure of its sovereign did not play a marked role in the religion of the Greeks. Also associated with the underworld of souls was a whole series of other mythological images of various origins: Pluto — initially the personification of wealth (Πλούτων — probably from Πλοῦτος "wealth," though among the Greeks there was a special mythological figure of Plutos); since, for the Greek farmer, wealth was embodied mainly in grain, and grain was stored in pits, Pluto became the underworld god. [22] Persephone is the goddess of fertility, a chthonic deity, the spouse of Pluto, who migrated together with him to the netherworld; Hecate is a complex mythological figure associated with black magic, a gloomy deity of night and of all kinds of subterranean terrors; Aeachos, Minos, and Rhadamanthos are otherworldly judges of human souls; Thanatos is the direct 'personification of death; Charon is the ferryman of souls across the underworld river Stix; Hermes is the conductor of souls, a figure that arose initially from an altogether different setting; Cerberus is a mythical monster, a dog guarding souls in the netherworld, etc.

The Romans held a vague notion of Orcus, ruler of the netherworld; this name (of unclear etymology) also served as a noun denoting the other world. But the souls of the dead themselves — the *manes* — were gods of the otherworld.

In the ancient Hebrew religion, wholly oriented to earthly life, funerary rites and customs in general were not important, and gods of the afterworld were completely unknown to the Hebrews — all the more so since the strict monotheism of the Jerusalem period did not allow any gods other than Jehovah. During the Talmudic period only a vague idea of "Sheol" — the world of the dead — developed.

In the Christian religion there were no individual and

independent images of sovereigns of the otherworld; but their functions were transferred to images of God and the devil, the two most important figure of the Christian pantneon. These two antagonistic beings emerge as sovereigns of two kingdoms into which, according to Christian ideas, the otherworld had been split: the heavenly kingdom of paradise, and hell, the kingdom of darkness and torment. But the sovereign of hell, the devil, is at the same time the universal evil force, the culprit of all evil in earthly life — the "father of sin"; God the "heavenly king" and the sovereign of paradise is at the same time the "Almighty," creator of the world and of man; he it is who created the devil himself. Jesus Christ — one of the "hypostases" of God, "the redeemer" and "savior" of men — is depicted, on the other hand, as the judge of souls: some he sends to hell for eternal torments and others to paradise for eternal bliss. Thus, in Christian dogma, these fantastic ideas, genetically associated with ancient mythological images which arose from the funerary cult, are blended in confused and contradictory fashion. Of course, their new conceptual role was not engendered by these ancient reminiscences, but by those social conditions which gave rise to Christianity itself, with its doctrine of retribution in the afterlife.

The Funerary Cult as a Form of Religion

Can we consider the funerary cult as a special form of religion? Is it not rather a component of any religion, entering as an element into its various forms at various stages of its development, much like, for example, the cult of the sun, of thunder, and of fire, or like animism, fetishism, and magic?

At first glance it can appear that this is the case, for the funerary cult — or, more precisely, ceremonials and beliefs associated with the dead — is actually present in the religion of any people, from the most backward to the most culturally advanced. The funerary cult exists among the Australian aborigines and among the Papuans; it is also found among the religions of the civilized peoples of Asia and Europe, in Christianity, Islam, and Confucianism.

But this interpretation would be incorrect. The funerary cult cannot be placed on the same taxonomic level with animism, magic, or the cult of fire or of the sun. The funerary cult has, in contrast to the categories just cited, its own basis, its own roots, in a specific sphere of human activity: attitudes toward the dead. Ceremonials and beliefs relating to the funerary cult are also closely interconnected. Though intertwined in many cases with other forms of religion, particularly at the latter historical stages, the funerary cult has always preserved its distinctiveness and independence.

In order to understand the characteristics of this form of religion as such, to elucidate for ourselves the ideas associated with it, and to grasp their genesis, we must examine funerary ceremonial not in the later modifications, but as far as possible in the earlier, unalloyed forms. Initially funerary ceremonials emerged as one of the forms of religion of primitive society.

This is very well seen in the funerary cermonials of the Tasmanians, the Australian aborigines, the Bushmen, the Fuegians, the Bororo, and other peoples of the middle and higher stages of savagery. Among all these peoples, death of any member of the community (horde) touches the entire community: all its members participate, according to specified procedures, in the funeral and memorial ceremonies; all to some extent are subject to established restrictions; among many tribes the entire horde, by custom, abandoned the camp where one of their fellow members had died. Special restrictions and mourning ceremonials placed upon the widow and closest relatives of the deceased are phenomena which only complicate, but do not eliminate, the *communal* character of the whole funerary ritual.

Comparatively early, at the close of the preclass period, as the paired family began to be separated out within the community, funerary ceremonials, while preserving their communal character, at the same time became attached to some extent to the family (special mourning restrictions placed on the widow of the deceased, etc.). Later, in early class society, funerary ceremonials were more or less intimately interwoven with family and clan worship, becoming part of the latter and losing their connection with public forms of worship. As part of the family and clan ceremonial, the funerary cult was preserved among many very advanced peoples. On the other hand, with the development, at the lower and middle stages of barbarism, of the cult of chiefs, funerary ceremonials entered as an element into this cult: funerals and memorial ceremonies for dead chiefs and rulers ramified into complex and lavish ritual, with profuse sacrifices, funeral banquets, and veneration of the deceased chiefs and their graves. Developing and becoming complex in both of these directions, and changing into a strictly regulated state system, the funerary cult attained — in ancient Egypt, for example — hypertrophied forms. Finally, it blended as an organic part, due to the teaching of the afterlife of souls, into the world religions: Christianity, Buddhism, and Islam.

* * *

From all the foregoing there follows, among other things, a practical conclusion. If funerary customs are not bound by their origion to religious beliefs, and if the latter themselves to some extent developed as a fantastic reflection of these customs in the consciousness of man, it follows that our contemporary funerary practice as well (cemeteries, crematoria, pantheons, mausoleums, grave monuments) must by no means be regarded as a survival of superstitious attitudes toward the deceased, or as a survival of religious beliefs and ceremonials. It is rooted, not in religious ideology but in motives common to all mankind embedded in man himself as a *social* being. The origin of these motives traces back to a period incomparably more ancient than the appearance of religion: more precisely, we inherited these motives from our animal ancestors. But in the course of history, these motives which determine our attitudes toward the deceased — the effort to remove them from the circle of the living, but at the same time, too, the attachment, the respect for their memory — not only do not disappear, but instead develop, are purified of their grosser features, are ennobled, or, in other words, *humanized* in the authentic sense of this word.

★ ★ ★

NOTES

1. See the studies of A. T. Lukachevskii, N. P. Tokin, V. I. Ravdonikas, V. K. Nikol'skii, P. P. Efimenko, M. O. Kosven, P. I. Boriskovskii, M. S. Butinova. etc.

2. For the objections of M. S. Plisetskii, see *Sovetskaia antropologiia,* 1957, No. 1. M. O. Kosven (1957: 35) has taken Plisetskii's view. On the other hand, P. I. Boriskovskii (1957: 204) agrees with Okladnikov, but shows greater caution, believing that the Mousterian burials "are still hard to associate with any well-defined primitive religious beliefs."

3. Cf. also *Akademiia nauk SSSR* 1955: 48, where the same author speaks less definitely, seeing the "basis" of ancient burial customs either in "concern over the fellow member of his collective" or in "false ideas" about man. P. I. Boriskovskii, who supports A. P. Okladnikov on these questions, also does not raise the question of whether Neanderthal men could have buried their deceased from some convictions other than religious ones.

4. V. F. Zybkovets (1956: 112-113) holds the primary motive of the most ancient (Neanderthal) burials to be the "maternal instinct." In his latest work, *Doreligioznaia epokha* [The Prereligious Epoch] (1959: 218, 220, etc.), Zybkovets makes his view more concrete: Neanderthal women, whom the age-sex division of labor made a great force in the community, strove to "restrain" the zoological cannibalistic proclivities of the men, and hid the "buried" from them, first the bodies of dead children, and then of elders, etc. There is probably some truth to this view, though much of it is very debatable.

5. For a summary of methods of burial among Australian aborigines, cf. Roheim 1925.

6. Richard Thurnwald correctly noted a whole series of factors determining the traditional methods of dealing with corpses among different peoples: the mode of life, the effect of climate, the influence of neighbors, such "sociological" factors as social stratification, forms of property, etc. (Ebert, ed. 1924-25: 365-366).

7. Different forms of burials are associated with the dual attitude toward the deceased: the effort to rid oneself of the corpse (instinct for cleanliness) and the striving to preserve it (instinct of social attachment). The successive development of methods of burial is shown on the diagram by arrows from the bottom up.

8. In some field ethnographic descriptions, clear mention is made of the lack of a direct tie between burial ceremonials and ideas about the soul of the deceased. Thus, Bronislaw Malinowski, in describing the funerary customs and rituals of the Trobriand islanders, notes: ". . . all these taboos, festivals, and ceremonials have nothing whatever to do, in the beliefs of the aborigines, with the spirit of the deceased. This latter has gone at once and definitely settled in the other world, completely forgetting about what is being done in the villages, and especially about what is being done in memory of his former existence" (Malinowski 1922: 490).

9. "I asked," writes Erhard Eylmann, "the Lurity'a, the western Arunta, and the Kaytit'ye, whether it was customary for them to bury any articles with the corpse. They all answered me that they knew nothing about this" (1908: 234).

10. A similar thought was recently expressed by the Italian Marxist historian Ambrogio Donini, but he was somewhat extreme in doing so: he holds that the most ancient funerary ceremonials were not religious, but that they became so only in class society (Donini 1962: 33-36). This is, of course, an excessively late dating of the transformation of funerary customs into religious ceremonial.

11. For criticism of the views of M. N. Pokrovskii, see Lukachevskii 1930: 81-86.

12. "The deceased person himself became frightening because in life this had been a most frightening person," correctly wrote A. T. Lukachevskii (1930: 86).

13. Adolf Jensen (1951: 351), defending this correct view, points out that it was first expressed (in 1906) by the student of Indonesian folk beliefs, Krejt.

14. The idea that the concept of the soul of the deceased is connected by its origin to funerary cermonial is by no means new, though it does not enjoy any particular popularity in the literature. It was Toland, at the beginning of the 18th century, who first expressed this hypothesis; in his view, "funerary ceremonials (of the ancient Egyptians) and the methods of preserving the memory of eminent personages may have been the cause which inspire the belief in immortality" (1927: 42, 53, 62). In more recent times Émile Durkheim, proceeding, it

is true, from altogether different considerations, concluded that the concepts of the soul of the deceased and dread in the presence of the corpse are not the cause, but the consequence of funerary customs: "It is not that they weep over the deceased because they fear him; they fear him because they weep over him" (Durkheim 1912: 573). Even Wundt, a stalwart adherent of the animist theory, cannot but note the effect of funerary practice on the rise of the belief in the soul: "Nothing could have so promoted the development of clearer ideas about the psyche (that is, the soul) as the annihilation of the body, as a result of which the substrate of the corporeal soul was altogether removed" (Wundt n.d.: 106).

15. This is how one of the early observers of Australian aboriginal life, Richard Howitt, explained the matter; cf. Howitt 1845: 189.

16. Rosalind Moss (1925: 7-13) views the matter in approximately the same way and, apparently, correctly.

17. Cicero was the first to express this idea.

18. G. Elliot Smith and W. Perry ascribed it to "children of the sun," emigrants from ancient Egypt, who supposedly spread advanced civilization over all the world; cf. Perry 1923, Part 13.

19. Max Ebert (1921-22) expressed a similar idea.

20. But the belief in "happy hunting-grounds," etc., was not known among all Indian tribes; cf. Dorsey 1894: 484-485, etc.

21. Usually these two ideas about the next world are contraposed: the "theory of continuation of existence" and the "theory of retribution" (Tylor 1939: 330). Actually they are not mutually exclusive.

22. This is a very plausible, in my view, suggestion of Martin Nilsson, one of the best experts on ancient Greek religion. (Nilsson 1925: 123). Other students, by the way, have not paid attention to the similarity of Pluto and Ploutos, and have noted the difference between them in the mythological concepts themselves: Ploutos — son of Demeter; Pluto — spouse of her daughter Persephone-Kore (Bogaevskii 1916: 141, 145-146).

LITERATURE CITED

Afanas'ev, A.
    1865-1869   *Poeticheskie vozzreniia slavian na prirodu* [Poetic Views of Nature Held by the Slavic Peoples]. Moscow. 3 Vols.

Akademiia Nauk SSSR
    1955   *Vsemirnaia istoriia* [World History]. Moscow, Vol. I.

Artsikhovskii, A. V.
    1954   *Osnovy arkheologii* [Fundamentals of Archeology]. Moscow.

Basedow, H.
    1925   *The Australian Aboriginal.* Adelaide.

Bogaevskii, B. L.
    1916   *Zemledel'cheskaia religiia Afin* [Agrarian Religion of Athens]. Petrograd.

Bogoraz, V. G.
    1939   *Chukchi* [The Chukchi]. Leningrad, Vol. II.

Boriskovskii, P. I.
    1957   *Drevneishee proshloe chelovechestva* [The Remotest Antiquity of Mankind]. Moscow.

Bouyssonnie, A.
    1927   "La religion des temps prehistoriques," in: *Christus, manuel d'histoire des religions,* by J. Huby. Paris.

Breasted, J.
    1915   *Istoriia Egipta s drevneishikh vremen* [History cf Egypt from the Earliest Times]. Moscow, Vol. I.

Bromilow, W.
    1929   *Twenty Years Among Primitive Papuans.* London.

Codrington, R.
    1891   *The Melanesians.* London.

Craighill-Handy, E.
    1927   *Polynesian Religion.* Honolulu.

Cunow, Heinrich
    1925   *Vozniknovenie religii i very v boga* [The Origin of Religion and Belief in God]. Moscow. 4th ed.

Curr, E.
    1886   *The Australian Race.* Melbourne-London, Vol. II.

de Landa, Diego
    1955   *Soobshchenie o delakh v Iukatane* [Report on the Situation in Yucatan]. Moscow.

de Rochas, V.

    1862   *La Nouvelle-Caledonie et ses habitants.* Paris.

Donini, A.

    1959   *Lineamenti di storia delle religioni.* Rome.

Dorsey, J. O.

    1894   "A study of Siouan cults," *Eleventh Annual Report of the Bureau of Ethnology.* Washington.

Durkheim, Émile

    1912   *Les formes elementaires de la vie religieuse.* Paris.

Ebert, Max

    1921-1922   "Die Anfange des europaischen Totenkultes," in *Prähistorische Zeitschrift.* Vols. XIII-XIV.

    1924-1925   *Reallexikon der Vorgeschichte.* Berlin, Vol. XIII.

Efimenko, P. P.

    1953   *Pervobytnoe obshchestvo* [Primitive Society]. Kiev.

Engels, Friedrich

    1952   *Dialektika prirody* [The Dialectics of Nature]. Moscow.

Eylmann, Erhard

    1908   *Die Eingeborenen der Kolonie Sudaustraliens.* Berlin.

Fison, Lorimer, and Howitt, A. W.

    1880   *Kamilaroi and Kurnai.* Melbourne.

Fox, C. E.

    1924   *The Threshold of the Pacific.* London.

Frazer, James G.

    1910   *Totemism and Exogamy.* London, Vol. II.

Frobenius, Ludwig

    1904   *Das Zeitalter des Sonnengottes.* Berlin.

Glaumont,

    1888   "Usages, moeurs et coutumes de Neo-Caledoniens," *Revue d'Ethnographie.* Vol. VI, Nos. 1-2.

Hillebrandt, A.

    1929   *Vedische Mythologie.* Breslau, Vol. II, 2nd ed.

Howitt, A. W.

    1904   *The Native Tribes of South-East Australia.* London.

Howitt, Richard

    1845   *Impressions of Australia Felix, During Four Years' Residence in That Colony.* London.

Jensen, A. E.

    1951   *Mythos und Kult bei Naturvölkern.* Wiesbaden.

Kharuzin, N.
1903 *Etnografiia* [Ethnography]. Moscow, Part IV.

Kosven, M. O.
1957 *Ocherki istorii pervobytnoi kul'tury* [Outlines of the History of Primitive Culture]. Moscow.

Krasheninnikov, S. K.
1949 *Opisanie zemli Kamchatki* [Description of the Land of Kamchatka]. Leningrad.

Krieger, M.
1899 *Neu-Guinea.* Berlin.

Kroeber, A. L.
1927 "Disposal of the dead," *American Anthropologist.* Vol. XXIX, No. 3.

Lippert, Julius
1881 *Der Seelenkult in seinen Beziehungen zur althebräischen Religion.* Berlin.

Lowie, Robert
1924 *Primitive Religion.* New York.

Lukachevskii, A.
1930 *Proiskhozhdenie religii* [Origin of Religion]. Moscow.

Lunarcharskii, A. V.
1924 *Vvedenie v istoriiu religii* [Introduction to the History of Religion]. Moscow. 2nd ed.

Malinowski, Bronislaw
1922 *Argonauts of the Western Pacific.* London.

Martin, J.
1818 *An Account of the Natives of the Tonga Islands.* London, Vol. II.

Melland, F.
1923 *In Witch-bound Africa.* London.

Miklukho-Maklai, N. N.
1950-1954 *Sobranie sochinenii* [Collected Works]. Moscow.

Montandon, G.
1934 *L'ologenése culturelle.* Paris.

Moss, Rosalind
1925 *Life After Death in Oceania and the Malay Archipelago.* Oxford.

Nilsson, Martin P.
1925 *A History of Greek Religion.* Oxford.

Obermayer, G.
   1913   *Doistoricheskii chelovek* [Prehistoric Man]. St. Petersburg.

Okladnikov, A. P.
   1952   "O znachenii zakhoronenii neandertal'tsev dlia istorii pervobytnoi kul'tury" [On the significance of the Neanderthal burials for the history of primitive culture], *Sovetskaia etnografiia*, No. 3.

Osborn, G.
   1923   *Chelovek drevnego kamennogo veka* [Man of the Old Stone Age]. Moscow.

Palmer, E.
   1844   "Notes on Some Australian Tribes," *Journal of the Royal Anthropological Institute*, No. 3.

Parker, K. L.
   1905   *The Euahlayi Tribe.* London.

Parkinson, R.
   1907   *30 Jahre in der Sudsee.* Stuttgart.

Perry, W.
   1923   *The Children of the Sun.* London, Part 13.

Plisetskii, M. S.
   1952   "O tak nazyvaemykh neandertal'skikh pogrebeniiakh" [On the so-called Neanderthal burials], *Sovetskaia etnografiia*, No. 2.

Pokrovskii, M. N.
   1923   *Ocherk istorii russkoi kul'tury* [Outline of the History of Russian Culture]. Moscow. 5th ed.

Popov, P. S.
   1907   "Kitaiskii panteon" [The Chinese Pantheon], *Sbornik MAE.* Vol. I, No. 6.

Powers. S.
   1877   *The Tribes of California.* Washington.

Priestley, Joseph
   1934   *Izbrannye sochineniia* [Selected Works]. Moscow.

Rattray, R. S.
   1927   *Religion and Art in Ashanti.* London.

Ravdonikas, V.
   1939   *Istoriia pervobytnogo obshchestva* [History of Primitive Society]. Leningrad, Part I.

Rivers, W. H. R.
1914 *The History of Melanesian Society.* Cambridge, Vol. II.

Roheim, G.
1925 "The pointing bone," *Journal of the Royal Anthropological Institute*, Vol. 55.

Roth, W. E.
1903 *North Queensland Ethnography Bulletin.* No. 5. Brisbane.

Routledge, W. S., and Routledge, K.
1910 *With a Prehistoric People.* London.

Sarasin, Friedrich
1917 *Neu-Caledonien und die Loyalty-Inseln.* Basel.

Schebesta, P.
1941-1950 *Die Bambuti-Pygmäen vom Ituri. Ergebnisse Forschungreisen zu den Zentral-Afrikanischen Pygmaen.* Part II, Brussels.

Schneider, K. M.
1956 *Mutterliebe bei Tieren.* Wittenberg.

Semenov, Iu. I.
1962 *Vozniknovenie chelovecheskogo obshchestva* [Origin of the Human Society]. Krasnoiarsk.

Shternberg, L. Ia.
1936 *Pervobytnaia religiia v svete etnografii* [Primitive religion in the light of ethnography]. Leningrad.

Skvortsov-Stepanov, I. I.
1959 *Izbrannye ateisticheskie proizvedeniia* [Selected Atheistic Works]. Moscow.

Solov'ev. V. S.
n.d. "Pervobytnoe iazychestvo, ego zhivye i mertvye ostatki" [Primitive paganism, its living and dead traces], in *Sobranie sochinenii* [Collected Works]. St. Petersburg, Vol. VI.

Speiser, F.
1923 *Ethnographische Materialien.* Berlin.

Spencer, Baldwin, and Gillen, F. J.
1899 *The Native Tribes of Central Australia.* London.

1927 *The Arunta.* London.

Spencer, H.
1876 *Osnovaniia sotsiologii* [Fundamentals of Sociology]. St. Petersburg, Vol. I.

Stefansson, W.
1925   *Das Geheimniss der Eskimos.* Leipzig.

Strehlow, C.
1907   *Die Aranda und Loritja-Stamme in Zentral-Australien.* Frankfurt-am-Main, Vol. II.

Toland, J.
1927   *Izbr. soch.* [Selected Works]. n. p.

Turaev, B. A.
1935   *Istoriia drevnego Vostoka* [History of the Ancient East]. Leningrad, Vol. I.

Tylor, E. B.
1939   *Pervobytnaia kul'tura* [Primitive Culture]. Moscow.

Vaillant, George C.
1949   *Istoriia atstekov* [History of the Aztecs]. Leningrad.

Vandier, J.
1944   *La religion égyptienne.* Paris.

Vatter, E.
1925   *Der Australische Totemismus.* n. p.

Wirz, P.
1924   *Anthropologische und ethnologische Ergebnisse der Central-Neu-Guinea Expedition.* Leiden.

1925   *Marind-Anim.* Hamburg, Vol. I, Part 2; Vol. II, Part 3.

Wundt, W.
n.d.   *Mif i religiia* [Myth and Religion]. St. Petersburg.

Yerkes, R.
1929   *The Great Apes.* New Haven-London.

Zelenin, D. K.
1916   *Ocherki russkoi mifologii* [Outlines of Russian Mythology]. Petrograd, Part I.

Zuckerman, S.
1932   *The Social Life of Monkeys and Apes.* London.

Zybkovets, V. F.
1956   "Opyt interpretatsii must'erskikh pogrebenii" [Attempt at an interpretation of Mousterian burials], *Voprosy istorii religii i ateizma,* IV.

1959   *Doreligioznaia epokha* [The Prereligious Epoch]. Moscow.

(S. A. Tokarev, *Rannye formy religii i ikh razvitie,* Moscow-Leningrad, "Nauka" Publishing House, 1964, pp. 155-212)

THE COMMUNE IN THE ANCIENT EAST AS TREATED IN THE WORKS OF SOVIET RESEARCHERS[1]

I. M. D'iakonov

Slave labor is not the sole distinguishing characteristic of the epoch of slavery. As we know, slave labor was widely employed in feudal and capitalist societies as well. What is characteristic of the slave system is the combination and the counterposition of free labor and involuntary labor in production itself. Often, in our attempts to find mass slavery in a particular ancient society (efforts which are sometimes in vain), we have not given thought either to the question of whether slave labor would have been economically advantageous under the particular conditions we are studying, or to whether the particular society possessed sufficient means of compulsion to make the mass employment of slave labor possible. For example, in the early Sumerian city-states, where the standing means of compulsion consisted merely of the small group of the ruler's henchmen, armed with copper axes and having no armor, it was impossible to employ slaves in the field tasks requiring large numbers of hands. This was so not because the society had not matured to the point of the creation of surplus products by slave labor, but because the mass of former soldiers, now slaves with copper hoes in their hands, could not physically be compelled to work in the fields, and it was dangerous to attempt to compel them. Therefore, for a long period, it was preferred to kill male prisoners and to employ the labor of slave women and their children in the home, under supervision and in crafts, thereby freeing the labor of free persons for field work

519

(Tiumenev 1956: 52; D'iakonov 1959a: 160). Slave labor in *agricultural* production should not necessarily be considered characteristic of the first type of class system (Il'in 1951: 52), which we call the slave-owning system of production. With the exception of certain special cases, the use of slaves for agriculture becomes possible only when the slave system is well advanced. On the other hand, in places where the goal of production was not the mass-scale output of commodities (and this was the case in the majority of ancient societies), slave production, requiring not only that the resistance of the enslaved be overcome but that capital — not immediately recoverable — be invested for the acquisition of slaves whose productivity was lower than that of free workers, did not always prove to be economically more advantageous. Therefore, no ancient society ever attained, or could attain, the complete replacement of free labor by slave labor. Alongside slave production, there always existed small-scale subsistence production by independent free producers. Here we disregard the work of hired laborers and that of individuals who are personally, but not hereditarily, unfree, although this kind of labor also existed in ancient times. However, in the present essay we do not attempt to provide a general survey of the economy of ancient societies and are therefore compelled to disregard a number of important economic factors, these included. Hired labor and the work of personally unfree people might or might not be present in various specific ancient societies,[2] depending upon circumstances. However, free subsistence production, primarily agricultural production, always existed in the ancient world.

Therefore, in order to study the socioeconomic system of the ancient world, the question of the status of the free producer of material goods is in no way less important than that of the position of the slaves. One might even say that in certain respects the question of the free individuals in ancient society is of greater importance. For the fact is that the slaves, as we know, were not a class in themselves; they stood outside social life. The blind and spontaneous resistance which the slaves offered to their exploiters was, of course, an exceedingly important social background to the historical development of the ancient world. Sometimes this resistance defined the boundaries and nature of social movements among free men, and on occasion it was employed by them in the course of the social struggle. But the slaves appear as an actively operating force only at a few critical moments in history, and even then their actions were never successful in the immediate sense, although they influenced the direction of development of future events.

The force acting directly in the social history of the ancient world — although the very existence of slavery had a decisive influence upon its action — was provided by various strata of free persons, and the determining factor in their struggle and interaction was their relative place with regard to production, not only with respect to slave production but, in particular, their position in subsistence production by free labor — primarily agricultural production, as we have stated. Therefore, the agrarian history of free producers is one of the most important factors in the history of the ancient world. The words of Marx on Roman society — "Its internal history may plainly be reduced to the struggle of small against large landownership, naturally with the modifications due to the existence of slavery" (Marx 1931: 89) — may also be applied to any ancient society.

A distinctive feature of the slaveholding era is also the fact that intensive development of slaveholding on a large scale is characteristic primarily of societies with a substantial development of commodity production or even of those in which commodity production plays the dominant role. True, we do know, for example, of the pseudo-latifundial economy of late Sumer of the third millennium B.C.E. (Struve 1934e: 495-507; 1934a: 211-222; 1919: 149-184; Tiumenev 1956: 244-413). However, its distinctive feature was that this was a state-owned economy, and its existence was possible only because of the monopoly position of the despotic state in Sumerian society, and even then only for a very short period (about a hundred years), for we no longer find it even under Hammurabi (D'iakonov 1956b: 37-62). Enormous state-conducted economic operations such as these are much more often

521

characterized by the working of their lands by producers conducting small-scale subsistence economies on parcels of land not belonging to them. This, for example, was precisely the use made of slaves belonging to the state economy of Egypt at the time of the New Empire (Lur'e 1955c: 16-26), among the Hittites (D'iakonov and Magaziner 1952: II, Commentary; Menabde 1956; 1961: 45), in Assyria (D'iakonov 1949b: 104, 108, 117, etc.), and in Urartu.[3] Therefore, it is only societies such as Corinth, Athens, or Rome of the late Republic and the early Empire — i.e., only a few societies of the ancient world in which commodity production was dominant — that may be cited as examples of the intensive development of non-state slaveholding on a large scale.

I do not at all wish to underestimate the fundamental significance of the pseudo-latifundia of ancient Sumer. Its significance is found primarily in the fact that the data it provided enabled Academician V. V. Struve to demonstrate irrefutably the existence of slaveholding production in the ancient East. His work was later confirmed by other data. Nevertheless, slaveholding economies of this particular type were not common among the ancient economies. If we exclude this special case, the investigations of Soviet historians demonstrate clearly that slaveholding production attained its greatest development in private economies, and the development of large private slave ownership depended in the ancient world upon the degree to which a commodity economy had been developed.

However, as already stated, production for the market in the ancient world was the exception rather than the rule. Of course, commodity-and-money relationships achieved a certain degree of development at a very early stage, as is demonstrated particularly by the fact that usury was highly developed everywhere. However, this also testified to the fact that commodity-and-money relationships were a fundamentally superficial phenomenon and had little to do with the sphere of production.

This hypothesis is developed as follows. The ancient non-state operation employing free labor (alone, or combined with slave labor on a small scale) was, as a rule, a subsistence economy whose purpose essentially was that of satisfying its own needs. However, the development of the productive forces led to intensification and specialization of branches of agriculture and the crafts, and to a division of labor, producing conditions in which exchange became a necessity. Nevertheless, the goal of production continued to be not the production of commodities, but merely the satisfaction of the needs of one's own economic unit for those products which, as a consequence of the division of labor, were not produced in it. This means that, within given limits, commodity circulation did exist, but commodity production as such did not — i.e., there was no system having as its object the creation of profit by the production of commodities specifically for the market. Hence, no accumulation of capital took place and the establishment of circulating capital was limited, thus producing a need for credit, with the usurer acting as mediator. However, although the appearance of usurious capital was a consequence of the needs of production, we know nonetheless that usurious capital does not stimulate further development of production, but acts as a parasite on it. Therefore, the ancient economies were and remained of a subsistence nature (Marx 1950: 623-624).

Moreover, under the conditions of the level of development of the productive forces existing in the ancient world, a subsistence economy could not be strictly private — i.e., individual. As a rule, such an economy could not exist without mutual aid. Inasmuch as it pertains to societies based on irrigation, this has long since been known and taken into consideration by all. But this is also true for non-irrigating societies. Fluctuations in the harvest had an exceedingly marked effect upon ancient agriculture. No less important were the losses caused to the economy by virtually uninterrupted military operations and, subsequently, by usury. Therefore, the mutual assistance of farmers was an indispensable condition for the existence of agriculture in ancient times. This mutual aid occurred not only in the sphere of production (in the period of written history, this has been manifested chiefly in the organization of irrigation) but also in the economy (for example, in the form of solidarity against the usurer) (Iankovskaia 1959: 16) and in the sphere of politics, in the form of the establishment of a particular organization unifying the free agricultural owners and guaranteeing their rights. The forms taken by this multifaceted system of mutual aid were the various types of communes.

The commune could take a number of forms. In the first place, the commune might appear as a system for jointly bringing the land under cultivation. The existence of the commune in this form was broken down by the individual nature of agricultural production, which came into being with the appearance of the hoe and, to an even greater degree, the plow. Therefore, I find dubious the suggestion advanced by L. S. Vasil'ev to the effect that joint land utilization existed in China in the Yin period, when, according to his statement, the wooden plow was in use, and not only "a class of exploiters" but "a stratum of craftsmen, servants, and slaves serving this class" existed "at the expense of the surplus labor of the communal landowners" (Vasil'ev 1961a: 61). Whether joint land utilization, without specific allocation to individuals, is possible under these circumstances, is something that social anthropologists will have to tell us. It seems to me that the root of Vasil'ev's error — I am convinced that we are faced with an error here — is the fact that he has not adequately gone into the problem of the clan commune, but I shall speak of this below.   •

A second form of commune was that which existed as an association for acquisition and utilization of water — an association determined by the collective nature of the labor required for irrigation.

Third and finally, the commune may be a civil entity guaranteeing the rights of its members — primarily the right to participate in governing the commune and the right to mutual assistance and to land tenure. It may well be that this form of commune was the most important. People united for mutual aid long before the beginning of land utilization, and such unions continued to exist after the end of communal land tenure — as long as small-scale free subsistence production continued. Gradually, this union took on the nature of a political organization. Therefore, an essential condition for membership in the commune was performance of the duties of a member in the form of participation in joint work and obligations, payment of taxes, etc. (D'iakonov and Magaziner 1952: I, Commentary, 265-270; Iankovskaia 1959a: 7-8; 1959b: 47). Carrying out these duties gave the member the right to participate in the joint tenure of the land, and later to a share when the communal land was periodically redistributed. Frequently, the possession of such a share and membership in the commune became so indissolubly intertwined that the loss of such a share also meant surrender of one's civil rights. This is why, in Asia Minor of the second millennium B.C.E., a man preferred even to put up his children or himself as security to the usurer rather than allow his share in the land to serve as security (Iankovskaia 1957a: 24 and passim).

Soviet students of the ancient East, from the very beginning of their treatment of socioeconomic problems — i.e., from the beginning of the work of Academician V. V. Struve in the early 1930s (Struve 1934d, 1934c) — have directed attention to the commune.[4] However, at the outset we based ourselves primarily upon the general comments found in the writings of Marx and Engels. Unfortunately, these observations do not bear directly upon the data available to us, inasmuch as no documents on the socioeconomic history of the ancient East were known in the 19th century. Marx's observations pertain primarily either to the commune of the feudal period or to the commune of those countries which, because of the rather high worldwide level of development of the productive forces, experienced a transition directly from the primitive to the feudal system during the period under consideration.[5] Specifically, this applied to the Germanic *mark* and the Slavic commune. Therefore, it is entirely natural that at first we were unable to find in our data the commune in the forms described by Marx. As a consequence, some historians held that the communes had disappeared at an extremely early date in the leading countries of the ancient East, although the late N. M. Nikol'skii opposed this view (Nikol'skii 1938; 1948: 131-135; 1953). This is, of course, true to some degree with respect to the commune in its initial form — i.e., the commune as a joint landowner — inasmuch as joint landownership (and, to an even greater degree, joint land utilization) is incompatible with the development of classes.[6]

On the other hand, we regarded the ancient commune in a somewhat one-sided fashion — to wit, only as a further development of primitive society and, to some degree, as a survival of it. We did not sufficiently take into consideration the fact that the existence of the commune was a consequence of the laws of the economics of slaveholding society itself or, to be more exact, of those of a subsistence economy. Therefore, the ancient commune does not necessarily have to be regarded as having developed out of the primitive commune. It could develop and has developed, *de novo*,[7] under the pressure of the indispensable conditions of economic existence.

Specific studies of the last fifteen years have provided us with a great deal of material for arriving at a judgment on the nature and laws of development of the ancient Eastern commune, at least in the Near East. Here special note must be taken of the research of Academician V. V. Struve, particularly his very last and as yet unpublished work, which casts a bright light upon the interrelationship of state, temple, and commune in Sumer. A certain amount of data on the Sumerian commune may also be derived from the works of the late Academician A. I. Tiumenev.[8] N. B. Iankovskaia (1957a, 1957b, 1959b, 1959a, 1961) employed extraordinarily vivid, clear, and specific data, derived from the lives of individual clans and families over a period of several generations, to treat the problem of the commune in the countries of the Near East which did not have river irrigation: Arrapha, Alalakh, etc. There is much of significance in the works of M. L. Gel'tser on Ugarit and Phoenicia (1952, 1954b, 1956a), of I. D. Amusin on Palestine (1955), and, to some degree, in those of Iu. B. Iusifov on Elam (1960, 1961), of G. Kh. Sarkisian on late Babylon (1952, 1953), and of D. G. Reder (1950) on early Babylonian and I. S. Katsnel'son (1960) on Nubian communal administration. I myself have written a number of papers on the commune in Sumer, Babylonia, Assyria, among the Hittites, and in Iran (D'iakonov 1959a, 1946, 1955; D'iakonov and Magaziner 1952: I, Commentary, 264-271; II, Commentary, 228-239,

285-295). My work on the early Babylonian commune has not been published, but a good deal of data specifically on the commune of this period has long been well known from the studies of Western scholars.[9] On the question of communal self-government, the works of the Danish-American scholar T. Jacobsen (1943, 1957) are exceedingly important. For Parthian and Sassanid Iran, in addition to the well-known writings of N. V. Pigulevskaia (1940, 1956, and others), there are the data of A. B. Perikhanian (1952, 1959), which have been published only in part. There are also a few things to be found in the book by M. M. D'iakonov (1961: 167-174, 194-206, etc.). Unfortunately, the works of V. O. Tiurin, M. A. Dandamaev, and myself on the Achaemenian period have as yet shed entirely too little light upon this question, although work here is progressing successfully and good results may be expected. The findings with respect to the Chinese communes in the works of Rubin (1960), Perelomov (1962), Vasil'ev (1961a, 1961b), as well as in the essay on the ancient history of China by Stepugina (1950; *Vsemirnaia istoriia* 1955-: II, 459-461, 500-501), are quite interesting. Nor should I fail to mention the work of our Sinologists Simanovskaia (1940), Duman *(Vsemirnaia istoriia* 1955-: I, 437, 610, 615, etc.), Its (1954) and Kriukov (1960: 53; 1961), although some of the suggestions advanced by certain of these writers, as well as those of L. S. Vasil'ev, as I have already observed, do not fit entirely into the concepts of the commune which we had developed by the beginning of the 1960s.

All this permits us to pose, at this point, the question of a theory of the ancient Eastern commune and to offer a certain synthesis of the results of the work. Of course, Egypt and India, for example, will in all probability provide a great deal that is new and unique. Nevertheless, the material already accumulated does, it seems, permit us to contend even now that the commune had certain characteristics in common throughout the ancient world. In this connection, we must not disregard the classical material (particularly that of K. M. Kolobova, O. V. Kudriavtsev, S. Ia. Lur'e, Ia. A. Lentsman, and E. M. Shtaerman) inasmuch as this form was identical.

Under those conditions, too, there was a commune differing little from that which we observe in certain countries of the East. Here, it is true, the commune existed almost entirely in only one of its respects, the civil. Much will also be yielded by analogies from ethnographic data, particularly African (it is not accidental that the chairman of this session is D. A. Ol'derogge), inasmuch as a number of African societies were similar to those of the ancient East in the nature of their development. This is true, of course, of all so-called "prefeudal" societies, inasmuch as a class society like that in Scandinavia at the time of the Vikings or in Kievan Rus' is nothing but an early slaveholding type of society which, because of the high level of development of the productive forces on a worldwide scale, has taken the path of feudal development and has therefore bypassed the stage of advanced slaveholding.

I shall not cite concrete data, for neither the occasion nor the time available permits it, but these data may be found in the writings of the authors I have listed. I shall attempt only to generalize those facts established by our researchers.

To begin with, what preceded the commune in the ancient world? If we disregard the paleolithic horde, of which we know very little, the most ancient form of commune that might interest us here is the clan-and-tribal organization based upon actual or imaginary kinship relations. It is characterized by common utilization of productive land, a far-reaching system of mutual aid in productive labor, the collective nature of distribution within the clan, and a system of self-administration in the form of a general meeting of all members of the clan, but primarily a council of elders. The priest leader and military leader were elective officers who in no way exercised rights of landownership or of hereditary succession.

The stages traversed by this stable system, with many thousands of years of tradition behind it, are determined by the nature of production and the nature of distribution associated with it. This system presupposed the lack of any division of labor within the clan. As soon as such a division of labor appeared — whether it took the form of specialization of individuals within the clan on particular agricultural crops or crafts, or the form of outside economic activities, etc. — the equalizing collective distribution became a hindrance to further development. Persons who did not desire to contribute their share to the common pot split away from the clan. However, this did not at all mean the appearance of individual economies, which would have been completely impossible under the conditions of that time. The family that split away did not subsequently divide, and grew into a joint family, economically unified in the form of a household commune. But this household commune might then have consisted of the descendants of the split-off pair in the paternal line and thus constituted the economic nucleus of a new type of clan — the patriarchal clan. For a long period, such a household commune did not make a final break with the old matriarchal clan. It calculated degree of relationship matrilineally, engaged in religious observances jointly with its matrilineal relatives, etc. But in the final analysis all ties are broken.

Hereafter, when we speak of the household commune, we will be dealing solely with the economy of a joint family constituting a *patriarchal* clan of a low order or forming part of a patriarchal clan. Household communes, as family-cum-economic organizations of people dwelling in a matrilineal clan, are virtually unknown to the ancient East, inasmuch as the data at hand refer primarily to the agriculturalists of the period of early class society, where the existence of a matrilineal clan organization, with its equalizing collective distribution, was no longer possible![10] B. B. Piotrovskii constantly insists upon the importance of pastoralism in the development of class society. But under the conditions of pastoralism, the patriarchal clan comes into being at an even earlier date, and our data provide absolutely no instances of primitive-communal pastoral societies with matrilineal clans.

If we return to the question of the agriculturalists, it must be noted that there is no predeterminate stage in the development of society at which the patriarchal clan must of necessity appear. Everything depends upon specific circumstances and the nature of production, and upon the need, under given concrete conditions, to violate the principle of collective distribution, upon the degree of development of natural areal division of labor and the exchange associated with this, etc.

The household commune is a unit of insufficient strength to exist quite independently, particularly under conditions of the general level of development of the productive forces and the accumulation of material goods characteristic of the last stage of primitive-communal society. Therefore, as a rule, it is part of a large communal unit based on the neighborhood principle. Usually, an enlarged communal settlement is established, having its own system of self-government — the Sumerian *uru* (D'iakonov 1959a), the Accadian *alu* (D'iakonov 1937, 1949b: 18, 44, etc.; Nikol'skii 1938), the old Hebraic *'ir*, (Nikol'skii 1937: viii), the Chinese *yi*. Moreover, the first forms of government are established, for the most part, on the basis of such unions of communes (and not on the basis of tribal alliances) as the transition to class society occurs. This is quite obvious from all the materials of classical antiquity and Near Eastern and Iranian data.[11]

Depending upon specific circumstances, such a neighborhood union of communes — the ancient rural commune — may or may not be united by kin or tribal ties. This is a secondary factor. One even sees situations in which a greatly enlarged patriarchal family or patriarchal clan comes to include a number of neighborhood communal unions or several village communes (Iankovskaia 1959a: 72).

One phenomena that appears very vividly in all the Sumerian, Hurritic, Ugaritic, and Iranian data — and, I would add, relying on the results obtained by L. S. Perelomov,[12] in the Chinese data as well — is that the patriarchal clan and the village commune are not two *successive* and mutually exclusive stages in the development of the commune. They coexist.[13] The same conclusion has been arrived at by our young students of early class society in Afghanistan, according to a communication to me from L. R. Gordon-Polonskaia.

A second conclusion that emerges unmistakably from all these data is the fact that (given essential dominance of a subsistence economy) nuclear families, consisting of a single married couple and their children, which appear sporadically, do not yet constitute a later stage in the development of the family, in comparison with the household commune as the basic economic unit in patriarchal-clan organization. Any joint family, having the nature of a household commune and having expanded, usually attains — usually by the third generation — such size that a joint economy without a division of labor (leading to economic dissolution of the family) becomes impossible. Such a family dissolves into individual couples, but each of these again develops into a joint family. Moreover, if the matrilineal clan ties have already broken down at this stage, it is possible that a patriarchal religious cult (for example, worship of paternal ancestors) may be retained in common by a number of such separated families; there may also be a common fund of land upon which they all draw, and even, to a limited degree, the duty of mutual aid.[14] Thus, the communal system grows into a complex clan-and-communal hierarchy where the bottom level represents either a joint family or a smaller one that has not yet grown into a joint family. Above this in the hierarchy are several levels of unions related by kinship, constituting, as it were, the hollow shell of household communes no longer existing as real productive units — that is, clans of the second [15] and higher orders (Iankovskaia 1959b: 44 and passim; D'iakonov 1959a: 81; 1949b: 48-49 and passim). All these factors may be combined at any given level in a neighborhood commune[16] while this commune or group of united neighborhood communes may, as a consequence of class stratification, appear at the appropriate moment as a primary state as well (the *polis* or *noma)* until larger state units are established.

Another picture is drawn for us by L. S. Vasil'ev in his book *Agrarian Relations and the Commune in China* [Agrarnye otnosheniia i obshchina v drevnem Kitae] and in his very interesting article, "The Problem of the Ching T'ien" [Problema tsin tian']. It seems to me that from a theoretical point of view this picture is mistaken, although I am not competent to judge it from the standpoint of a Sinologist. L. S. Vasil'ev sees no fundamental difference between the patriarchal household commune and the patriarchal clan, on the one hand, and the primitive-communal clan-tribal organization, existing primarily in the form of a matriarchal clan, on the other. The household commune is the economic form that must be taken by the patriarchal family (or by a first-order patriarchal clan), and therefore exists for the same period of time as does the patriarchal family, even — or even primarily — in class society.[17] However, what is apparently a patriarchal cult of male ancestors is regarded by Vasil'ev as evidence of the existence of group marriage, which allegedly existed side by side with an exploiting class and a state bureaucracy in the person of the hsiao-ch'ên and others, while he regards the absence of land allotments to small families on the communal land as evidence of collective land utilization. From my point of view, this is actually possible when the land is worked with a digging-stick, but not when the wooden plow is used, and in a primitive, not in a class society (Vasil'ev 1961a: 56-61, 77, 80, etc.). The division of communal land under the *ching t'ien* system into from eight to ten or a maximum of twelve lots also confuses him inasmuch as he does not predicate the existence of joint families (patriarchal clans) alongside the rural commune.

Within the household commune, complete power is held by the patriarch: the head of the house, the father, *pater familias.* [18] However, the neighborhood (commune) is ruled by an assembly of heads of households. Moreover, communal self-government under the conditions of class society (and even earlier, under the conditions of military democracy) usually changes in the direction of development of a council of elders, which now comes to include primarily not all the heads of household communes, but only those of the richest clans, representing, as a clan nobility, those second- and third-order clan unions into which their own clans fall. In addition to the council, there is a general assembly of all free arms-bearing individuals (Jacobsen 1943: 159 ff.; 1957: 104 ff.; Wolf 1947; Reder 1950; D'iakonov 1959a: 127 ff.; Rubin 1960: 23 ff.; Amusin 1955; and many others). However, this usually plays a rather passive role in the council of elders, which is natural under the conditions of organization we have outlined, inasmuch as the majority of warriors are in patriarchal dependence upon the clan aristocracy.[19] However, a military leader or "tyrant" may sometimes base himself upon the general assembly with the purpose of weakening the power of the clan elders, as we see in the Sumerian epic or in Greece.

The household commune owns its own means of production; power is exercised by the patriarch.[20] The right of ultimate ownership of the land is exercised by the neighborhood commune. This is expressed, in the first place, in the regular re-allotments of land within the neighborhood commune. Furthermore, such lots may, it appears, also exist within the bounds of second- and higher-order patriarchal clans, as a consequence of which land re-allotments may, in all probability, occur nonsimultaneously and even only partially. On the other hand, more than one household commune may come to occupy a particular lot. Thus, the lot may be larger or smaller than the clan land allotment (D'iakonov 1949b: 49; Iankovskaia 1959b: 42).

In the second place, the fact that the village commune is the ultimate landowner is expressed in the need for *participation* by representatives of these clans as witnesses in any transaction involving the land carried out by a single household commune or its members, and in the requirement that such a transaction be confirmed by a clan communal organization of higher rank and, if the transaction is sufficiently important, by the *neighborhood commune* as a whole, and subsequently by *the emperor*.[21] But we should emphasize the exceedingly important fact that, as a consequence of the individual nature of agricultural production and the growing inequality of property, the ultimate ownership of the land by the commune does not exclude the possibility of alienation of family land allotments or portions thereof. In Sumer, for example, this occurred as far back as we have been able to follow with the aid of the materials available to us — almost earlier than the establishment of class society and the state. [22]

Furthermore, one may speak of the right of ownership of the rural commune only in rather guarded terms, inasmuch as the very concept of property presupposes the opposing concept of propertylessness. The land is of the god — i.e., common — inasmuch as this god is the ancestor and protector of the entire commune. When, however, outcasts appear — people separated from the commune and deprived of property (which permits the acquisition of land by the members of the commune to be apprehended as membership) rural-communal ownership of the land usually breaks down, and the exercise of this property right is transferred to the heads of the household communes and is apprehended by us as private. But the rural commune continues as the collective owner of water and as a civil group, outside which neither civil rights nor rights in the land may exist.

What is the relationship between this communal organization and the developing class stratification? This latter phenomenon is doubtless based on property stratification. But inasmuch as collective distribution occurs within the household commune, it is not individuals who become rich or poor, but the household commune. Poor and rich clans appear[23] as a result of inequality of harvests or division of labor, or the success or failure of their raids. However, production cannot in all cases provide a surplus product, and not every household commune can utilize the labor of slave women, which is the source of accumulation. In the earliest stages, however, it is not the exploitation of slaves that makes it possible to sustain inequality of property, but the fact that rich households are able to keep poorer households dependent upon them by the use of provisions for communal mutual aid, these poorer households being related to them by patriarchal kin ties of the second and higher orders.[24] Poorer clans need the support of the rich and, therefore, themselves turn to the latter for "patronage."[25] The exploitation of war refugees, outcasts from other communes, etc., who come to form a clientele for the heads of the noble clans, constitutes a significant element in this picture.[26] With the development of the division of labor, as is clearly demonstrated by data from Asia Minor, the need for credit circulation is added, giving rise to usury, whimsically combined with patriarchal dependence and using clan institutions (Gel'tser 1956a: 17; Iankovskaia 1959a: passim). From a very early date, and not at all merely from the beginning of the feudal system, as certain Sinologists maintain, land rent appears, often as a means of enlarging the landholdings of the rich households, and by no means always as a form of exploitation.[27]

Only when the prosperous clans have achieved a given level of well-being, attainable only when there is a sufficient level of division of labor, and deriving from it and from the specific conditions of an economy of property inequality, does it become possible to supplement the economy of the household commune with slave labor (Engels 1933: 128). The exploitation of slaves makes it possible to increase the accumulation quickly and most intensively not only out of the surplus time, but from the necessary labor time of the slave. However, this involves economic complications of its own (labor power is rapidly exhausted, and labor productivity is low); therefore, ancient society never refrained from the use of other, less intensive, non-slave forms of exploitation, when they were possible and profitable, and according to the concrete conditions of the time and place.[28]

The more intensive the division of labor and the more pronounced the property stratification even within the clans, the greater were the stimuli to fragmentation of the household communes and the more frequently small families appeared, until finally the nuclear family consisting of a single marital unit became the rule in commodity-producing, slaveholding societies. However, retrogression is sometimes seen in this field. Thus, as a result of the impoverishment of the members of the commune of old Babylon by usurers and — as was established by T. Jacobsen (1958) — because of a temporary catastrophic drop in harvests due to salinization of the land, the market value of goods produced by the Babylonian economy dropped sharply and, at the same time, the nuclear families, which had begun to play the major role under Hammurabi, again yielded place to the household communes of the Kassitic period.

But the village commune as a civil collective of free citizens continued to exist under all circumstances. Here it becomes necessary to turn our attention to the interrelationship between the commune and the state.

I omit discussion of the postulate, obvious to Marxist scholarship, that the state arises as a consequence of the need to hold the exploited in subjection by force, inasmuch as nobody agrees voluntarily to the establishment of an unequal distribution of goods in society. I shall also assume as given the well-known signs of the existence of a state: territorial-administrative divisions, means of compulsion separate from the people, etc. I note only that the existence of a system of writing is a reliable secondary index of the existence of a state.

As already indicated, the state came into being initially within the limits of the commune or of intimately related communes. At the outset it continued to be governed, *pro forma*, as the commune had previously governed itself — i.e., by a council of elders with the participation of a general assembly of the citizens along with the war leader and the high priest. Most often the war leader gradually usurped the office of the priest and came to take his place: thus, in Sumer, the high priest *(en)* yields place to a new functionary, the head of state with priestly functions *(ensi)*, and then the ensi is pushed out by the *lugal*, formerly an elective military leader, but later an absolute monarch for whom the function of priest is already only one of a number of functions. When this is the case, the council of elders now represents not the commune in its entirety but, at point of fact, only the clan nobility, the developing class of slave-owners.

The most common is the *first* course of development, which we shall arbitrarily title the average. Under this system, we see the development of societies in which historical and natural conditions do not favor either highly productive agriculture based upon the upon the river system of irrigation, or early development of commodity production and money-and-commodity relationships, while a greater role is played by military plunder as an attempt to create accumulation (moreover, under the conditions of small commune states, accumulation by means of plunder is a deception, and the development of the productive forces was slowed down). The council of elders, adapted to the needs of constant warfare, was now inadequate for further exercise of state compulsion. The role of the war chief who was simultaneously king, of his retainers, and of an extensive royal officialdom, increased. The king's people here stand in opposition to the members of the communes, and the royal administration to communal self-administration. The role of the king and his personnel is also very great in the economy. Sometimes, he has a monopoly over crafts, particularly those producing commodities, over foreign trade, and over mining[29] — in short, over everything the commune itself cannot handle. A stratum of slave-owners not related to the clan nobility comes into being. But the condition and guarantee of economic independence is the existence of clan holdings, and the upper class of the king's henchmen merges with the upper aristocracy. Here, no large independent royal landholding is usually established. The king's henchmen, to the degree that they are not themselves part of the clan nobility, and the king's retainers are maintained from lands set aside (in the form of a special tax) from the land lots belonging to the communes. This was the situation among the Hittites (D'iakonov and Magaziner 1952: I, Commentary, 293 ff.), in Assyria (D'iakonov 1949b: 57, 76), and apparently in Ugarit, judging from the works of M. L. Gel'tser (1954b: 73) and others. It is in this category that we must, it would seem, place the "well system of fields" or the "*ching t'ien* system" in China.[30] However, throughout Asia Minor, it is possible to distinguish clearly the king's henchmen from members of the commune, since as the former are denoted in documents only by name and profession, while the latter are called "sons" of a given commune, either by name and patronymic, or by name and *pisba* (the name of the commune).

The *second* (historically the most ancient) course of development is in the countries of river irrigation, primarily Sumer. Here, a necessary condition for the development of production is the establishment of irrigation structures of a type which, from the very outset, were more than the individual clan communes could handle, and subsequently became greater than the neighborhood communes could manage (Struve 1934d: 36). At the same time, the execution of such extensive irrigation measures was something that could be carried out only with the use of force, just as the very existence of societies based on property stratification requires state force. Here the major role begins to be played by that officer who, under the conditions of ancient society, had the duty of assuring the welfare of the commune by all available means — to wit, the high priest and his people. An extensive system of temple agriculture comes into being. At first, it employs members of the communes, but they are later increasingly displaced by persons who have been separated, or who gradually come to be separated, from the commune and whose position ultimately is reduced to that of slaves.[31] Gradually these farms cease to be controlled by the responsible officers of the commune (even of its priests) and become the property of the king. But this is only the beginning. It is in this area that we see the early development of large state units embracing entire river valleys. These units are established by the state through the armed strength of the personal retainers of the priest-king, who thus rises above the individual communes and personifies their unification, while the agencies of communal self-government are reduced to the role of local self-rule (D'iakonov 1959a: 131). But the commune as a form of civil organization of free men and of slave-owners remains in existence, in this variant as well, to the very end of the existence of the slaveholding system. The communes may become village communes, which under the conditions of the latest military-administrative unions such as those of Assyria, Persia, or the Seleucid monarchies turned out to be fiscal unions of the population residing on the royal lands (D'iakonov 1959b: 119-121; Ranovich 1950: 157) "won by the spear," and might also grow into privileged, self-administering, slave-owning commercial and craft towns or temple unions like the Hellenistic *polis* (Sarkisian 1952: 68-83; Perikhanian 1959). But these communes always exist, and in them self-administration in the form of councils of elders — and usually general assemblies as well — also is found everywhere, and membership in the communes is the condition for full civil and economic rights.

Here it is also possible to draw a sharp line between

the members of the communes and the king's people, or between the *awīlum* and the *muškēnum*, to use the terminology of the Hammurabic Code (D'iakonov 1956b: 37-62; 1958). However, it must be noted that this line of demarcation is not absolute. Inasmuch as full civil rights were related to membership in the commune, to that degree only the lowest strata of the king's people were outside the communes, while major figures in the administrative apparatus — the bulk of the slave-owning class in states of this type — acquired land not only from the king but also in the communes, and in addition to being "slaves of the king," they were "sons" of some particular commune — i.e., they were *awīlum*. The same holds for the first of the types of states we are describing. Of course, major royal officials, priests, and military leaders, as well as the richer and higher-born of the members of the communes, did not directly serve the king and perform duties in the commune, but sent their slaves or indentured members of the poor household communes dependent upon them to do this in their stead. This established the basis for the division of society into persons subject to taxes and duties (members of the commune) and those not so subject (D'iakonov 1949b: 73; Stepugina 1956: 501).

In seeking to emphasize in every possible way the difference between royal land and communal land, between the king's people and the members of communes, I omitted from consideration, in my preceding works, the very close interweaving that occurred, particularly at the earlier stages, between the temple agriculture and that of the commune, despite all the differences between them. This close interconnection has been magnificently illustrated in the latest and as yet unpublished work of V. V. Struve. It would appear that it is along these lines that we will find the solution to the puzzles we still face in studying the socioeconomic history of Egypt. The enormous role played here in daily life by distinctive forms of the cult of the dead led to an even more complex interweaving between the economies of the free households and the temple economies, and between the economies of the temple and the state. Moreover, here the supreme power of the king over the entire country developed earlier and to a considerably higher level than in Babylonia, and this might have been the reason why there was not as clear-cut a division of the royal from the communal. But if we leave Egypt aside, for which this problem has not yet been resolved, it must be stated quite definitely that the ultimate ownership enjoyed by ancient kings of the East over all the land, which our own textbooks still speak of, is no more than a myth. To this day, no single piece of evidence has been presented in support of the existence of ultimate ownership of the land by the king, while there is a great deal of proof to the contrary. References to Marx do not help here; everything Marx wrote on this subject was built on the data then available to him — i.e., data almost exclusively dating from medieval times. Moreover, it is found primarily not in works published by Marx himself, but in rought outlines, fugitive thoughts, and correspondence with Engels at a time when the theory of the historical process was only first being developed by them in their discussion with each other. It is characteristic that in *The Origin of the Family, Private Property and the State*, a work in which, in Lenin's words, "there is not a single careless sentence," (Lenin n.d.: 436) a work specially devoted to early forms of the state, there is not a single word about ultimate ownership of land by the king. Even in Seleucid times, when the king's power was at its greatest, his property did not extend to the lands of the urban communes in the countries of Asia Minor (Sarkisian 1953: 65; D'iakonov 1961: 167). Everything that has been presented in proof of the alleged existence of the ultimate property right of the king in all the land pertains either merely to his prerogatives in the field of public law (such as, for example, confiscation of land for failure to pay taxes or to perform duties, or for other violations of the law, the need for his sanction for land transactions, expressed in the required formalities, the payment of taxes thereon, etc. — that is, to acts falling within the purview of every sovereign government) or to royal lands as such, and not to lands in general.

A third course of development is characteristic of those societies in which, because of various historical circumstances — in particular the clear-cut regional division of labor and a relatively high level of development of the productive forces, created by neighboring and more ancient societies — commodity-and-money relationships are widely developed at an early stage. This results in a disruption of clan ties even before the state machinery has been fully developed, in the elimination of royal power, and in a struggle between democracy and oligarchy. After a period of dictatorship of the "early tyranny" type, a republican system is established, offering maximum support to the development of individual, private, slave-owning enterprise. Membership in the commune — although it is a new and reorganized commune, i.e., the *polis* — remains an absolute condition for full civil and economic rights. The *polis* or *municipium* is retained here as a form of civil organization of the slave-owners and the free, even during the period when empires are established. However, private property *(ager privatus)*, which is counterposed to *ager publicus*, is not private property in the capitalist sense and can exist only within the framework of communal relationships. We see all this in Greece, in Rome, to some degree in Asia Minor (Perekhanian 1959), and in Phoenicia (Gel'tser 1954a; 1958: 69).

The large states established in the East in remote antiquity on the basis of a unification of entire river basins by single irrigation systems should be differentiated from the later empires. The reasons for the development of the latter are brilliantly demonstrated by N. B. Iankovskaia (1956) on the basis of data from Assyria and also presented by M. M. D'iakonov and myself on the basis of other empires of the Near East, [32] and therefore I shall not give detailed consideration to this process here. I shall state only that it relates to the non-uniformity of economic development of individual areas under the conditions of dominance of a subsistence economy and to the appearance of compulsory, non-equivalent exchange in the form of tribute, since under these circumstances normal commercial exchange cannot exist on the necessary scale.

I have come to the end of my lengthy introduction and should like to draw some of the most important conclusions. They may be formulated in three points.

1. The existence of a patriarchal-clan commune does

not rule out the existence of a neighborhood commune; both types of communes exist under the conditions of a subsistence economy. The patriarchal household commune is, under the conditions of early class subsistence economy, an economic form of existence of the joint patriarchal family, or a first-order patriarchal clan. The neighborhood commune includes a number of household communes and, consequently, a number of families or first-order clans connected by patriarchal-clan relationships within the limits of clan organizations of various orders, which may either be embraced entirely by the neighborhood commune or extend beyond its framework.

2. As distinct from the medieval commune, which was an organization of peasants who did not enjoy full rights as citizens and were personally dependent and exploited, the ancient rural, neighborhood or urban commune (and these were merely forms of a single type of organization) was primarily a civil organization of free citizens and slave-owners enjoying full rights. Its function of collective landownership could disappear in some cases, but it existed as a civil organization as long as the slaveholding system existed.[33] The expression, typical of our textbooks, about exploitation in the ancient East "of slaves and peasant commune members" is a vestige of a compromise that arose during the 1930s in the course of the discussion between the partisans of the concept of slaveholding and those of feudalism as the typical form of society in the ancient East. There can be no doubt that members of the commune may be subjected to exploitation — for example, by usurers; but the exacting of a tax by the government, be it in kind, money, or labor (in the form of duties), is not exploitation in itself, inasmuch as these taxes may be paid by the ruling class and, all the more, by a class not basic to the social system, which is obviously true of the free members of the commune who are not slave-owners — the numerous remnant of the free masses of primitive society. A certain analogy to its position may be seen in the peasantry of the capitalist epoch, often constituting a majority of the population, but no longer constituting the basic class, and undergoing a continuous process of stratification into rural capitalists and

rural proletarians. In the same way, the free members of the communes of ancient times underwent a constant process of stratification into slaveholding members of the commune and indentured poor who gradually merged with the slave class. [34] But as a *whole*, the free farmers were not a class subject to exploitation. Even the richest and most highly placed people of the ancient world were citizens of urban and rural communes and therefore commune members.

3. A characteristic of the ancient commune is civil self-administration through a council of elders and a general assembly. Its existence can be demonstrated in ancient Mesopotamia at all times. For the ancient Babylonian period, in particular, this discovery was made by bourgeois scholars as far back as the 1910s. It may be readily traced in all the other countries of the Near East in the second millennium B.C.E., as well as in the cities during the first millennium. It has recently been demonstrated by V. A. Rubin and L. S. Perelomov to have existed in China, and in India by G. M. Bongard-Levin. With respect to the classical portion of the slaveholding world, there has been no question of this at least since the time of Fustel de Coulanges.

In the small early commune-states, communal self-administration, seized by representatives of the rich clans, is directly a form of state administration, while in the kingdoms and empires it is a form of local self-government by the ruling class and members of the communes. But this self-government did not extend to the king's people themselves, who were not simultaneously members of communes. This is why it is difficult to discover in studying the archives of temple and state in Sumer.

Communal self-government and participation by commune members in the affairs, duties, and income of the commune are major criteria by which it is possible to recognize the neighborhood (i.e., urban or rural) commune in any period of ancient society, while the existence of free individuals enjoying full rights, and of exploiters, among the commune members demonstrates in any case that what we are dealing with is not a feudal but an ancient society.

These are the data on the communes in the ancient East which it has been possible to extract to date from the writings of Soviet researchers thus far publisned. The present discussion should have the purpose of refining and correcting these data.

* * *

EDITORS' NOTE

a. The source PBS in Note 22 below could not be identified.

NOTES

1. Introductory paper read May 18, 1962, at a discussion on the problem of the clan and rural commune in the ancient East, held at the Second All-Union Session on Study of the Ancient East, in Leningrad. A condensed stenographic report of the discussion is published below in the section, "Scholarly Activities." [See VDI 1963 in Literature Cited.]
2. Thus, they appear no earlier than the time of the Akkad dynasty in Mesopotamia, according to V. V. Struve (1934b: 53; 1948: 13-33) and D'iakonov (1959b: 222).
3. See D'iakonov (1952) and Melikishvili (1958: 46-47). The situation was somewhat different in Achaemenian Persia, for which see Dandamaev (1960); compare also Iusifov (1958); D'iakonov (1959b).
4. Also compare Avdiev (1934). [There is apparently an error in this reference, but no way of telling how it should read — Editors.]
5. That the principal production relations must correspond to the level of development of the productive forces is an immutable law; therefore it is impossible to entertain the hypothesis that two different socioeconomic systems — the slaveholding and the feudal — could have appeared on the basis of an identical level of development of the productive forces. Therefore, if any society progresses from the primitive-communal to the feudal system, completely bypassing the slaveholding stage, this signified that this progression became possible due to the existence of a higher level of development of the productive forces than that which corresponds to long-term existence of the slaveholding stage. If we oversimplify, we

might say that the feudal socioeconomic system (as distinct from the hierarchical state structure, resembling the feudal hierarchy) is impossible in the Bronze Age. In actuality the situation is more complex: soft alluvial soils permit the establishment of an elaborate irrigation system and, accordingly, of the surplus product essential to the appearance of class society even under the conditions of the early eneolithic period. But where rock must be hewn to permit irrigation, bronze tools are often inadequate, and even the tools of the Early Iron Age do not permit an excess of agricultural products to be produced in the forests of the northern portion of the Old World. On the other hand, the adoption of the higher productive and military skills created by neighboring slaveholding countries permits primitive tribes in certain instances not to have to spend a period in a slaveholding form of production, but to progress directly to the more productive economy based upon noneconomic compulsion of individual personally dependent farmers.

6. In Sumer, collective ownership of the land by a neighborhood cannot be traced farther than the Akkad dynasty (24th to 23rd centuries B.C.E.); see D'iakonov (1959a: 80-83). In Assyria it cannot be traced beyond the Mid-Assyrian Period (16th-12th centuries B.C.E.); see D'iakonov (1949b: 47,76). In Arrapha it still existed in the 15th and 14th centuries B.C.E.; see Iankovskaia (1959a: 8). But it no longer existed in Elam as far back as the beginning of the second millennium B.C.E.; see Iusifov (1960, 1961).

7. See, for example, D'iakonov (1949b: 120). The classical *polis* was, in our view, just such a newly developed type of commune.

8. Particularly in the first chapters of his *Gosudarstevnnoe khoziaistvo drevnego Shumera*. See also Tiumenev (1950).

9. Thus, certain information on communal self-government may be found in A. Walther (1917), J. G. Lautner (1935), and others.

10. Cases are known to modern ethnography in which the breakdown of clan ties under the influence of commodity-and-money relationships occurs right in a matrilineal clan which has been affected by higher — say, capitalist — economic conditions, in which case the matrilineal household commune displays characteristics entirely analogous to those we observe in the patriarchal household commune during the period of dissolution under the influence of commodity-and-money relationships in slaveholding society. But I know of no such in-

stances in the ancient East.

11. See, for example, D'iakonov (1959a: 166; 1956a: 154, 189, 192, etc.). For Syria, Phoenicia, and Greece this is obvious.

12. For the role of elders at the heads of clans, see Perelomov (1962: 66 ff.).

13. This is also clear from data on Sumer (D'iakonov 1959a: 81), Assyria (D'iakonov 1949b: 48-49), Arrapha, Alalakh, the Hittites (Iankovskaia 1959b: 48-51), and Crete (the clan communes — *voikii* — within the neighborhood commune at Gortyna). See Kolobova (1957). In Southern Arabia, patriarchal clans of a higher order apparently played the role of neighborhood communes, as is suggested by the data offered to us by A. G. Lundin.

14. This is clearly evident from material of Sumer, of Assyria during its middle period, and of Arrapha. See the above-cited works of I. M. D'iakonov and N. B. Iankovskaia.

15. A first-order clan is identifiable with a joint family, which usually constitutes a single household commune in the economic sense.

16. In certain historical conditions, a clan commune of one or another order may appear as a neighborhood commune.

17. In addition to the researches adduced above, the existence of a patriarchal household commune and a patriarchal clan in, for example, Babylonia of the 19th to 17th centuries B.C.E. is evident from Nikol'skii (1948: 56-70), while its existence in Babylonia of the 4th and 3rd centuries B.C.E. may be seen in Sarkisian (1952: 72-73). The household commune and the patriarchal clan were entirely real social factors as far back as the Parthian and Sassanid states, as is evident from the Sassanid code, *Matakdan-i khazar Datastan* (communication from A. G. Perikhanian); see also Perikhanian (1959).

18. Up to and including the right to mortgage and sell members of the family, for which see, for example, a number of the articles of Hammurabi's Laws (i.e., Sec. 117) and the Middle Assyrian Laws, as well as the typical provision of Hittite law, under which the head of a family may pay for his own crimes with the heads of members of his family (not only slaves but the free) (D'iakonov and Magaziner 1952: I, Commentary, 287-292; II, Commentary, 242-246, 300). Compare also Biblical (for example, *Deuteronomy*, 21: 18-21) and the Sassanid legislation.

19. Each freeman-warrior was at the same time a member of some clan, the heads of which sat in council and were linked by clan solidarity and discipline.

20. This is clear from the land sale transactions on the "Manishtusu Obelisk." See D'iakonov (1959a: 69-79; Tiumenev (1946).
21. D'iakonov (1959a: 81, 1949b: 58). Compare *Zakony Manu* (VIII: 245-266) and many others.
22. The most ancient records of transactions are in pictographic writing; for a list see D'iakonov (1959a: 46). The oldest document yet deciphered dates from the 28th or 27th centuries B.C.E. (the Enkhegal' document, PBS,[a] IX, No. 2; A. Deimel 1924: 282 ff.; D'iakonov 1959a: 47).
23. They may be identified readily from the Sumerian transactions on purchase and sale of land.
24. Iankovskaia (1959b: 44 ff.), where specific examples are cited.
25. Iankovskaia (1961) (case of clan communes dependent upon Kissuk commune).
26. Iankovskaia (1959a: 12). Compare the supplementing of the personnel of the Sumerian temple farms by refugees from other communes (D'iakonov 1959a: 101-163).
27. The letting of land from one's share was practiced as far back as by the early Sumerian temple farms *(uru$_4$-lal* lands), but this was not rental in the direct sense, inasmuch as those who held these lands were, as a rule, temple people; see Struve (1934c: 16). Renting as such was widely practiced in Old Babylonian times; see D'iakonov and Magaziner 1952: I, Commentary, 280. Here rent was, for the most part, not a form of exploitation.
28. In this category we have, in particular, patriarchal exploitation of poor clan members — members of destroyed and impoverished clans who have fled to "protection" and similar "clients" (not only "clients" of rich clans, but, in the first place, "clients" of the king and the temples — up to this point, conditions did not permit them to be converted into slaves, whose exploitation is more intensive) — the exploitation of certain subjugated communes in their entirety. These forms of exploitation have much in common with early feudal types. However, when feudal relationships have completely taken shape, the ruling class is successful in completely combining the advantages of *intensive non-economic* compulsion of the *entire* mass of the peasantry, which in ancient society was *free* for the most part, with the advantages of more highly productive *non-slave* labor. This presupposes a higher labor productivity than that which was, as a rule, possible under the conditions of the development of the productive forces characteristic of ancient society. It is possible that it is specifically the level of

the ratio between the surplus and necessary labor obtainable at this level of development of the productive forces that might here serve as one of the distinguishing criteria.

29. Gel'tser (1952: 34-35); Stepugina (1956: 494); Batsieva (1953: 20-21); and many others.

30. For the latest and most detailed description of this system, see Vasil'ev (1961b).

31. For the history of this category of enterprise, see Tiumenev (1946).

32. *Vsemirnaia istoriia,* AN SSSR, I, "Vvedenie k chasti IV" (I. M. D'iakonov); M. M. D'iakonov (1961).

33. Breakdown of urban communes is a very characteristic feature of the transition to a feudal economy. This was demonstrated very vividly by G. Kh. Sarkisian, employing Armenian data (1960, Chap. V).

34. This idea is by no means a new one in scholarship in our country. See, as an example, G. F. Il'in (1950b: 178) citing D. A. Suleikin (1949: 188-189).

(Soviet Anthropology and Archeology,
1963, II, No. 2.)

ON THE CHARACTER OF THE MOST ANCIENT CLASS SOCIETIES

G. A. Melikishvili

(Academician of the Academy of Sciences, Georgian SSR)

The most ancient class societies, as we know, arose in the East, and the question of the nature of these societies was first acutely posed in Soviet science in the discussion about the Asiatic mode of production that took place at the end of the 1920s and in the early 1930s; as a result, the view prevailed that the Asiatic mode of production cannot be considered as denoting a separate socioeconomic formation distinct from slaveholding and feudalism. Acceptance of the existence of such a formation in the East, in the opinion of specialists holding this view, involved the denial of general laws of mankind's development, and the acceptance of special paths of development followed by eastern societies and of the existence of "perpetual slavery" or "perpetual feudalism" in the East. However, the following question naturally arose: if no specific Asiatic formation existed in the East, then how should these ancient eastern societies be characterized? A prominent role in the solution of this question was played by the view of Academician V. V. Struve, based on the study of a large body of concrete data (Ancient Babylonian commercial texts), to the effect that the personnel of the royal landed estates widespread in the Third Dynasty of Ur worked on the estates year round, and consequently consisted of workers without their own means of production; the scholar placed them in the category of slaves

549

(Struve 1934d; 1934c; 1934e; Postovskaia 1961: 80-82, 98 ff.). Thus, it began to appear that, by studying the factual material, the leading role of slave labor in production could be demonstrated both in other ancient eastern countries and in other eras. Accordingly, the attention of researchers began to be drawn especially to numerous reports in ancient eastern sources about the seizure of prisoners of war and their enslavement, as well as the sharp distinction between free men and slaves in the documents of ancient eastern law (the Code of the Ancient Babylonian King Hammurabi, the Hittite laws, etc.). In this way the view was formed that a slaveholding formation existed in the ancient East, but at the same time several investigators still emphasized that eastern slaveholding had not attained as high a level of development as ancient Greece and Rome. The reasons for this state of affairs were seen as the stable maintenance in the East of the institution of communal landholding, etc. The entire complex noted by Marx and Engels as characterizing eastern societies and the Asiatic mode of production, was commonly mentioned as constituting specific features of eastern slaveholding (Ter-Akopian 1965; Garushiants 1966).[1] Adherents to the view that a slaveholding formation existed in the ancient East relied also on some statements made by V. I. Lenin in his famous lecture, "On the State" (first published in 1929), where slavery was called the first form of exploitation, and the society based on slavery was called the first class society. The assertion of the slaveholding nature of ancient eastern society and the first class societies became conclusively entrenched after publication, in 1938, of *Kratkii kurs istorii VKP(b)* [A Short Course in the History of the All-Russian Communist Party (Bolshevik)], which listed the socioeconomic formations in the following order — primitive-communal, slaveholding, feudal, capitalist, and socialist — and said nothing about any Asiatic mode of production.

In postwar Soviet historiography, ancient eastern society, as a rule, is designated as "early slaveholding" or "communal-slaveholding" and is sharply differentiated from Classical slaveholding. In particular, its distinguishing feature is held to be the weak development of slaveholding and the quite restricted use of slave labor in production. The bulk of the producers of material goods are held to be ordinary commune members.

Acceptance of the slaveholding (early slaveholding) nature of ancient eastern societies has become so general that few now understand the necessity for validating this conclusion. True, researchers holding this view were sometimes still forced to explain why we call societies slaveholding which had few slaves, and where the sphere of use of slave labor was very restricted (as a rule, the labor of free commune members predominated in agriculture, the main branch of production). One group of researchers sharply attacked the use of "the quantitative criterion" in defining the mode of production of a given society, maintaining that this question must be resolved starting from the forms of ownership and methods of exploitation (Utchenko and Shtaerman, 1960: 9 ff.; Borshch 1961: 165-169). Reference was often made in this connection to the statement of I. V. Stalin (made, incidentally, in an altogether different context, in relation to another question) that one must be guided not by those strata of society which were strongest at a given moment, but did not develop, but rather by those that did develop and had a future, even though at a given moment they were not preeminent (Zel'in 1953; Eremian 1953: 20-21). In *Vsemirnaia Istoriia* [World History] (1955-: I, 140) the numerical strength of the mass of the free populace compared to the slaves is explained by the assertion that in the ancient East the free populace had not yet been transformed into slaves, but were dependent on the slaveholding aristocracy. In other words, it was noted that slavery in the East "for thousands of years did not directly constitute the basis of the economy, though it was a leading and progressive institution" *(VDI* 1947: 4). Finally, in the view of several scholars, ancient eastern society is justifiably called slaveholding, since exploitation of slave labor was prominent on the estates of society's ruling circles *(VDI* 1963: 191).

Thus, the dominant concept in Soviet historiography viewed ancient eastern society as "early slaveholding"[2] and characterized "early slaveholding" as the first, lowest stage of the slaveholding socioeconomic formation, the highest degree of development here being ancient Greek society. But despite the almost total prevalence of this concept, from time to time divergent points of view on the nature of ancient eastern, and generally the most ancient class, societies were still expressed. S. Iushkov, for one, advanced the idea that prefeudal "barbarian" states once existed. He regarded as examples of such states, in particular, the Kievan state up to the 11th century, the Mongol states prior to their consolidation by Genghis Khan, and the Anglo-Saxon kingdoms up to the 9th century; doubtless, ancient eastern states were also regarded by him in this way (Iushkov 1946).[3] In these states Iushkov noted the coexistence and the conflict of three different economic systems — primitive-communal, slave-holding, and feudal — among which the feudal was the leading mode. In the 1930s, I. M. Lur'e, sharply attacking the recognition of ancient eastern societies as slaveholding, regarded them as feudal; later, however, agreeing with the dominant viewpoint, he did not deem it possible to contrast ancient eastern society both with the "early slave-holding" society of ancient Greece and Rome and with "developed slaveholding" societies, and proposed that they be viewed not as successive stages of development but as two different, coexisting types of slaveholding society (Lur'e 1952: 172-173; VDI 1953: 233). In the opinion of A. I. Tiumenev (1957: Pt. I, 51), "The difference in character of the social order and in historical destiny between eastern and Classical slaveholding societies can in no way be reduced to a difference between states of development. This is above all a difference in the very paths of development." Citing, in confirmation of his judgment, extensive material mainly from the history of Ancient Mesopotamia and Egypt, on the one hand, and from Ancient Greece on the other, Tiumenev showed that in the ancient East the basic producing population was the primary object of exploitation by the slaveholders. True, he added, "such 'universal slavery,' to use the words of Marx, in the East did not of course preclude use of the labor or prisoners of war as well," but this latter (since the entire labor force was in the hands of the ruling class) can only be supplementary and secondary in significance. Debt bondage was also not of key significance, and Struve, basing himself on Tiumenev's viewpoint, vainly tried to attribute to it a large role in the exploitation of the broad masses through the slaveholding system (Tiumenev 1957: Pt. I, 54, 55). It cannot be denied that Tiumenev is logical: one can perhaps speak of the slaveholding character of ancient eastern societies only if exploitation tantamount to slaveholding actually existed there. But (this will be dealt with below) there are strong doubts on the latter point. Some researchers (particularly I. M. D'iakonov) not only refuse to view commune members in ancient eastern countries as slaves, but in general are disinclined to regard them as exploited masses (D'iakonov 1963a: 33-34; *VDI* 1963: 179 ff.). Contributions like those cited did not attract due attention when made, and found a very weak response. The discussion associated with this set of problems was resumed in Soviet historiography only quite recently, in the early 1960s. These problems, particularly the Asiatic mode of production, began to be widely discussed in the foreign Marxist literature, which entailed examination of problems of the periodization of the universal-historical process, of the typology of the most ancient class societies, etc.

Having amassed much experience and performed enormous work in studying diverse concrete material, Soviet oriental studies can now fully enter into broad generalizations on a stronger scientific basis. The bold and creative attitude of Soviet historians toward the investigation of general sociological and concrete historical laws has also established favorable conditions for elucidating the nature of the socioeconomic order of the ancient eastern societies and of the most ancient class societies in general, on both the concrete historical and the general sociological levels. In particular, we can now evaluate more definitely than at the outset of the 1930s the proportions of labor performed by slaves and by free commune members in the productive activity of ancient eastern societies, and the ratio between different forms of exploitation. Information found by V. V. Struve in documents of the Third Dynasty of Ur (Babylonia) about the numerous workers employed the year round on royal landed estates[4] suggested that such exploitation of broad strata of the local populace may subsequently be found everywhere, both in other countries and in other periods. But further research showed that the large slaveholding landed estates of the Third Dynasty of Ur represented an exception even in Babylonia itself and, having existed for only one to two centuries, disappeared altogether after the fall of that dynasty. Their lands were passed out as allotments to soldiers and government officials, and also to small tenants of royal lands on condition that part of the harvest be paid to the owner (D'iakonov 1952: 91-92). Studies also showed that the labor of slaves in countries of the ancient East was used on a very limited scale. In agriculture, the main field of production, the labor of the free population unquestionably predominated everywhere. The labor of slaves was used relatively more widely in trade and construction (though in the latter, and also in irrigation, free labor was also widely used). But the largest number of slaves was among servants, domestic workers, and sometimes also in the army (slaves, as we know, were also widely used as soldiers in the medieval East). Slaveholding occupied an insignificant place in Egypt; only in certain periods did the number of slaves reach any sizable proportion, and even in the Classical period the use of slave labor did not become widespread among Greeks living here (Tiumenev 1957: Part II). Slavery is also not found to have been widespread in China, where it was mainly domestic, and only women were slaves initially (Erkes 1954; Pokora 1963). Slave labor played almost no role in agriculture; even in periods of special influx of slaves, their labor was mainly employed for services to the nobility (Rubin 1959: 21). Slavery also was not the basis of social production in ancient India. Free persons were chiefly encountered as artisans here, and in agriculture the main role was played by persons belonging to the category of *shudras* (Vid'ialankar 1959: 44). Although on the lowest rung of the caste hierarchy, *shudras* were in no way slaves, as is implied by some students, but were the local populace exploited by the elite of society (Il'in 1950a: 107, etc.). The slave *("desa")* in India was in general held to be a person standing outside the *varna* (castes). Such

554

slaves were found as servants in the homes of the very wealthy; a similar kind of slavery, and not at all on a smaller scale, also existed in the early medieval period (8th-12th centuries) in India (Vid'ialankar 1959: 52). The slaves alluded to in ancient Indian sources (in general, converted into such for some crime) were employed also in mines. Slaves were also occasionally encountered in royal military contingents (Il'in 1951: 42). The highly restricted spread of slavery in ancient India is also shown by the fact that the famous Magasthenes (3rd century B.C.E.) held that there were no slaves at all in India.

True, a large number of war prisoners sometimes appeared in given ancient eastern countries as a result of victorious wars, but by no means were these used in production; nor were they transformed into typical slaves and subjected to typical servile exploitation. Exploitation of slaves on large farms was so complex and unprofitable an operation that their owners preferred to convert to a system of small farms, a step in the transformation of slaves into serfs (Rubin 1955: 120). In late Assyria, for example, the settling of prisoners of war on the land as independently operating state slaves, who paid their master (or the state) part of the harvest, became a widespread phenomenon. The Hittite kings earlier operated in the same way (D'iakonov 1952: 92); and in Egypt in the period of the 19th-20th dynasties, the population transferred from conquered lands also were often settled on the land (Lur'e 1955b: 26). In Assyria, as in Urartu, war prisoners were included in the army, formed into military settlements, etc. (D'iakonov 1952; Melikishvili 1958). In late Babylonia, on the other hand, release of slaves on condition of payment of "quitrent" found wide acceptance in agriculture, in the crafts, and in trade. Thus, in countries of the ancient East we often encounter the conversion of slaves into independently operating workers who fulfilled definite obligations to the master (share of harvest, part of earnings) — that is, we find a certain approximation of the form of their exploitation to the feudal type. Broad strata of the local population were drawn to a still greater extent into exploitation of this ("feudal") type in the countries of the ancient East.

Especially abundant material about exploitation of the local free population is found, as we know, in the history of ancient Egypt and ancient China. In Egypt, in various periods, there were large estates of rulers, nobles, and temples employing the labor of a whole army of compatriots who, in addition, were recruited into various other governmental and public activities, paid heavy taxes, and were severely exploited by the ruling circles of society and the widely ramified state bureaucratic apparatus. Even in a later — for example, the Hellenistic — period, the principal producers in agriculture were not slaves, but the local population, the so-called *laoi basilikoi*. In Egypt during this period, the strengthening of private-property elements through state landholding, and the attachment of farmers *(laoi*-commune members) living on the lands of the ruler, temples, nobles, or cities (the same applied to military colonists) to the commune at their places of residence (Tiumenev 1957: Part II, 39-48) — all these are quite obvious. In ancient China, chieftains began very soon to be transformed into managers of communal lands, on which, in addition to private allotments, plots worked jointly by commune members began to be parceled out, but the harvest from them belonged to the ruler. Extensive material exists on the distribution of lands by kings or rulers of particular territories to representatives of the bureaucratic and military machinery, and about the cruel exploitation of their countrymen by the latter. It is known that many students are inclined, on this basis, to view the social order of ancient China as feudal or, in any case, to begin the feudal period in China very early — from the 5th or 7th century before Christ.

We have already spoken about the predominance, in the productive life of ancient India, of the labor of exploited lower strata of the local populace. Here the labor of commune members was predominantly used not only in agriculture, but also in public services on the state level. The existence of the ruling class in India was primarily founded, in addition to exploitation of domestic slaves, on primitive feudal exploitation of commoners (tribute, state taxes, and public services) (Osipov 1948: 37). Forms of exploitation approximating the feudal were widespread also in ancient Mesopotamia (Sumer, Babylonia) (Semenov 1965: 72-75, etc.), along with the exploitation of slaves who were fairly widely used here in certain periods. In ancient Sumer, for example, commune members — holders of allotments on temple (or royal) estates — usually worked four months a year on these estates, and bore the yoke of heavy taxes and other obligations. In the Hittite kingdom, there was a widespread practice by which representatives of the ruling group were granted land tracts by the king to be worked by local free farmers (Menabde 1965: 60, etc.).

Since a criterion other than the proportion of the labor of slaves in the production process can scarcely exist, one cannot by any means conclude, on the basis of this sole criterion, that slaveholding socioeconomic relationships prevailed in ancient eastern countries. The labor of war prisoner-slaves, under conditions in which almost all of a country's labor force was at the disposal of the ruling circle, could be — and actually was — of only secondary, auxiliary, supplementary significance (Tiumenev 1957: Part I, 54). At the same time, as Tiumenev correctly noted, it is incorrect to ascribe a large role to debt bondage in the countries of the ancient East. Transformation of the propertyless debtor into a slave was in general quite rare, and was not a source of mass slavery. It doubtless met with sharp resistance from broad strata of the populace. Besides, mass enslavement of fellow countrymen by debt bondage weakened a state's ability to resist outside incursions, which under those conditions could bring the given society to wholesale catastrophe. That is why the government itself was forced to restrict debt bondage by legislative acts (the laws of Hammurabi, the legislation of the Hebrew king Josiah, etc.).

Correctly assuming that neither the existence of slaves who were war prisoners nor the conversion of fellow countrymen into slaves through debt bondage could have transformed ancient eastern society into a slaveholding society, Tiumenev still asserted that this society was slaveholding inasmuch as here (particularly in Egypt and Babylonia) the entire local populace, broad strata of fellow countrymen, and commune members were the object of servile

557

exploitation by the elite. In fact, Marx characterized the situation in the countries of the East as "universal slavery" (Tiumenev 1957: Part I, 53-54). However, this expression of Marx was doubtless figurative, and must not be taken literally. And while in the East a free man often proved to be economically and legally no better placed than a slave, this does not at all mean that the boundary between slaves and freemen must be erased. The difference between them in the ancient East, and in fact in ancient times generally, was very far-reaching: the slave stood outside of society, outside the juridical community of people, outside the law altogether; a slave was a man whom a master could with impunity, murder, mutilate, punish, sell, etc. But all this could hardly apply to free commune members, who were by no means regarded as anyone's property, and were not themselves wholly deprived of property rights over means of production. But, in fact, slaveholding generally consists of precisely these two features. Consequently, the exploitation of the broad layers of the populace by the ruling circles cannot be viewed as servile. Moreover, as has been noted, in many cases the exploitation of foreign slaves tended to be transformed into a feudal type of exploitation: slaves were settled on the land; they worked the farms independently and paid taxes to the master or the state; some had families; and sometimes the law gave them specific protection.

The exploitation of a broad circle of rank-and-file free commune members by the state and the military-bureaucratic machinery was essentially closer to early feudal and protofeudal dependence than to slaveholding. Even in the lands of Western Europe the beginning of feudalization was associated at times with the transformation of free commune members into an object of fiscal exploitation by the state, and with their subsequent involvement in different forms of landed and personal dependence. But the core of the feudal order consisted precisely in the appropriation, via taxes or rent, by the ruling class of the surplus labor product of the direct producers, and the later transformation of land and the person of the producer into the property of the ruling class. The surplus labor product of the free commune member (peasant), appropriated through taxes or other obligations to the state, essentially did not differ from rent collected from a dependent population which had lost the right to ownership of land and personal freedom. A similar process of the maturing of feudal relationships, observed in several countries of Western Europe, emerges still more clearly in countries of Asia and Africa, in the formation of feudal relationships (Beliakov and Kolesnitskii 1964). Here, in the East, in many places especially in the early medieval period, as we know, the state form of ownership of land and water flourished, and the state carried out, via its machinery, the exploitation of the peasantry who had allotments on state lands.

Along with exploitation of slave labor, and the proto-feudal type of exploitation of broad strata of the local populace in countries of the ancient East, we also encounter — at times on a very wide scale — exploitation of hired labor. Thus, various forms of exploitation coexisted in the most ancient class societies of the East, and as a rule each type of exploitation took on fairly undeveloped forms (Semenov 1965: 81), which appeared as the corresponding socioeconomic order. The predominance of undeveloped forms of exploitation here was caused primarily by the closeness of the level of social development to the primitive-communal order, whose heritage was communal land tenure and a numerous stratum of free commune members who retained their economic independence and personal freedom. This closeness also determined to a large extent the nature of the ruling strata of the population. The latter retained to a substantial extent, at least externally, the functions of head, organizer, and leader, whether of the economic, military, or cultural activity of the society. The main source of their privileges was precisely this. Traditions of the primitive-communal order often made themselves felt in both political and governmental organizations, etc.

Thus, the basic characteristic feature of societies of the early eastern type was the coexistence of different forms of exploitation, different socioeconomic modes, with the preservation, by broad strata of the population, of economic independence and personal freedom, and with the presence of significant survivals of the primitive-communal order. Heterogeneity of forms of exploitation, and the coexistence of various socioeconomic orders, are generally characteristic of societies of transitional type. We see this situation in the period of the transition from Roman slaveholding society to feudal; we encounter it in the transition from feudalism to capitalism. It is obvious that the societies of interest to us are also transitional societies, but differ from other similar societies in that they are in transition, not from one class-antagonistic social order to another, but from the classless, primitive-communal order to a certain form of *developed* class society; consequently, the content of these changes was more profound, more substantial than that of those which occurred within the framework of the stage-by-stage development of class-antagonistic society.

What is the place of such early class societies in the sociohistorical development of mankind? Do they represent a certain stage in this development? The history of social development is one of the manifestations of the dialectical development of the universe. Initially human society (societies) appears before us as unified. The next stage is its breakdown into antagonistic classes, into a ruling elite and an enslaved, subjugated, exploited mass; and the battle between these social forces determines the entire future development of society. In the struggle of the classes, the fundamental law of dialectics is manifested: the law of unity and struggle of opposites. Subsequently it leads to the formation of a new, higher unity: the developed classless society. Thus, primitive classless society, class society, and developed classless society are the main stages of social development, which are directly connected and united with the development of the material productive forces of society, and which express the relationship of the latter to nature. An extremely low level of productive forces, an exceptionally low labor productivity, which did not allow man to produce more than was necessary for the maintenance of his existence, corresponded to the primitive classless order. Later, the development of productive forces opened up the possibility of production of surplus product, and this created the objective conditions for the appropriation, by some persons, of the products of the labor of others, the exploitation of man by man (period of class society). Finally, there comes into being a development of productive forces so high that exploitation of man by man becomes senseless and unnecessary, since one cannot appropriate anything that another does not have.

If the dialectical process of social development in general includes three fundamental stages (unity on a primitive basis; schism into antagonistic classes; unity on a new, higher level), into what main stages must the period of antagonistic class society be subdivided? It is natural to base the periodization on the principle according to which the period itself is differentiated and, having recognized as such the extent to which society is divided into antagonistic classes, to distinguish, according to this principle, stages of early class or undeveloped class society, developed class society, late class society, and society in transition to developed classless society. Many types, many forms of society, can exist in history, but they all must necessarily embody one of these stages of development of class society. If one takes, as the criterion for defining a given class society, the extent to which it is divided into opposing parts, into ruling and subjugated groups, the early class and the undeveloped class levels must naturally subsume those conditions in which such a breakdown had not been completed: the main bulk of the people still retains economic and personal independence, and the position of the ruling group is still not strong enough to permit it to place the main bulk of its fellow countrymen under the yoke of hereditary personal and economic dependence. The function of organizer, head, and leader, rooted in the primitive-communal order, still served as the source of privileges — whether this position of leadership concerned the relationships of man with nature, with religion, with other societies, or among the members of a given society — that is, whether economic, religious, military, or intrasocietal activity was involved. As we have seen, this was the situation most commonly found in the ancient East — in the most ancient class societies of the world. As we know, Engels held that one of the two ways in which the "relationships of dominance and subjugation" arose was precisely the formation of a ruling class with organizing functions, and here he named first of all eastern and then other (Greek, Celtic) early class societies. The second way was the emergence of a society based on slavery — slave-holding Greece and Rome (Engels 1950: 167-169).

The division of labor in society lies, as we know, at the basis of the subdivision of society into classes. In itself, the institution of organization or administration emerged not on the basis of coercion, but on the basis of the division of labor in society stemming from social necessity. In itself, leadership in public life also does not involve obligatory domination or exploitation of anyone. It begins to do so when these functions begin to be used to set up, preserve, or consolidate the leaders' own (economic or political) privileges, and to oppress, rob, or subjugate other members of society. Such trends obviously begin to manifest themselves very rapidly. Herodotus, for example, shows excellently *(Her.* I. 96-101) how among the Medes a sovereign king appeared in the person of Deiocus, and how rapidly he changed from the people's servant to its sovereign and lord! In a society where the right of ownership of all means of production and of the main bulk of the people was not yet in the hands of the ruling group, where its privileged position rested mainly on the functions of head of social, economic, military, or cultic activity, the forms of exploitation had their distinguishing features. These were state taxes; participation in public works (which ultimately is also used for the preservation, expansion, and consolidation of the privileged position of the ruling strata); work on the estates of the king, the officials, and the temples as a matter of state and public obligation; and participation in expeditions with unequal distribution of spoils and prisoners. Of course, the economic and property supremacy attained in this way by the ruling elite was later transformed into a supplementary factor for intensifying exploitation by methods of economic coercion as well. For this purpose, the letting of land for rent (or under other conditions) to land-poor or landless members of the society, the hiring of persons wholly or partially deprived of means of production, and the granting of loans at high interest rates (whether in money, foodstuffs, etc.) were practiced. This kind of exploitation could be carried out not only by the ruling military-bureaucratic aristocracy, but also by the stratum that was advancing economically through trade or usury.

Naturally, the greater the authority held by the ruling (governing) stratum and the more extensive its field of activity, the more easily was the exploitation of the broad masses of the population carried out in such forms. Therefore, the power of the ruling, governing elite that carried out organizing functions depended directly on the scale of the "public economy" and its ratio to the total economic activity of the society. It is precisely this situation which was created in the large societies of the East based on irrigation, which once attracted the special attention of Marx: owing to the characteristics of the natural setting, the need arose here to conduct economic life on a large scale, sometimes on the scale of the whole country, with large groups of producers. Hence the combination of surviving communal (state) forms of property and management of the economy with concentration of broad powers and vast despotic authority in the hands of the state and the state bureaucracy. This "Asiatic mode of production," as Marx called it, was quite clearly one of the modifications, one of the variants of early-class, undeveloped class society.

If war — one of the forms of "production" characteristic of antiquity, which spawned the so-called "military-parasitic" and "barbaric" states encountered both in ancient times and in the Middle Ages — had been pushed into the foreground, this might have led in another case to similar results, in terms of the consolidation of the position of the ruling stratum and its exploitation of broad strata of the population in similar forms. When, however, functions of management of the economic activity of society were concentrated in the hands of religious practitioners, of temples, one of the widespread forms of society in antiquity was instituted: temple or theocratic societies (amalgamations). Finally, in several ancient societies, where intense development of intermediary trade between different countries was observed due to favorable conditions, a distinctive complex of social relationships took form, in which a trading and moneylending elite arose. These societies were characterized by a sharper property and economic differentiation.

Early class societies and their ruling strata, as a rule, also exploited other societies through war or inequitable trade. If such exploitation was carried out on a large scale by a weakly differentiated or even wholly undifferentiatec society, a type of exploiting society (commune, tribe, clan) emerged (for example, Sparta). But if this exploitation was carried out by a fairly well-differentiated society, it generally resulted in still greater consolidation of the economic and political might of the ruling, leading stratum of the exploiter society, which appropriated the lion's share of tribute, spoils, slaves, etc., coming from the enslaved societies, even though in absolute terms some improvement in the position of the ordinary members of the ruling society may have been observed here.

What, then, are the paths of the further development of the early class or undeveloped class society? Evidently, these paths might vary, depending on the ensemble of internal and external conditions, including the disposition and struggle of forces within the society. The ruling circles, of course, strove to consolidate their privileged position, to further enslave their fellow countrymen, economically and politically. But fierce resistance by the latter, and other conditions interfering with this, might severely hinder this process: in many cases the military chieftain, judge, and ruler did not succeed in becoming hereditary owners and masters, and then society followed the path of "eastern feudalism"; only in those cases where almost total enserfment of the local populace was achieved did feudalism of the Western European type develop. Of course, the ruling circles, especially in a situation of fierce resistance from the lower layers of society, always strove to shift the main severity of exploitation to the outside — to transfer it to other, alien societies. Under especially favorable conditions, this led to the development of the slaveholding order, to the maturing of early class society into developed slaveholding society.

However, can we view early class societies as early

slaveholding — as the first, lowest stage of the slaveholding order? It appears to us that this would be incorrect. Undeveloped class societies can be viewed as the transitional step, not only to the developed slaveholding but to the developed feudal order. It is not fortuitous that the vast majority of such societies actually developed precisely in the direction of feudalism, and not of developed slaveholding. The latter, conversely, occurred rather rarely and was brought about by an exceptional situation, by specific causes, both internal and external. For the ancient world this situation, evidently, consisted, on the one hand, in the preparation of internal conditions for the broad use of slave labor in production (individualization of the economy; its rapid development owing to the large scale of commodity-money relationships, trade, crafts, and navigation, the institution of private property, and the breakdown of communal relationships; impoverishment and pauperization of much of the free population, etc.); and, on the other, in the existence of a broad backward environment to which the more developed society could shift the main force of exploitation, pumping out vast material resources and easily acquiring large masses of slaves (Kuzovkov 1954). In this way the situation produced as a consequence of the acute inequality of development in a given area of the world was evidently a necessary condition for the emergence of a developed slaveholding society. But this situation was fairly rare in the ancient world. We encounter it, for example, in Phoenicia, Greece, and Rome. In certain periods it may have developed in other places as well. But this only confirms that development of an early class society in the direction of the slaveholding order was more the exception than a necessary stage. Consequently, early class society cannot be viewed only as the initial, the lowest stage, in the development of slaveholding society.

In general, early class society becomes slaveholding if slaveholding elements or early feudal elements begin to predominate in it, and when forms of exploitation of the feudal type predominate therein. However, side by side with such early class societies, there could — and did — exist societies with a decided predominance of forms of the Asiatic mode of production, that is, in which both forms of exploitation and both socioeconomic ways of life coexisted, with no especially pronounced tendency for the society to change into one of the slaveholding or feudal type (Vasil'ev and Stuchevskii 1966: 62, 70).

The mainstream of social development lay in the breakdown of society into antagonistic classes owing to internal socioeconomic differentiation. History, plainly, known no case of the formation of a developed slaveholding society via such socioeconomic differentiation within the given society itself. The transformation of broad strata of native inhabitants, in the presence of substantial survivals of the primitive-communal order, into slaves lacking any rights was extremely complex and was not caused by the necessary requirements of the preservation and development of material productive forces of society — those ultimate rulers of destiny in social development. Therefore, under the conditions of antiquity, a particular, relatively strong slaveholding society could be formed, only in exceptional cases, by some internal unification of the society itself *(polis,* slaveholding community-state) and by shifting of the main burden of exploitation outside, onto other societies. This situation leads to ruin as soon as the ratio of forces between the slaveholding community-state and its exploited external hinterland changes. The basic contradiction of developed slaveholding societies was obviously expressed precisely in this. It is not surprising, then, that the onslaught of the barbarian hinterland against the citadel of slaveholding exploitation — ancient Rome — emerges as the fundamental factor in the breakdown of ancient slaveholding, along with internal difficulties of the functioning of the slaveholding mode of production (the low productivity of slave labor). After this, society returns to the mainstream of its development — the feudal path. Under conditions of the feudal exploitation of the mass of producers, the serf peasantry proves to be not so much the heir of the slaves of Classical society as the immediate successor of the free commune members of early class societies — the next step in the development of this social stratum enmeshed in the bonds of different kinds of dependence and exploitation.

From all the foregoing it becomes understandable why feudalism is so widespread, so universal an antagonistic formation: feudal society is in fact the highest actually existing form of the developed precapitalist class society. Precisely by virtue of this it became the starting point for formation of a new, higher stage of social development: the basis of development into bourgeois, capitalist society. Theoretically, from the viewpoint of the development of antagonistic classes, the next step in the movement of society could have been the transformation of serfs into slaves; however, not only did this not occur, since it is in sharp conflict with the needs of development of the productive forces, but, on the contrary, the powerful onslaught of the latter, together with the revolutionary battle of the enslaved part of the population, victoriously smashed the fetters forged by centuries of legal and economic inequality, creating first juridical — at least formal — equality (capitalism) and then actual equality between individuals (socialism).

The ancient world and the Middle Ages were acquainted with all those stages of social development about which we have spoken: early class (in which different socioeconomic orders coexist or one of them predominates — the Asiatic mode of production, early slaveholding or early feudal societies); developed slaveholding or developed feudal societies. However, it could hardly be that any one of the cited stages of social development was necessarily associated with a specific level of development of labor implements. It is obviously incorrect to seek a direct correlation between the predominance of slaveholding or feudal relationships and the level of development of material production, and to hold that feudal socioeconomic relationships necessarily represent a higher level. We know that the transition from slaveholding to feudalism in Western Europe occurred more rapidly under conditions of decline than upsurge of production. The predominance of a particular form of socioeconomic relationships obviously does not depend mechanically on the level of development of tools and the technology of production. The same tools, obviously, can serve as the basis of both slaveholding and feudal orders, and, in individual cases, even of the primitive-communal order, just as the same technology serves as the basis, in one case, of a capitalist society and in another of a socialist one. It is hardly possible that over the span of antiquity and the Middle Ages such a leap occurred in the development of productive forces as would decisively influence the predominance in the society of a given form of exploitation. Therefore, we cannot exclude a priori the existence in antiquity, along with the early class (including early slaveholding and early feudal) societies most universal there, of individual well-developed slaveholding or feudal societies: when and where, in what varieties, etc. — all this must be decided in each individual case on the basis of concrete historical material.

Of course, a line must be drawn between the above-mentioned main stages of social development and socioeconomic formations. The latter are commonly individual types or forms of society. They are characterized by a certain socioeconomic structure of society, by an entire complex system of production relationships intimately interrelated with a specific condition of the productive forces. The fundamental criterion for defining the character of a society, for classifying it into a particular formation, is represented by relationships of production — relationships established between people in the process of production. They, of course, subsume not the place of a particular person in the production process, but the "relationship of the owners of the requisites for production to the immediate producers" (Marx 1950: 804). Obviously, as the main types of these relationships are, so also must be the main forms of exploitation of man by man and, consequently, the main types of class society, the main antagonistic socioeconomic formations (in conformity with the form of these relationships which has become dominant in the society).

Marx pointed to four main modes of production underlying the four main types of class society, the four antagonistic socioeconomic formations. Along with the slaveholding (Classical), feudal, and capitalist modes, the Asiatic mode of production can be viewed as a socioeconomic formation, inasmuch as it is characterized by a particularly specific economic structure and by social relationships and a state structure corresponding to it. Obviously, along with the well-known three types of "dominance and enslavement," the three forms of exploitation, a fourth can be singled out, in spite of its proximity at times to feudal and protofeudal — and at other times to slaveholding — forms of exploitation. In three antagonistic socioeconomic formations — slaveholding, feudal, and capitalist — the owner of the requisites for production emerges as the owner of means of production and, on this basis, exploits a person fully owned (slave) or partially owned (serf) by him, or even a person in no kind of personal dependence on him at all (wage labor). However, as we have already noted, at the early class stage, under conditions where the instituion of property is weakly developed, still another type of society based on the exploitation of man by man takes shape. The characteristic features of this type of society were excellently noted by Marx precisely in describing the distinguishing features of eastern societies: the ruling stratum appears in the person of the state, its machinery, and all persons associated with it as the personification of the unity of society; the ruling stratum appears as the head that governs society and its productive activity (including also war); it appears as the collective owner and manager of the means of production and of the country's labor force as a whole. On this basis, there arises severe exploitation of broad strata of the populace, which takes on specific forms, as well as a specific political organization of society, characterized by a high degree of centralization. This type of society, revealed by Marx from materials of the history of Asia, and described by him in greatest detail in the work *Formy, predshestvuiushchie kapitalisticheskomu proizvodstvu* [Precapitalist Forms of Production], is characteristic, as is now clear, by no means of Asia alone, and should therefore be called by some other name.

The existence of such trends, generally characteristic of early class societies, was caused by their transitional nature, their closeness to the primitive-communal order, the preservation of many of its traditions, the weak development of the institution of private property, and the still extremely low level of productive forces. However, this does not mean that "Asiatic" forms of exploitation gained a dominant position in all early class societies, and that all these forms, and particularly all ancient eastern societies, must be viewed as belonging to the Asiatic socioeconomic formation. This must be spoken of only in those cases where similar trends, similar relationships, between the "owners of the requisites for production and the direct producers" became dominant and determined the aspect of society. And since types of exploitation appear not only in the form of formations, but also as ways of life, there may quite possibly have been, and doubtless were, class societies in which different socioeconomic ways of life coexisted, even without pronounced pure dominance of one of them. In fact, historical conditions are so varied that an infinite number of varieties of societies can appear. "The same economic basis," said Marx, "the same basis as far as the basic conditions are concerned — owing to infinitely various empirical circumstances, natural conditions, racial relationships, historical influences operating from outside, etc. — may reveal in its manifestations, infinite variations and gradations, which can be understood only with the aid of analysis of these empirically given circumstances" (Marx 1950: 804).

The "Asiatic" mode, and "Asiatic" forms of exploitation, as we have seen above, can quite justly be viewed as "protofeudal," since they were formed in particular conditions favorable to the development of society in the direction of feudalism. However, it is incorrect, on this basis, to view the "Asiatic" way of life and the "Asiatic" formation as varieties of the feudal way of life and the feudal formation. They were transformed into early-feudal and then into feudal relationships when the nature of the relationship of owners of the conditons of production[5] to the immediate producer changed radically — that is, when the first of the managers and leaders, the representatives of state authority, began to be transformed into the actual owners of the means of production and of the person of the producer. As was noted above, it is quite possible that under the conditions of the ancient

East all the main precapitalist forms of society were formed: early class (and its specific varieties — "Asiatic," early slaveholding, early feudal, societies with coexistence of various ways of life), and also developed slaveholding (cf., for example, Phoenicia) or developed feudal (China?). Obviously, it is necessary — through profound study of the economic structure of society, of the entire complex system of relationships of production, political and state structure, forms of ideology, and taking account of the level and state of the productive forces — to define the concrete types and varieties of society, to define socioeconomic formations, their stages of development and varieties. This concrete study can open up better prospects for historical research than the tendency, long observed in our country, to bring together societies of wholly disparate types under the heading of the same socioeconomic formation, and the effort, in particular, to see feudalism everywhere after the fourth century following the fall of the Western Roman Empire, and, prior to this, to see only slaveholding.

It seems to us that, in the course of the discussion, the impossibility of viewing all the most ancient class societies as slaveholding has emerged in an increasingly definite way. It has also become clear that there was a need for a clear definition of the place occupied in the course of social development by the Asiatic type of society, which bears the impress of the clear-cut individuality that once attracted the interest of the founders of Marxism. We are in agreement with those authors who have noted the combination, in the most ancient class societies, of various forms of exploitation; it is also legitimate that many scholars have cast doubt on the universality of the course of development, as attested from Western Europe; this was caused, it seems to us, to a large extent by the interaction of societies at different steps of development, and by the unevenness of development, which played a large role in the foundation and development of Graeco-Roman slaveholding and Western European feudal societies, and then of capitalist society. The causes for the distinctiveness of the Western European path, which brought about the high rate of development of this society, must be sought in the duration and intensity of developed class relationships — of the stage of developed class society, characterized by a high degree of class division, and by the polarization of the latter and the deepening of class contradictions.

Of course, as yet only the first steps have been taken in the solution of the problems posed above. We still confront a great deal of work in the concrete, profound study of individual societies, as well as in the processes of the functioning and development of society as a specific structure, a system of interrelated and mutually conditioned elements and phenomena, the beginning of which was laid down so brilliantly in the classics of Marxism-Leninism.

* * *

NOTES

1. As early as 1934, A. V. Mishulin suggested that the socioeconomic order of ancient eastern societies be defined as early-slaveholding (Postovskaia 1961: 105). In the second edition of his book *Istoriia Drevnego Vostoka* [History of the Ancient East] (Moscow-Leningrad, 1941, p. 6), V. V. Struve, who initially wrote about "developed slaveholding society" in the ancient East, agreed in large measure with the view of his opponents on the specific nature of ancient eastern societies.

2. The slaveholding nature of ancient eastern society was unreservedly admitted even by those researchers who in the early 1930s, in the course of the discussion, spoke and wrote against this idea (Academician A. I. Tiumenev, Professor I. M. Lur'e, and Professor N. M. Nikol'skii).

3. For criticism of these views, see Ranovich 1947: 29.

4. A number of problems associated with these latifundia still remain unclear: how they were set up, how the body of workers employed on them and receiving compensation was formed, juridical status of the latter, whether the latifundia embraced the entire economy and the entire land supply of the country. In Struve's view, rural communes — collectives of small farmers who paid taxes to the royal estate — existed along with royal latifundia (Struve 1948: 32). But A. I. Tiumenev regarded them as also employees of the royal estate

who were given small tracts in compensation for their services (cf. A. I. Tiumenev 1950: 49 ff.).

5. Probably in the broad sense: sovereign, manager, *actual* owner, etc.

(Voprosy istorii, 1966, No. 11)

THE PROBLEM OF THE SOCIOECONOMIC ORDER
OF THE ANCIENT NEAR EAST

Iu. I. Semenov

In almost all works examining the history of the
ancient Near East, we find the assertion that ancient Near
Eastern society was slaveholding. But we learn from these
same studies that, at least in the early stages of development of ancient Near Eastern societies, there were very
few slaves, that they constituted an insignificant minority
of the population, and that during the entire historical
span of these societies the bulk of the producers of material goods were people who cannot be classed as slaves.
"The bulk of the working population of this time," states
V. I. Avdiev (1953: 192) in his characterization of the
Old Kingdom of Egypt, "was made up of free cultivators,
members of the ancient rural communes." "In our opinion," writes I. A. Stuchevskii (1958b: 204), "in Egypt the
elements of slavery were at first weakly developed; in the
age of the New Kingdom they were much strengthened."
"Most of the population of Mesopotamia — not only at
the beginning of the third millennium before our era, but
also much later — were doubtless commune members,"
noted V. V. Struve (editorials in *Vsemirnaia istoriia* 1955[a]:
I, 196). "In the ancient East," we read in one of the
editorials in *Vestnik drevnei istorii* (hereafter, *VDI*),
"peasants constituted the bulk of the laboring populace.
Slavery here for millennia did not directly constitute the
basis of the economy, though it was a leading, progressive
institution" *(VDI* 1947: 4). Similar statements can
be cited ad infinitum.

But if there were few slaves in the ancient East, slavery may have been at the same time the only or, at least, the predominant form of exploitation. If this were so, the description of ancient Eastern societies as slave-holding would then be justified. However, the very opposite is stated in all studies on the subject. Of course, the views of different scholars are not in full agreement with respect to the situation of those direct producers who were not slaves. Some see them as a more or less homogeneous mass. Others differentiate among them *free commune members* who farmed independently and persons who were in some way involved in the households of the ruler, the temples, and the elite — *semifree, dependent* persons. But scholars agree on the major issue: all direct producers who were not slaves, both dependent and free farmers, were subjected to exploitation (Nikol'skii 1938: 77, 80, 97; 1939: 68 ff.; Struve 1940: 16-19; Struve 1961a: 25, 29; *VDI* 1951: No. 1, 8-9; Melikishvili 1951: 31; Tiumenev 1956: 3, 20, 21, etc.; *Vsemirnaia istoriia* 1955: I, 196, 258, etc.; Gel'tser 1956b: 15; 1960: 17; D'iakonov 1959a: 38, 264, etc.; Vasil'ev 1961a: 6, 218-219; Kriukov 1961: 21; Menabde 1963: 86, and many other works). Here it is admitted that even the number of only those producers directly dependent on the ruler, temples, and elite considerably exceeded the number of slaves: "The numerical predominance over slaves of the group of persons not yet enslaved, but dependent on the slaveholding elite, is one typical feature of early forms in the development of the slaveholding society — in Egypt and Mesopotamia of the third millennium before our era in particular, and in part even later" (I. M. D'iakonov and G. F. Il'in, *Vsemirnaia istoriia* 1955: I, 140). If we add to dependent producers the exploited "free commune members," we get a picture of a clear, complete, and repeated predominance, in the societies of the ancient East, of non-slaveholding forms of exploitation over slaveholding forms. And this picture emerges even on the basis of generalizing statements by scholars firmly convinced of the slaveholding nature of these societies.[1]

The paradox of characterizing as slaveholding a society whose economy was based on non-slaveholding

forms of exploitation cannot fail to strike us. Hence the attempts at explanation. For example, in writing about ancient Sumer, I. M. D'iakonov (1959a: 118) writes: "We must not be embarrassed by the fact that in this society, which we define as early slaveholding, slaves were relatively few and were not chiefly engaged in the leading branches of production, that not only the number of the free but also the number of clients subject to not wholly slaveholding, semipatriarchal forms of exploitation exceeded the number of slaves, and that the economic importance of clients was evidently greater." The author proceeds to explain why there were few slaves in ancient Sumer and why they were not engaged in the leading branches of the economy. But what causes embarrassment and requires explanation is not at all the small number of slaves in ancient Sumerian society, but the description of this society as slaveholding. Some scholars, attempting to demonstrate the thesis of the slaveholding nature of ancient Eastern societies, sometimes try to designate as slaves those representatives of the local population who to some extent belonged to the estates of the ruler, the temples, and the elite, and sometimes even some of the "free commune members." However, the vast majority of historians do not support these attempts and characterize them as unfounded and contradictory to historical facts (VDI 1951: 7). The most widespread argument favoring the prevalent point of view on the nature of ancient Eastern society is that, while slavery was not the quantitatively predominant mode of exploitation, it was nevertheless the leading mode and determined all the others (VDI 1947: 4; D'iakonov 1959a: 118, etc.). Unfortunately, however, there is no substantiation of this position in a single study.

The thesis of the leading role of slavery cannot be demonstrated without subjecting to detailed theoretical analysis every form of exploitation that existed in the ancient East, and without revealing the entire complexity of their relationships. In this connection, we encounter a fact that is truly amazing: literally in not a single work do we find the slightest attempt at theoretical analysis of non-slaveholding forms of exploitation in the ancient East

— that is, of those forms which in the unanimous opinion of Soviet scholars were absolutely predominant in that era, at least quantitatively.

Some scholars, while noting in passing that "free commune members," who constituted the bulk of producers, were subjected to severe exploitation (just like slaves), do not return to the question at all and concentrate their attention exclusively on slavery. There is not a word about what this form of exploitation amounted to, what its character was. In the works of other scholars, these forms of exploitation, while described in more or less detail, are theoretically analyzed. In the best situation, we find certain terms used to designate different forms of non-slaveholding exploitation: "patriarchal," "semi-patriarchal," "clientele," "colonate," and "debt slavery." Unfortunately, this also does not help much in grasping the question, for the meaning of the terms remains very vague and indefinite.

One cannot find, in any single work published in the past 20 to 25 years, even an attempt to deal with what would appear to be the most demanding question: did the non-slaveholding forms of exploitation in the ancient East belong to those already known (slavery, feudalism, or capitalism), or did they constitute a special antagonistic mode of union of the worker with the means of production? This, in fact, is the only formulation of the question which can lead to a solution to the problem of the socio-economic order of the ancient East.

The largest amount of material available to scholarship on the ancient East concerns the forms of exploitation of immediate producers in the temple and state economies of ancient Sumer. This question has been the subject of works by eminent Soviet scholars: V. V. Struve (1934d, f; 1947a; 1948; 1949; 1960; 1961a; 1963; etc.); A. I. Tiumenev (1948a, b; 1950; 1954; 1956; 1957[b]; etc.); and I. M. D'iakonov (1948; 1949a; 1950; 1959a). Data on the initial stages of development of the temple estates of ancient Sumer are fragmentary. The earliest such estate about which the sources permit us to form a more or less clear idea is the estate of the temple to the main god of the city of Shuruppak (27th-26th centuries B.C.E.). The main branch of the economy was farming. The documents contain no indication that tilling of the land was done by the labor force of the estate. If this did take place, it was on an extremely insignificant scale (Tiumenev 1956: 105, 106). A large part of the temple lands was distributed in small plots for tilling by persons of the most varied callings, occupations, and qualifications. The direct producers also obtained working animals and grain for sowing from the temple administration. Part of the harvest from the sections went to the holder; the rest went into the temple granaries. Users of the sections were grouped under the supervision of special officials — responsible *engary*, who collected grain from persons in their charge and transferred it to the temple warehouses (Struve 1934f: 15; Tiumenev 1956: 40, 98-104, 121; D'iakonov 1959a: 103 ff.).

A large part of the temple estate personnel of Shuruppak, including users of land plots, were called *gurushy:* that is, they were denoted by the same term as were all free members of the city community in general. This is evidence that, in all likelihood, they were commune members, differing from the rest by their more intimate ties with the temple estate (Struve 1934f: 15 ff.; Tiumenev 1956: 103 ff.). Some *gurushy* who belonged to the temple estate received, more or less regularly, foodstuffs in kind. The temple estate personnel included (in addition to the *gurushy) dumu-dumu*, whose position was probably close to that of the slave, *aru*, (male slaves), and *gim* (female slaves). Slaves played no marked role in economic life. *Dumu-dumu* also had no prominent place. The main producers of material goods in the temple estate of Shuruppak were the *gurushy* — holders of plots of temple land (Tiumenev 1956: 99, 117-119, 121).

Analysis of the forms of exploitation to which holders of plots of temple land were subjected is no easy matter. This form of exploitation is primarily akin to the feudal. The cultivators worked an allotted section (more or less independently) and gave the temple part of the produce. There is evidence — very indeterminate, it is true — that at least part of the *gurushy* were in some measure personally dependent on the temple. In several documents, for example, temple *gurushy* were alluded to as "fugitives" (Tiumenev 1956: 115). But though the cultivator tilled his allotment, it would hardly be correct to characterize him as managing his own farm. First of all, the plot he worked was often changed. Secondly, he worked the land, using cattle obtained from the temple administration and sowing it with grain from the temple warehouse. The temple estate was the base for the economy of a petty producer. The farm of the holder of the plot of temple land was essentially nothing but a distinctive form of the existence of the temple estate, and the cultivator combined in himself features, on the one hand, of an owner and, on the other, of a worker on another person's farm. The fact that the cultivator received the basic means of production from the temple shows that he himself lacked them.

We know of two types of producers who lack means of production, two types of workers on someone else's farm: slaves and proletarians. To which of these did the features manifested by the cultivator of temple land belong? If we recall that we are speaking of an age removed from us by five millennia, then the answer automatically suggests itself that features of the slave were manifested in the cultivator. And such features were manifested — namely, the existence of personal dependence. But features of the wage worker, the proletarian, emerged far more distinctly in the cultivator of temple land. We can hardly doubt that holders of land were recruited in the main from the impoverished commune members who had lost the plot of communal land and other means of production belonging to them. The initial incorporation of the free man into the temple personnel was similar in many respects to his being hired for work in the temple estate. And after being transformed into a holder of temple land, a *gurush* remained basically a full-fledged member of the community. In particular, he bore military service. However, in the course of time his position inevitably changed. Features of personal dependence must have appeared in it, ever becoming stronger.

The next stage in the development of the temple economy of Sumer is most graphically represented by the economic documents of the temple to the goddess Bau in

Lagash related to the periods of Lugalianda and Urukagina (25th-24th centuries). During that time the land of the temple estate was divided into several categories. The larger consisted of "land of the priesthood." It was worked by teams of agricultural workers of the temple — *shublugals* — headed by overseers. All the harvest from this land went to the temple. For their labor the *shublugals* received plots of "feeding land," usually not directly. As a rule, their plots were part of the allotments given by the temple to the team overseers. Allotments of "feeding land" were also given to other categories of temple personnel. In addition to plots of land, the *shublugals* received allowances in kind (Struve 1934f: 15-17; Tiumenev 1956: 135-177; D'iakonov 1959a: 101-113). In Struve's view, in addition to the category cited, there was yet another category of *shublugals* who had allotments of land not included in the "feeding land" and who were not given produce. Finally, some of the temple land, as Tiumenev noted, was given for tilling against payment of a definite proportion of the harvest, and the rent was sometimes paid simultaneously with the receipt of the allotment (Struve 1961a: 49-51; 1963: 18; Tiumenev 1956: 152, 173). *Shublugals* and producers similar to them in status, particularly *ukuushy*, constituted the main labor force of the temple economy (Tiumenev 1956: 139, 152-159, 175, 195, etc.; D'iakonov 1959a: 51, 110). Slaves *(gim, dumu*, perhaps also some of the *iginudu*, and the porters) were not employed in the leading branches of production. Some served the household of the queen, and others constituted an auxiliary labor force (Tiumenev 1956: 159, 160, 195, 425; D'iakonov 1959a: 103).

There was a similarity in the position of the *shublugals* to that of feudally dependent workers. They themselves tilled plots assigned to them, sometimes even using animals that belonged to them personally and not to the temple (Tiumenev 1956: 155; Struve 1961a: 48, 96). Above all, however, they were workers on the temple estate. The slavelike features noted even in the *gurush* — the cultivator of temple land in Shuruppak — were unquestionably manifested more distinctly in the *shublugal* of Lagash. The *shublugal* was considered the property of the temple, and was in personal dependence on the temple administration, including his immediate superior, whose allotment he was obliged to till along with his own (D'iakonov 1959a: 109, 112). The temple administration could, without compensation or with compensation at its discretion, take from the *shublugal* his livestock and house (D'iakonov 1959a: 107-108; Struve 1961a: 36).

At the same time, the *shublugal* approximates the free worker in a number of respects. These traits are so pronounced that Struve describes the *shublugals* as free commune members (1934f: 15, 17, 21; 1961a: 38, 49-51; 1961b: 171). Other researchers view the *shublugals* as persons who had already lost their ties with the commune and had altogether left it. However, all these scholars, like Struve, view the *shublugals* as personally free people (Tiumenev 1956: 155-175; D'iakonov 1959a: 82, 103, 110). Together with the entire free population, they were subject to military service. A comparison of the *shublugals* of Lagash in the 25th-24th centuries B.C.E. with the *gurushy* — cultivators of temple land in Shuruppak in the 27th-26th centuries — shows that the change in the status of the main category of temple workers in the estates of Sumer tended to bring this status closer to the servile.

A new level in the development of the temple and state economy of ancient Sumer is seen in the royal economy of the Third Dynasty of Ur (late 22nd and 21st centuries B.C.E.). The main producers of material goods in this economy were the *gurushy*, who in their great majority were part of the local population (Struve 1947b: 241-242; 1953: 81-91; Tiumenev 1956: 268-270, 299). Like the *shublugals* of Lagash, they worked in teams under the supervision of overseers; but in contrast to the *shublugals*, they did not receive land allotments. The *gurushy* worked the year round, without interruption, on the royal estate, and were fully provided for in kind. Their status differed little from that of slaves (Struve 1934d: 54-56; 1947a: 720-742; 1949: 159-179; Tiumenev 1956: 266-276). Their in-kind provisions cannot be viewed as wages. That this is so is particularly evident if we compare the status of *gurushy* with that of wage workers, whose labor was quite widely used in the royal economy of the

Third Dynasty of Ur (Struve 1934d: 57; 1948: 13-33; 1949: 179-182; Tiumenev 1956: 306). Wage workers obtained from special agencies wages substantially exceeding the in-kind provisions of the *gurushy* (Struve 1934d: 57; 1948: 18-21; 1949: 179-182). This fact convincingly shows that the *gurushy* of the royal estate were personally dependent workers. Yet, in our view, they cannot be called slaves in the full and precise meaning of the word. To some extent they were regarded as free. In all probability, they could never be bought or sold (Tiumenev 1956: 276 ff.). They could and did have families (Struve 1934d: 56, 57, 100; 1953: 85-90). The *gurushy* of the royal estates were workers on the very borderline of servile status.

It would be logical to expect that the next stage in the evolution of forms of exploitation in the state economy of ancient Mesopotamia would consist of transformation of the bulk of its workers into slaves, in the full and precise sense of the word. If this presupposition proved valid, this would be a weighty argument in favor of the position that slavery held the leading, determining role in ancient Mesopotamia, and thus an argument in favor of characterizing Sumerian society as slaveholding. The simple preservation, in more or less unmodified form, of the economic system developed in the royal estate of the Third Dynasty of Ur would also be a rather weighty argument in favor of this position.

However, in fact, after the fall of the Third Dynasty of Ur, the above-described system of exploitation gradually came to an end (D'iakonov ed. 1952: Pt. 1, 262; Tiumenev 1956: 431-432). In the period of the first Babylonian dynasty, royal land was not used for crop farming for the royal estate. Some of it was divided into allotments for representatives of the royal administration, and for priests, warriors, artisans, etc. Another part was distributed among petty direct producers — the *ishshakkums*. The latter, in addition to land allotments, also received sowing grain, draught animals, and implements, and were obligated to give up part of the harvest (D'iakonov ed. 1952: Pt. 1, 265-267, 270-271; D'iakonov 1956b: 40-46; Tiumenev 1957: 60-61).

The *ishshakkums* are very reminiscent of the holders of plots of temple land in Shuruppak, who have already been considered. Their status combined just as contradictorily the features of feudally dependent producers, wage workers, and slaves; and the features of personal dependence emerge most distinctly in their case. The *ishshakkums* were divided into teams under special bosses. If one of the latter was transferred to another locality, all the *ishshakkums* in his charge had to follow him. It was possible that the core of the *ishshakkums* was made up of former *gurushy* settled on the land. Under Hammurabi the number of *ishshakkums* was increased by the addition of impoverished commune members who lacked plots of land and other means of production.

It is difficult to answer the question of who worked the fields of the Sumerian elite. D'iakonov assumes that those who labored on the lands of the elite were "dependent, but personally free workers whose status was similar to that of the temple *shublugals*. They differed from the *shublugals* only in that they were dependent not on the temple, but on private persons, and were 'clients' of the latter" (D'iakonov 1959a: 48-49, 110-111).

In the private estates of the Old Babylonian Kingdom, land was rented chiefly in small lots and for short periods of time (one or two years). Usually, ruined commune members rented land. Most commonly, the tenant obtained sowing grain, draught animals, and implements from the owner of the land. The position of such a tenant was characterized by features peculiar to the wage worker. In essence, he obliged himself for a specific — but not very long — period to till someone else's land with the means of production of the latter. However, one cannot call him a completely free wage worker. During the rental period he actually fell into personal dependence on the landowner. In the event of a negligent attitude toward his obligations, he was severely punished: his fingers could be cut off, he could be gored by bulls on the land he worked (D'iakonov ed. 1952: Pt. 1, 255-256; Struve 1940: 19-21). The foregoing makes this kind of tenant more similar to the slave. Additionally, there are features that make him resemble the feudally dependent worker:

the tenant managed a farm on someone else's land, and for this he paid the landowner part of the produce he raised. Hired labor was used in private estates of the First Babylonian Dynasty. Slave labor was almost never used in agriculture (Tiumenev 1956: 62).

The tilling of a plot of temple, royal, or private land for a share of the harvest, or on any other conditions (the *shublugals* of Lagash) was by no means the sole means which could and did lead to the transformation of a personally free individual into a dependent worker of one of the above-described types. Another means was to place oneself under the patronage of an economically powerful person (D'iakonov 1959a: 114-116; 1956a: 335). A free person could, for example, assume an obligation to work on someone else's estate in exchange for the promise of maintenance. This inevitably entailed personal dependence on the patron. However, such a worker could abandon his patron. In Assyria of the 16th-11th centuries B.C.E., the placing of oneself under patronage was often officially registered as "adoption," which made the personal dependence strong and permanent. In the contracts for "adoption" that have come down to us, it was usual to include a condition by which the adopted person was obligated to work for the adopter. It was not only persons without means of production who were adopted; in some cases the record tells of the "adoption" of a person together with his field and house. In the Middle Assyrian period a form of transformation of a free man into a dependent one, called "revival in an impoverished state," was also known (D'iakonov 1949b: 64-66). The existence of "revival" as a form of enslavement of a free man is also noted during the Hittite Empire (D'iakonov ed. 1952: Pt. 2, 285).

During the first two millennia B.C.E., one of the most widespread modes of transforming a free man into a dependent person in the countries of the ancient East was debt bondage. Its forms were uncommonly diverse. The loan was made against the person of the debtor himself or against those of members of his family, and also against movable and immovable property. The "hostage" was obligated to work the creditor's estate. In several countries — for example, in Babylonia (second millennium

B.C.E.) — the authority of the creditor over persons who fell into servitude was limited by law. Thus, under the Code of Hammurabi, the "hostage" who had worked in the estate of the creditor for three years was deemed to have paid his debt and was considered free (D'iakonov ed. 1952: Pt. 1, 240; Struve 1959: 5-17). In Alalaha, Arrapha, and other countries the "hostage" was obligated to work on the creditor's estate until he had paid the full amount of the debt. As a result, debt bondage often became a lifelong status. But even in these cases, debt-dependent persons did not generally become slaves. They retained certain rights. Cases are known from the history of Alalaha in which not individual persons, but entire communities, fell into debt bondage (Gel'tser 1956b: 17-19, 25-26; Iankovskaia 1957a: 23; 1959b: 41). In Assyria (second millennium B.C.E.), as long as the person remained only a "hostage," the power of the creditor over him was restricted; in particular, he could not be subjected to corporal punishment. If the debt was not paid on time, the creditor acquired full power over the debtor, including even the right to sell him beyond the boundaries of Assyria. Nonpayment of debt entailed the transformation into the creditor's property of what was pledged by the debtor, including land (D'iakonov 1949b: 68-69, 72-73). In Arrapha this transition was formalized as the adoption of the creditor by the debtor. Frequently, in this case, the former owner (and sometimes even his relatives) continued to till the plot of land which no longer belonged to him, paying part of the harvest to the new owner (D'iakonov 1949b: 72, 73, 77; Iankovskaia 1957a: 23). It is difficult not to see that here again we see a combination of features of a person managing his own economy with those of a worker on the estate of another, and that, depending on conditions, either the features of a slave or those of a hired worker could be predominant.

This kind of exploitative relationship can be described endlessly, for, as some Soviet researchers directly admit, it was unusually widespread in all "early slaveholding" societies and was characteristic of them (D'iakonov ed. 1952: Pt. 2, 287; Gel'tser 1956b: 18). Let us attempt to interpret the above data. In the first place, we must regard as firmly established the fact of widespread occurrence, in countries of the ancient East, of forms of exploitation of man by man which contradictorily combine features of slavery, feudalism, and wage labor.

It is important to underscore that we are confronted not with a mechanical union of individual features of antagonistic relationships of the above-indicated three types, but with a nondiscrete, undifferentiated organic unity of these types: and this constitutes a special form of exploitation which differs from the slaveholding, feudal, and capitalist forms, and is neither the first, nor the second, nor the third. This is a special nondiscrete, undifferentiated antagonistic mode of exploitation, potentially containing all known antagonistic modes of production. It is wholly understandable that the type of productive relationship which we have isolated needs a name.

Antagonistic relationships of the type described are very widespread — and not only in the ancient East. They are found in all class societies in process of formation and at early stages of development of all class societies. It is natural that they cannot remain unnoticed. We find descriptions of them in the works of both ethnographers and historians, and not only of the ancient East. We also encounter in these works the use of different terms to designate these relationships. They include "clientella" (Tolstov 1934: 183-186; Averkieva 1941: 74; Tokarev 1945: 111 ff.; Tokarev and Tolstov, eds. 1956: 618, 698-699, etc.; D'iakonov 1959a: 111-118; 1963b: 28-29; El'nitskii 1964: 15, 50, 95, 106, 117 ff., etc.) and "colonate" (D'iakonov 1949b: 118, 120, 138; El'nitskii 1964: 138-139). But the term "debt-slavery" is the most widely used (Tokarev 1933: 72-73; 1945: 103, 149-152, 182, etc; Tolstov 1935: 201, 202, 210; Averkieva 1941: 74-76; Kolobova 1939: 39, 50-56, etc.; Mavrodin 1946: 144; Tokarev and Tolstov, eds. 1956: 445; Pershits 1961; 121 ff.; El'nitskii 1964: 123, 127 ff.; Zel'in 1964: 236 ff., and many other works). It is used throughout the works on the ancient East, especially when indebtedness [?] and other related phenomena are being referred to (see, for example, Struve 1934b; 1959: 15 ff.; D'iakonov 1949b: 33, 67-76, etc.; *Vsemirnaia istoriia* 1955: I, 296 ff., 321 ff.;

587

Amusin 1955: 26; Gel'tser 1956b: 17-78, 25-26; Iankov-skaia 1957a: 23-24; Nikol'skii 1959: 120, 130-131; and many others). It is used also in works on ancient Eastern history and in characterizing the position of the tenant-sharecropper and other kindred categories of direct producers (Nikol'skii 1938: 98; 1959: 130; D'iakonov ed. 1952: Pt. 1, 286, Pt. 2, 285; Lur'e 1955b: 146; Tiumenev 1957: 55; D'iakonov 1963b: 33, etc.).

All this taken together allows us to suggest the term "debt-slavery" to designate the above-described nondifferentiated form of exploitation. We will call the exploited producers *debt-bondsmen* and the exploiters *bond-holders.* Correspondingly, we will speak of debt-slave production relationships, and the debt-slave mode of production and mode of exploitation. Use of the term "debt-slavery" to designate a nondifferentiated mode of exploitation is fraught with certain inconveniences, for the circle of phenomena embraced by it — in the sense we have proposed — as we will see below, is considerably wider than the circle of phenomena that it usually denotes. But we must reconcile ourselves to this.

Discovery of the existence of debt-slave productive relationships makes it possible to untangle several complex and confused problems of socioeconomic history and, in particular, to understand the actual position of certain categories of direct producers in the structure of ancient Eastern society.

One of the most controversial is the question of the status of producers of material goods in the estates of temples and the elite in Egypt of the Old Kingdom — expecially those denoted by the term *meret.*

T. N. Savel'eva, author of one of the recent works in which this problem is dealt with, characterizes the *meret* (whom she views as the main producers in the estates of members of the royal family, temples, and the elite) as slaves. On this ground she concludes that Egyptian society of the Old Kingdom is unquestionably slaveholding (Savel'eva 1962: 183-186, 207). The arguments cited by the author in favor of the position that the main bulk of workers on estates of temples and the elite were slaves boil down to the following.

Above all, Savel'eva emphasizes, these producers lacked the means of production. They tilled the land of their master, used livestock and farm implements belonging to him, sowed the master's seed, and received supplies in kind from the landowner. They worked in gangs. The book states that the master had the right to dispose of his workers as if they were movable property belonging to him, either with the land or without it. However, from the same work we learn that the bulk of workers on estates of temples and the elite were Egyptians, that these workers had families and lived in villages, and that these villages supplied the landowner with various kinds of produce, livestock, etc. ("deliveries" and "gifts"), and paid "assessments and taxes" to his "personal estate." We also discover that the *meret* participated in the funerary cult of their master and brought him gifts. The effort to find a way out of this contradiction led Savel'eva to the conclusion, first, that not all *meret* were slaves and, secondly, that at least some of the workers on estates of the elite were settled on the land and farmed more or less independently, using the means of production belonging to the magnate (Savel'eva 1962: 121-128, 171-189, 207-208).

A more cautious characterization of the position of the bulk of workers on estates of the ruler, temples, and the elite is given by Iu. Ia. Perepelkin in the chapter on the Old Kingdom of Egypt in the first volume of *Vsemirnaia istoriia*. He also points out that these producers worked as teams headed by overseers, that they tilled the master's land, using cattle and implements belonging to him, and that they obtained from him provisions in kind, temporarily or permanently; and he indicates that the land belonged to the master, along with the sowing grain and all of the harvest collected from his fields. At the same time, the author notes, at least some of the workers on the lord's estate had some property and could dispose of it. As a whole, however, Perepelkin writes of them as Egyptians "who, though exploited by the elite who used slaveholding methods, differed from slaves proper" *(Vsemirnaia istoriia* 1955: I, 164). "Such a direct producer of material goods," he indicates, "while in fact lacking means of production, still retained certain charac-

teristics of the former state and could own some property"
(Vsemirnaia istoriia 1955: I, 164).

In our view, even the above data afford sufficient
grounds for the conclusion that the bulk of workers on
the estates of temples and magnates in Old Kingdom
Egyptian society were debt-bondsmen, close in status to
debt-bound producers of the temple economy of ancient
Sumer, but differing from the latter by considerably more
pronounced features of personal dependence. The fact that
the status of the *meret* combined the features of slaves,
feudally dependent producers, and free workers afforded
various authors the opportunity to treat them at once as
slaves, as serfs, and as free producers. A one-sided
approach to the solution of the problem is determined in
many respects by its formulation. The point is that researchers had assumed in advance that producers of material goods in ancient Eastern society could only be slaves
or free producers. Even the possibility that they could
prove to be feudally dependent workers was excluded.
Therefore, some researchers, having convincingly demonstrated that the *meret* could not be characterized as free
producers, concluded that they were of servile status
(Struve 1934d: 38, 46, 93-96; Cherezov 1949: 66; 1951:
40-46; 1952: 123-126; 1960: 269; Katsnel'son 1954:
19-25). Others, having demonstrated no less convincingly
that the *meret* were not slaves, arrived at the conclusion
that they were of free status. Thus, in the opinion of
I. M. Lur'e, the *meret* were free persons estranged from
the commune, working in the estates of temples and
nobles and receiving plots of land for their work. Their
status was compared by this author with that of the
shublugals of Sumer (Lur'e 1952: 73-80; 1955a: 147-151).
It is interesting to note that in the 1930s, when the
question was formulated somewhat more broadly, Lur'e
viewed the *meret* as feudally dependent producers, as
serfs (1939: 121-125, 133-136). Finally, some researchers
have asserted that their ranks included both free persons
and slaves (Stuchevskii 1958b: 202; 1960: 9).

Whereas the debt-bound producers of the Old Kingdom of Egypt were most reminiscent of the *bondsmen* of
ancient Sumer, in Middle- and New-Kingdom Egypt the

predominant forms of debt-slave exploitation were similar to those existing in Babylonia — above all, sharecropper tenancy (Stuchevskii 1958a; 1962: 43; Lur'e 1955b; Tiumenev 1957: 66-68).

The undifferentiated nature of debt-slave relationships of exploitation is a consequence and a sign of their undeveloped state, their immaturity, and is reflected in the low level of development of the productive forces. In the period of the Copper and Bronze Ages, not a single one of the three known forms of exploitation could come to maturity, not even the slaveholding. It is precisely for this reason that the nascent relationships, as they developed in the state economy of ancient Sumer to the slaveholding relationships, was upset.

The assumption that during the Copper and Bronze Ages debt-slave relationships could not have developed into slaveholding appears, at first glance, to be strange at the very least. In fact, there is no doubt that, in the societies of the ancient East, actual slaves also existed, in addition to *bondsmen*. But slavery itself in the ancient East was immature and therefore most intimately fused with debt servitude. Slaves were mainly employed in the household; in all other domains of economic activity they were employed only as an auxiliary labor force. *Bondsmen* could and usually did play the very same economic roles as slaves. Therefore, it is extremely difficult to draw a line between the former and the latter. Here we are helped only by the fact that most slaves were foreigners. They were taken into captivity or were bought, which accounted for their lack of any rights. *Bondsmen*, however, were for the most part representatives of the local population. Therefore, even though completely deprived of means of production, they did retain certain rights. Nevertheless, in the process of development, the difference between slaves and *bondsmen* engaged in domestic and auxiliary work gradually was increasingly erased. Identical working conditions promoted the equalization of their social status. On the one hand, a change toward the servile state occurred in the status of *bondsmen;* on the other, a change in the position of slaves toward that of *debt-bondsmen*. The *bondsmen* found themselves in greater personal dependence than before, and lost part of their rights. Slaves, on the other hand, acquired certain rights, analogous to those enjoyed by *bondsmen*. As a result, the two groups actually fused into a single mass of dependent persons, in which all shades of personal dependence were observed — from the true servile state to the condition of the almost free person. This mass of dependent persons was viewed as something homogeneous, which was often expressed in the existence of a single term to designate it. This fact often puzzles researchers who operate from the premise that all workers, including domestics, were in the category of either slaves or free men. In this case, they have had to speak of a twofold meaning of these terms, and of a lack of socioeconomic meaning in them (Savel'eva 1962: 192-194, 208, etc.).

In certain periods, wars supplied much greater numbers of prisoners than could be used in household and auxiliary work. What happened to them? The answer to the question of their fate is vitally significant, for it allows us to determine the productive relationships that prevailed in ancient Eastern society.

In our view, a direct, unconditional identification of prisoners of war with slaves is erroneous. Prisoners of war, in and of themselves, are not yet slaves; they are still only people torn out of the system of relationships existing in the society to which they belonged, and thus separated from the means of production. What these persons became depended at this point on whether they were given means of production and, if they were, by precisely what method. As a rule they were given means of production by the method dominant in the given society.

In ancient Eastern societies of the second and first millennia B.C.E., prisoners of war, when there were more of them than could be used in domestic and auxiliary work, were usually settled on the land. They were supplied with implements and managed their own farms, paying part of the harvest to the owner — usually the state in the person of the ruler. The population of conquered countries could even be driven as prisoners for forced settlement in other areas of the state. It is wholly understandable that not only prisoners, but also persons who previously had the status of slaves, could be allotted land and means of production. The settlement of prisoners of war on the land was widely practiced in Egypt of the New Kingdom, in the Hittite Empire, in Assyria, and in Urartu (Melikishvili 1951: 27-28; D'iakonov 1952; 1963b: 62; Tiumenev 1957: 65; Lur'e 1955b: 25-26; Stuchevskii 1960: 18; D'iakonov ed., 1952: Pt. 2, 285, etc.).

In the works of Soviet researchers, war prisoners who were settled on the land are usually called slaves. Still, this use of the term "slave" essentially deprives it of any clear-cut socioeconomic meaning. Only that producer of material goods can be called a slave who, first of all, is somebody's complete property and, secondly, works on somebody's farm, most commonly that of his owner. Prisoners of war settled on the land managed their own farms. In this respect alone they differed qualitatively from slaves. This distinction is so precise that it could not but capture attention. Therefore some Soviet researchers, while by tradition relegating prisoners settled on the land to the category of slaves, point to their qualitative difference from slaves proper — slaves in the full sense of the word (D'iakonov 1949b: 102-107). Characterization of this form of dependence as primitive serfdom is also encountered in our literature (Zel'in 1937: 187-201).

Undoubtedly, the position of war prisoners settled on the land included features which make them resemble slaves. Their economy, especially at first, took on the appearance, in many respects, of a form of someone else's operations. Their status combined features of the master with features of the worker on the farm of another. This circumstance permits us to call them *debt-bondsmen*. At first glance, it appears strange to characterize prisoners of war settled on the land as being in debt-bondage, for the concept of debt-bondage is usually linked with the idea of economic dependence. However, as has already been stressed, this term is used by us in a broader sense to denote an undifferentiated, immature mode of exploitation. In the given case, we are dealing with precisely this sort of undifferentiated exploitation. Therefore, the characterization of prisoners of war settled on the land as *debt-bondsmen* is altogether correct. By the way, it must be noted that we are dealing not only with extra-economic but also with economic dependence on the owner of the means of production.

As *debt-bondsmen*, war prisoners settled on the land essentially did not differ economically in any way from *debt-bondsmen* belonging to the local population. Identical economic status in the course of development inevitably led to a leveling of their social status in general. Prisoners of war settled on the land, in gaining a measure of economic self-sufficiency, also acquired certain civil rights and obligations. As a result, the line between them and the *debt-bondsmen* of the local population was erased, and they were merged into a single mass. This is especially what occurred in Assyria. "Enslavement of the peasantry," writes I. M. D'iakonov, "led in the second and first millennia B.C.E. to a profound internal crisis, as a result of which we observe, by the 8th century B.C.E., the formation of a single class of farmers settled on the land, but as a rule lacking means of production. This class is deemed to be made up of slaves, but slaves possessing several rights that they did not have earlier. By their origin, these are, first, debt-bound peasants; secondly, inhabitants of conquered countries resettled on new land; and thirdly, slaves settled on the land. They represent the bulk of the population of the nation . . . and bore all general state obligations, including military service" (D'iakonov 1949b: 148). On the one hand, these producers were considered the property of the ruler, temples, and private individuals, and could as a rule be sold with the land; on the other hand, they had their own property and were accorded certain civil rights. Thus, together with features of slaves and feudally dependent producers, they also exhibited certain features of free workers. The contradictoriness of their status also accounted for D'iakonov's contradictory characterization. On the one hand, D'iakonov calls them slaves; on the other, he emphasizes their sharp difference from true slaves. Ultimately, he settles on designating them as "coloni" (1949b: 106, 118), a term he subsequently rejected. Actually, they were debt-bound persons. D'iakonov convincingly showed that *debt-bondsmen* constituted the main bulk of the exploited population both in the Middle Assyrian and in the New Assyrian periods — that is, Assyria, at least during this period, was not a slaveholding state.

We must emphasize that other researchers also point a very strong trend toward the merging of prisoner-of-war slaves and local exploited population into a single general mass (Tiumenev 1957: 54, 57; Stuchevskii 1960: 8 ff.; Savel'eva 1962: 208). And we can hardly name one Orientalist who does not see, in the absence of any clear line of demarcation between free persons and slaves, one of the most characteristic features of ancient Eastern society.

The persons whom researchers call slaves generally have families, own some property, and enjoy certain rights (Tiumenev 1957: 57; Iankovskaia 1959a: 24, 31; D'iakonov 1959a: 255; 1963b: 18). In Egypt of the New Kingdom we encounter "slaves" who lease land or even own it under the same rights and conditions as free men; they transfer it by inheritance to their children, sell this land — sometimes even to their own masters — have dependent persons, enter into various kinds of transactions, appear in court, etc. (Lur'e 1955b: 22-26; Stuchevskii 1960: 3-10). In our view, this kind of "slave" must be characterized in most cases as a *debt-bondsman*.

Slaveholding relationships in the ancient East, in our opinion, did not form an independent order of social production; they existed only as an element of the dominant socioeconomic order of debt-bondage. By virtue of this, these relationships showed a constant tendency to be transformed into debt-bondage relationships, to merge into the dominant order. Slavery in the ancient East, in essence, emerged as the most extreme, the most arduous form of debt-bondage.

Relationships of hired labor, also showing a tendency toward transformation into debt-bondage, toward dissolution into the dominant order, also existed as an element of the dominant debt-bondage order in the ancient East. Wage labor was not wholly free; it was always to some extent debt-bound and emerged essentially as a relatively mild form of bondage (Struve 1948: 17 ff.; *Vsemirnaia istoriia* 1955: I, 213, etc.).

The bulk of debt-bondsmen were not represented by prisoners of war and their progeny, but by the local population. It is therefore impossible to understand the structure of ancient Eastern society without examining the position of the social stratum from which debt-bound persons were mainly recruited. Representatives of this social stratum are usually called "peasant commune members," "free commune members," or simply "commune members." They were petty producers, possessed means of production, and formed their economies independently, being mostly subsistence-oriented. A petty independent subsistence economy may have existed in two main forms: first, as a separate, self-sufficient order of communal economy — the petty subsistence or family-communal order; and second, as the most necessary and most important component of the feudal socioeconomic order (Semenov 1964). Which of these do we encounter in ancient Eastern society?

Petty independent producers in the ancient East were subject to severe exploitation by the state, the principal landowner. They paid assessments and bore obligations. The taxes they bore were essentially a distinctive form of feudal land rent. Therefore, the given form of exploitation can be characterized only as feudal. Thus, there are definite grounds for viewing the petty independent subsistence economy in societies of the ancient East as a component of the feudal socioeconomic order, and petty independent producers as feudally dependent. In addition, this petty subsistence economy emerges in several respects as a special order of social production, and the petty producers in question as free. At their discretion, they could dispose of means of production, including land; they could alienate them, mortgage them, take out loans by pledging their movable and real property, including land, and also by pledging their persons and the persons of members of their own families. A continuous process of property and social differentiation — a process of class formation — took place among them. A very small number of them grew wealthy and were transformed into *bondholders*. The greater part became impoverished, were ruined, lost their means of production, and ultimately replenished the class of *debt-bondsmen*. Thus, the petty independent subsistence economy combined, on the one hand, features of an independent order of social production and, on the other, elements of the feudal socioeconomic order. Correspondingly, the position of the petty independent owner combined, in an equally contradictory manner, features of feudally dependent and free producers. All this can show only the extreme immaturity of the feudal relationships in the ancient East. Since, due to their undeveloped state, they differed greatly from the feudal relationships of the Middle Ages, we will call them *protofeudal;* as to the socioeconomic order which they formed, we shall accordingly term it *protofeudal.*

Usually the state emerged as the protofeudal lord in the ancient East. The fact that the right to receive assessments from given villages was often passed on to specific persons, most commonly state dignitaries, does not change matters (Nikol'skii 1939: 72; Gel'tser 1956b: 14 ff.; 1960: 86 ff.; 1961: 51 ff.). At the level of development of productive forces attained by the ancient Eastern societies, a sufficient amount of surplus product could be squeezed from petty self-sufficient producers only if a sufficiently powerful apparatus of direct coercion — the state — came into play. The state in the ancient East not only stood behind the existing production relationships, but also served as the direct weapon of exploitation of workers.[2] With the aid of this machine, not only was the resistance of the laboring masses suppressed, but a sizable mass of surplus product was extracted, both from petty independent and from debt-bound producers. This role of the state was connected with the immaturity of antagonistic relationships that stemmed from the low level of development of the productive forces.

Thus, two orders of social production existed in ancient Eastern society: the *debt-bondage* and the *protofeudal.* No sharp line between them or between the classes of debt-bound workers and protofeudally dependent petty self-sufficient producers existed.

Debt-bondage relationships were undifferentiated, immature antagonistic production relationships. An unusual diversity of forms is typical of these relationships.

The status of the debt-bondsman combined in a contradictory manner the features of the slave, the feudally dependent producer, the wage worker, and frequently also, let us add, of the free independent producer. At least some of the debt-bondsmen owned some property and could freely dispose of it, and to a sizable extent managed their own economic life independently. It must not be thought that all these features always emerged in a well-defined way. Some of them might be dominant, others remained in the background, or even existed only potentially. Their existence can sometimes be determined only by examining debt-bondage relationships in their development. In analyzing them, we encounter all possible degrees of personal dependence, from complete and unconditional to the almost complete absence of any dependence. Debt-bondage relationships shaded off, on the one hand, into slaveholding and, on the other, into capitalist relationships. We observe here all possible nuances of the relationship of the worker to the means of production, all the way from simple use of implements secured from the master for the period of performing labor operations to well-nigh complete ownership of the means of production, including land. Debt-bondage relationships imperceptibly shaded into the *protofeudal.*

Debt-bondage relationships were not merely diverse, but also underwent constant change. These changes might tend to approximate the status of debt-bondsmen to that of slaves, as was observed in the state economy of ancient Sumer. Under conditions of the development of commodity-and-money relationships, debt-bondage relationships could tend to approximate those of capitalism. Under such conditions some of the ruined petty producers did not immediately fall into simple debt-bondage. During a certain period of time they appeared predominantly as wage workers — that is, essentially as temporarily debt-bound. We observe this in Babylonia. Finally, debt-bondage relationships could change in such a way as to approximate the feudal, as we have observed in Assyria. However, all these changes could not be brought to completion. The level of development attained by the productive forces in ancient Eastern society did not permit even slaveholding relationships to mature, not to speak of others.

But whereas debt-bondage relationships could not be transformed into true feudal relationships, their transformation into the *protofeudal* variety was possible. The trend toward conversion of debt-bondage relationships into feudal necessarily had as its basis the increasing economic independence of the worker, the approximation of his status to that of the petty independent producer. At the level of productive forces attained by ancient Eastern society, however, this inevitably meant the appearance and intensification in the worker of features of the free producer — that is, one who could dispose of means of production and of his own person. As a result, some *debt-bondsmen* could attain a position essentially differing in no way from that of the protofeudally dependent, petty self-sufficient producers. This is especially true of those who were dependent on the state and on temples.

As the *debt-bondsmen* approached the petty independent producers in status, the process of property and social stratification inevitably commenced among them. This process brought a minority of them into the ranks of the dominant class, but the majority were transformed into *debt-bondsmen.* Once again this makes understandable, for example, the evolution of the ancient Egyptian term *nemkhu*, which appeared in the period of the Middle Kingdom. Initially this word meant "poor peasant," "orphan." In the beginning period of the New Kingdom it acquired the meaning of "plebeian." *Nemkhu* was contrasted with *seram* (nobility). And finally we discover that the *nemkhu* included, on the one hand, persons possessing considerable wealth and, on the other, the impoverished, who fell into debt-bondage (Lur'e 1953: 9-16).

The most important factor governing the movement of debt-bondage relationships toward the *protofeudal* was class conflict. On the broadest scale, the transformation of *debt-bondsmen* into petty independent producers occurred in troubled periods of the history of ancient Eastern states, such as, for example, the periods of the first and second decline of Egypt (Anon. 1935: 35-37; Struve 1934d: 68-70. To a substantial degree the incursions of peoples at the lowest level of social development promoted this process. Thus, for instance, the social order of Babylonia in the Kassite period was more archaic than that of the Old Babylonian Kingdom (Struve 1940: 14).

Thus, there was a most intimate relationship between the protofeudal and debt-bondage-based orders in ancient Eastern societies. These orders existed in an inseparable unity, in which the leading role fell to the debt-bondage order, regardless of the relationship between the numbers of *debt-bondsmen* and petty independent producers. In the socioeconomic structure of ancient Eastern societies, shifts could and did take place in the most varied directions, but the trend toward transformation of all categories of direct producers, without exception, into *debt-bondsmen* was ultimately dominant. The debt-bondage order governed the entire socioeconomic structure of ancient Eastern society, and thus the entire order of its life as a whole. It was precisely the debt-bondage order that was the basis of the economic and political might of the exploiting class, and thus the basis of its dominance over the mass of petty independent producers. It is for this reason that the society of the ancient East must be characterized as a debt-bondage-based society. Thus, there existed in the ancient East a special antagonistic socioeconomic formation, differing from slaveholding, feudal, and capitalist formations — the debt-bondage-based formation. It constitutes historically the first form of existence of the class society — the first class socioeconomic formation. Its characteristic feature was the immaturity of antagonistic relationships. The servitude formation is a class society in which, owing to the immaturity, a process of class formation, the establishment of classes, proceeded throughout its history. Any class society emerging in the period of the Copper and Bronze Ages inevitably had to be immature. Therefore, the debt-bondage formation is not confined to the ancient East. This can be seen even from the example of Mycenaean society.

In works by Soviet researchers, Mycenaean society is characterized as slaveholding. However, from these same works we learn that in the Mycenaean society, as in the ancient Eastern, there was no sharp dividing line between free men and slaves, that in it there existed a number of direct producers whose position was intermediate between those of the former and the latter. These were, as a rule, dependent persons living on the land and managing their own economic life. Further, we discover that the majority of direct producers, who are designated by the term usually translated as "slave," differed substantially in status from slaves. For example, the persons called "slaves of God" were petty and largely independent tenants of both state-owned and private land (Lur'e 1957: 241-242, 254, 269-280; Lentsman 1963: 179-182). As one researcher remarked, if it were not for the term itself, we would have no grounds for considering them slaves (Lentsman 1963: 181). Finally, we are told that both free persons and slaves belonging to private individuals emerged as tenants of state-owned and private land. As for what the same authors call slaves "in the full sense of the word, true slaves," these, as the documents show, were engaged mainly in works serving the palace estate, and they were also probably used as auxiliary labor in several branches of production (Lur'e 1957: 254, 279; Lentsman 1963: 154-156, 180-182). All this taken together permits us to characterize Mycenaean society as debt-bondage-based. It must be noted that many scholars point to the close similarity of the social order of the Cretan and Mycenaean societies (Lur'e 1940: 47, 59; Sergeev 1948: 76, 98; *Vsemirnaia istoriia* 1955: I, 420; Lentsman 1963: 165-166, 187, etc.).

The hypothesis we have advanced to the effect that the debt-bondage-based socioeconomic formation was the first form of class society, preceding slaveholding society, may and probably will provoke not a few objections. In particular, it is not impossible that the reproach will be made that this conclusion contradicts the Marxist theory of historical development. But the assumption that there have been only three antagonistic socioeconomic formations — slaveholding, feudal, and capitalist — of which the first immediately replaces the primitive-communal, the tribal, is not an inseparable and integral part of the materialist interpretation of history, as is sometimes thought.

The essence of the materialist interpretation is that the evolution of human society is viewed as a natural-historical process of development and succession of socio-economic formations. As for the question of how many formations actually existed, and in what order they replaced each other, historical materialism, taken by itself and apart from concrete historical data, cannot give an answer to this. This problem has to do not so much with the general methodology of historical research as with historical research per se. This is a question of facts.

Historical materialism is not a ready-made diagram of the historical process, into which it remains only to fit the historical facts, but a method of interpreting historical facts, a method of cognizing social phenomena, a method of penetrating the core of the historical process. This fact has often been alluded to by Marx, Engels, and Lenin (Marx and Engels 1948: 315-316, 418, 421; Lenin 1958-65: I, 143-144, etc.).

Thus, even if the classical authors of Marxism-Leninism, in all their works, mentioned only three antagonistic social orders, this would not be sufficient grounds for characterizing the assumption we have advanced on the debt-bondage-based formation as being in contradiction to the materialist interpretation of history. But this is far from being how this matter stands. Without going into details, let us point only to the well-known statement by Marx, in his foreword to "Toward a Critique of Political Economy," about the Asiatic, ancient, feudal, and bourgeois modes of production and, correspondingly, about the Asiatic, classical, feudal, and bourgeois socioeconomic formations (Marx and Engels 1955-64: VII, 7-8).[3] As is clear from the context, Marx understood the Asiatic formation not as the first form of existence of human society in general, but as the first form of existence of class society. Other statements by Marx on this same question make it possible to establish that, in referring to the Asiatic formation, he had in mind the society of the ancient East (Marx and Engels 1955-64: XII, 732; XXIII, 89, 345; Marx 1940: 5-31). Thus, according to Marx's view, in the ancient East there existed a different antagonistic socioeconomic formation than in the classical world. It is well known that he viewed the ancient society as slaveholding. Hence it follows that Marx did not regard ancient Eastern society as slaveholding. In the ancient East, in his opinion, there existed a special antagonistic formation, qualitatively differing from the slaveholding (classical) and historically preceding it. In the works of Marx we do not find any concrete characterization of this formation. Historical scholarship at that time did not have access to data that would make it possible to determine the type of productive relationships which formed the basis of ancient Eastern society. It is precisely on this account that Marx called the mode of production dominant in the ancient East simply "Asiatic."

The material now available to science affords, in our view, the possibility of defining this mode of production as debt-bondage-based. Correspondingly, the Asiatic socioeconomic formation can be characterized as based on debt-bondage.

Class societies arose not only in the Copper and Bronze Ages (fourth to second millennia B.C.E.), but also in the Early Iron Age (first millennium B.C.E.) and in the Middle Iron Age (first millennium B.C.E.) and in later periods of man's history. It is wholly understandable that in different historical periods, characterized by a different level of development of the productive forces, the process of establishing a class society could not have taken place in completely identical fashion; in particular, it did not lead in every case to the emergence of a socioeconomic formation based on debt-bondage, as did occur in the ancient East. Nonetheless, establishment of the fact that a special, debt-bondage-based mode of production existed helps us to better interpret the socioeconomic structure of all early class societies, without exception. It compels reexamination of many established ideas concerning the initial stages of development of those societies, including the ancient Greek, the ancient Roman (first millennium B.C.E.), the ancient Russian (first millennium C.E.), and others (Semenov 1957; 1960).

In conclusion, we must stress that reexamination of the view of early class societies in general, and of the ancient Eastern in particular, as slaveholding is urgently dictated by the present state of science. This is sufficiently borne out by the discussions about the periodization of history and the Asiatic mode of production that have been unfolding in recent years in the pages of the Marxist press, in which both Soviet and foreign researchers have participated (Simon 1962; Varga 1962; Parain 1964; Tökei 1964; Chesneaux 1964; Suret-Canale 1965; Godelier 1965; Struve 1965).

★ ★ ★

EDITORS' NOTES

a. This source is listed in the Literature Cited section under the date 1955.
b. References to this source in this article involve only Part I.

NOTES

1. We will notate the statements of authors who are far from convinced of this. Here, for example, is how L. S. Vasil'ev characterizes the ancient Chinese society: "During this very period slaves appeared in society. But at this stage slavery still played a very subordinate role and did not constitute the basis of production. . . . The main producers were peasant-commoners; slaves in fact lived mainly on the labor of the commoners exploited by their masters" (Vasil'ev 1961: 6, 218-219).

2. This fact was reflected in the very structure of the state apparatus. See for example, Postovskaia 1947, as well as her article in *Kratkie soobshcheniia Instituta Narodov Azii* [Brief Reports of the Institute of the Peoples of Asia], 1962, No. 46.

3. See Marx and Engels 1955-64: XIII, 7-8. This problem is taken up in detail in Ter-Akopian 1965.

(Narody Azii i Afriki, 1965, No. 4)

LITERATURE CITED
in D'iakonov, Melikishvili and Semenov

Amusin, I. D.
1955 "Narod zemli." ["The people of the earth."] VDI, No. 2, 14-36.

Anon.
1935 *Rechenie Ipuvera. Leidenskii papirus no. 344. Sotsial'nyi perevorot v Egipte v kontse Srednogo tsarstva — vvodnaia stat'ia V. V. Struve.* ["The testament of Ipuver. Leiden Papyrus no. 344. A social revolution in Egypt at the end of the Middle Kingdom - introductory essay by V. V. Struve."] Moscow and Leningrad.

Avdiev, V. I.
1934 "Sel'skaia obshchina i iskusstvennoe oroshenie v drevnem Egipte." ["The rural commune and artificial irrigation in ancient Egypt."] IM, No. 6, 70-83. [Source in doubt.]

1953 *Istoriia Drevnego Vostoka.* [History of the Ancient East.] Moscow.

Averkieva, Iu. P.
1941 *Rabstvo u indeitsev Severnoi Ameriki.* [Slavery Among the Indians of North America.] Moscow and Leningrad.

Batsieva, S. M.
1953 "Bor'ba mezhdu Assiriei i Urartu za Siriiu." ["The struggle between Assyria and Urartu over Syria."] VDI, No. 2.

Beliakov, G. F. and Kolesnitskii, N. F.
1964 "Simpozium po probleme genezisa feodalizma" ["Symposium on the problem of the genesis of feudalism."] VI, No. 6.

Borshch, I. E.
1961 "Konferentsiia po istorii antichnogo rabstva." ["A conference on the history of slavery in classical antiquity."] VDI, No. 2, 165-169.

Cherezov, E. V.
1949 "K voprosu o pozemel'nykh otnosheniiakh v Egipte epokhi Drevnego Tsarstva." ["A contribution to the question of agrarian relations in Egypt in the epoch of the Old Kingdom."] VDI, No. 3.

1951 "Sotsial'noi polozhenie *mr.t* v khramovom khoziastve Drevnego Tsarstva." ["The social position of the *mr.t* in the temple economy of the Old Kingdom."] VDI, No. 2, 40-46.

1952 "K voprosu o znachenii drevneegipetskikh terminov

meret i *khentiushe* vo vremena Drevnego Tsarstva." ["A contribution to the question of the meaning of the Ancient Egyptian term *meret* and *khentiushe* at the time of the Old Kingdom."] VDI, No. 2.

1960 "Drevneishaia letopis' 'Palermskii kamen'" i dokumenty drevnego tsarstva Egipta." ["The most ancient chronicle, the 'Palermo stone,' and the documents of the Old Kingdom of Egypt."] *Drevnii Egipet* [Ancient Egypt], Moscow.

Chesneaux, Jean
1964 "Quelques perspectives de recherche," *La pensée,* No. 114.

Dandamaev, M. A.
1960 "Chuzhezemnye raby v khoziaistvakh akhemenidskikh tsarei i ikh vel'mozh." ["Foreigh slaves on the estates of Achemenaean kings and their high officials."] *XXV MKV.*

Deimel, A.
1924 *Sumerische Grammatik.* Rome.

D'iakonov, I. M.
1937 "K istorii znachenii odnogo termina." ["A contribution to the history of the meaning of a certain term."] *Lingvisticheskii Biulleten' studentov nauchnykh kruzhkov lingvisticheskogo fakulteta LGU,* No. 4, 117-132.

1946 "Vavilonskoe politicheskoe sochinenie VIII-VII vekov do n.e." ["A Babylonian political text of the eighth and seventh centuries B.C.E."] VDI, No. 4, 41-53.

1948 "Eshche o termine *guruš (KAL)* v shumerskom iazyke." ["More about the term 'gurush' (KAL) in Sumerian."] VDI, No. 1.

1949a "Kto takie 'gurushi' v khoziaistvennykh tekstakh III dinastii Ura?" ["Who are the 'gurushi' in the economic texts of the third dynasty of Ur?"] VDI, No. 2.

1949b *Razvitie zemel'nykh otnoshenii v Assirii.* [The Development of Land Relationships in Assyria.] Leningrad.

1950 "O ploshchadi i sostave naseleniia shumerskogo 'goroda-gosudarstva.'" ["On the area and population makeup of the Sumerian 'city-state.'"] VDI, No. 2.

1952 "K voprosu o sud'be plennykh v Assirii i Urartu," ["A Contribution to the question of the fate of prisoners in Assyria and Urartu."] VDI, No. 1, 90-100.

Ed. 1952 *Zakony Vavilonii, Assirii, i Khettskogo tsarstva.*
[Laws of Babylonia, Assyria, and Hittite Empire.] VDI,
No. 3-4, appendix.

1955 "K voprosu ob obshchestvenom stroe midiiskoi
derzhavy. ["A contribution to the question of the social
structure of the Median Empire."] *Trudy instituta istorii AN
Azerbaidjanskoi SSR.* VI, 4-23.

1956a *Istoriia Midii.* [History of Media.] Moscow.

1956b *"Muškēnum* i povinnostnoe zemlevladenie na tsarsk(
zemle pri Khammurabi." ['Muškēnum and service land tenure
on royal land under Hammurabi."] *Eos,* v. XLVIII, No. 1,
37-62.

1958 "Etnos i sotsial'noe delenie v Assirii." ["Ethnos and
social division in Assyria."] SV, No. 6, 43-56.

1959a *Obshchestvennyi i gosudarstvennyi stroi drevnego
Dvurech'ia. Shumer.* [The Social and State Structure of
Ancient Mesopotamia. Sumer.] Moscow.

1959b "Rabovladel'cheskie imeniia persidskikh vel'mozh."
["Slaveholding estates of Persian high officials."] VDI,
No. 4, 70-92.

1963a "The commune in the ancient East, as treated in the
works of Soviet researchers. SA&A, Vol. II, No. 2, 32-46.
[Included in this collection, pp. 519-548] [Page references to
this source in the text are to its original publication in VDI,
1963, No. 1.]

1963b "Nekotorye dannye o sotsial'nom ustroistve Urartu."
["Some data on the social constitution of Urartu."] *Problemy
sotsial'no-ekonomicheskói istorii drevnego mira.* [Problems in
the Socioeconomic History of the Ancient World.] Moscow
and Leningrad.

D'iakonov, I. M. and Magaziner, Ia. M.
1952 *Zakony Vavilonii, Assirii i Khettskogo tsarstva.* [Laws
of Babylonia, Assyria, and the Hittite Empire.] (Appendix to
VDI, Nos. 3 & 4.) [Commentary on D'iakonov, 1952.]

D'iakonov, M. M.
1961 *Ocherk istorii drevnego Irana.* [A Sketch of the History
of Ancient Iran.] Moscow.

El'nitskii, L. A.
1964 *Vozniknovenie i razvitie rabstva v Rime v VIII-III vv.
do n.e.* [The Origin and Development of Slavery in Rome in
the Eighth to Third Centuries B.C.E.] [Place lacking.]

Engels, Friedrich
1933 and 1950   *Anti-Dühring*. Moscow. [Variously cited by D'iakonov and Melikishvili, Eds.]

Eremian, S. T.
1953   *Rabovladel'cheskoe obshchestvo drevnei Armenii.* [The slaveholding society of ancient Armenia.] Author's abstract of doctoral dissertation. Moscow.

Erkes, Eduard
1954   *Das Problem der Sklaverei in China.* Berlin.

Garushiants, Iu. M.
1966   "Ob aziatskom sposobe proizvodstva." ["On the Asiatic mode of production."] VI, No. 1, 83-100.

Gel'tser, M. L.
1952   "Materialy k izucheniiu sotsial'no-ekonomichiskoi struktury Ugarita." ["Materials for the study of the socio-economic structure of Ugarit."] VDI, No. 4, 28-37.

1954a   "Klassovaia i politicheskaia bor'ba v Bible amarnskogo vremeni." ["The class and political struggle in Byblos of the Amarna period."] VDI, No. 1, 33-39.

1954b   "Novye dannye o sotsial'noi strukture Ugarita." ["New data on the social structure of Ugarit."] VDI, No. 4, 28-37.

1956a   "Novye teksty iz drevnego Alalakha." ["New tests from ancient Alalakh."] VDI, No. 3, 29-36.

1956b   "Novye teksty iz drevnego Alalakha i ikh znachenie dlia sotsial'no-ekonomicheskoi istorii Drevnego Vostoka." ["New tests from ancient Alalakh and their significance for the socio-economic history of the ancient East."] VDI, No. 1.

1958   "Zametki o istorii Finikii VIII v. do n.e." ["Notes on the history of Phoenicia in the eighth century B.C.E."] *Palestinskii sbornik* [Palestinian Collection] No. 3 (65).

1960   "Nekotorye voprosy agrarnykh otnoshenii v Ugarite." ["Some questions of agrarian relationships in Ugarit."] VDI, No. 2.

1961   "Sel'skaia obshchina i prochie vidy zemlevladeniia v drevnem Ugarite." ["The rural commune and other forms of land tenure in ancient Ugarit."] VDI, No. 1.

Godelier, Maurice [Godel'e, M.]
1965   "Poniatie aziatskogo sposoba proizvodstva i marksistskaia skhema razvitiia obshchestva." ["The concept of the

Asiatic mode of production and the Marxist model of the development of society."] NAA, No. 1. [Translated in SA&A, 1965, Vol. IV, No. 2.]

Gurevich, A. Ia.
1965 "Obshchii zakon i konkretnaia zakonomernost'."
["General law and concrete regularity."] VI, No. 8. [Translated in *Soviet Review*, Fall 1966, Vol. 7, 3-18.]

Iankovskaia, N. B.
1956 "Nekotorye voprosy ekonomiki Assiriiskoi derzhavy."
["Some questions of the economy of the Assyrian Empire."]
VDI, No. 1, 28-46.

1957a "Khurritskaia Arrapkha." ["Hurrite Arrapha."] VDI, No. 1.

1957b "Zavisimost' rasporiazheniia sobstvennost'iu v Arrapkhe ot osobennostei obshchestvennogo stroia." ["The dependence of the disposition of property in Arrapha on the features of the social structure."] Eos XLVIII, No. 2, 3-13.

1959a *Raspad bol'shesemeinoi domovoi obshchiny v Perednei Azii II tys. do n. e.* [The disintegration of the extended-family house-commune in Asia Minor in the second millennium B.C.E.] Leningrad: author's abstract of dissertation.

1959b "Zemlevladenie bol'shesemeinykh domovykh obshchin v klinopisnykh istochnikakh." ["Land tenure by extended-family house-communes in the cuneiform sources."]
VDI, No. 1.

1961 "Iz istorii khurritskogo obshchestva." ["From the history of Hurrite society."] XXV MKV.

Il'in, G. F.
1950a "Shudry i raby v drevneindiiskikh sbornikakh zakonov." ["Sudras and slaves in the ancient Indian law codes."] VDI, No. 2.

1950b "Vopros ob obshchestnoi formatsii v drevnei Indii v sovetskoi literatura." ["The question of the social order in ancient India in the Soviet literature."] VDI, No. 2.

1951 "Osobennosti rabstva v drevnei Indii." ["Special features of slavery in ancient India."] VDI, No. 1.

Its, R. F.
1954 "Sotsial'no-ekonomicheskie otnoshenia v Kitae v period dinastii In' (XIV-XII vv. do n.e.)." ["Socioeconomic relationships in China in the period of the Yin Dynasty (in

the fourteenth to twelfth centuries B.C.E.] VDI, No. 2, 9-18.

Iushkov, S.
1946 "K voprosu o dofeodal'nom ('varvarskom') gosudarstve." ["A contribution to the question of the prefeudal ('barbarian') state."] VI, No. 7, 45-65.

Iusifov, Iu. B.
1958 "Tsarkoe remeslennoe khoziaistvo v Elame midiisko-persidskogo vremeni." ["The royal handicraft operations in Elam of the Medo-Persian period."] Trudy instituta istorii AN Azerbaidjanskoi SSR. XIII, 80-106.

1960 "Kuplia-prodazha nedvizhimogo imushchestva i chastnoe zemlevladenie v Elame II tys. do n.e." ["Purchase and sale of real property and private land ownership in Elam in the second millennium B.C.E."] Klio XXXVIII, 5-22.

1961 "O chastnom zemlevladenii v Elame II tys. do n.e." ["On private land ownership in Elam in the second millennium B.C.E."] XXV MKV.

Jacobsen, Thorkild
1943 "Primitive Democracy in Ancient Mesopotamia." Journal of Near Eastern Studies, II, No. 3.

1957 "Early political development in Mesopotamia." Zeitschrift für Assyriologie und verwandte Gebeite. Neue Folge, 18(52).

Jacobsen, Thorkild, and Adams, R. M.
1958 "Salt and silt in ancient Mesopotamian agriculture." Science, 128, 1251-1258.

Katsnel'son, I. S.
1954 "O znachenii drevneegipetskogo termina meret." ["On the meaning of the ancient Egyptian term meret."] VDI, No. 2, 19-25.

1960 "Nekotorye cherty gosudarstvennogo stroia Nubii v VI-IV vv. do n.e." ["Some features of the state structure of Nubia in the sixth to the fourth centuries B.C.E."] XXV MKV.

Kolobova, K. M.
1939 "Revoliutsiia Solona." ["The revolution of Solon."] Uchenye Zapiski Leningradskogo Gosudarstvennogo Universiteta, No. 39, Historical Series, No. 4.

1957 "Voikei na Krite." ["The Voikii in Crete."] VDI, No. 2, 25-46.

Korsunskii, A. R.

1964 "Problema revoliutsionnogo perekhoda ot rabovladel'-cheskogo stroia k feodalnogo v Zapadnoi Evrope." ["The problem of the revolutionary transition from the slaveholding to the feudal order in Western Europe."] VI, No. 5.

Kriukov, M. V.

1960 "In'skaia tsivilizatsiia i bassein reki Khuankhe." ["Yin civilization and the basin of the Huangho River."] Vestnik istorii mirovoi kultury, No. 4.

1961 "Rod i gosudarstvo v In'skom Kitae." ["Clan and state in Yin China."] VDI, No. 2, 3-22.

Kuzovkov, D. V.

1954 "Ob usloviiakh, porodivshikh razlichiia v razvitii rabstva, i ego naivysshee razvitie v antichnom mire." ["On the conditions which gave rise to differences in the development of slavery and its highest development in the world of classical antiquity."] VDI, No. 1.

Lautner, J. G.

1935 Altbabylonische Personenmiete und erntearbeiterverträge. Leiden.

Lenin, V. I.

n.d. "O gosudarstve." ["On the State."] In Sochineniia [Works], Vol. XXIX, Moscow. Translated in V. I. Lenin, Collected Works, Vol. XXIX, 470-488.

1958-1965 Polnoe sobranie sochinenii [Complete Works]. Moscow.

Lentsman, Ia. A.

1963 Rabstvo v Mikenskoi i Gomerovskoi Gretsii [Slavery in Mycenaean and Homeric Greece]. Moscow.

Lur'e, I. M.

1939 "Immunitetnye gramoty drevnego tsarstva." ["Grants of immunity of the old kingdom."] Trudy Otdela Vostoka Gos. Ermitazha, No. 1, 121-125, 133-136.

1940 Istoriia drevnei Gretsii. [History of Ancient Greece.] Leningrad.

1951 "Drevneegipetskie terminy meret i khentiushe vo vremena Drevnego tsarstva." ["The ancient Egyptian terms meret and khentiushe at the time of the Old Kingdom."] VDI, No. 4, 73-80.

1952 "Zamechaniia po povodu prospekta 'Vsemirnoi istorii,' tt. I-II." ["Comments on the prospectus for the

'World History,' Vols. I-II."] VDI, No. 4, 172-173.

1955a "Eshche raz o termine *meret.*" ["More on the term *meret.*] VDI, No. 1, 147-151.

1955b ."Novye dannye o svobodnykh zemledel'tsakh i rabakh v Egipte Srednego tsarstva." ["New data on free farmers and slaves in Egypt of the Middle Kingdom."] VDI, No. 1.

1955c "Raby-derzhateli khramovoi zemli (po materialam novogo tsarstva)." ["Slave holders of temple land (on data of the new kingdom)."] VDI, No. 1, 16-26.

1957 *Iazyk i kul'tura Mikenskoi Gretsii* [The Language and Culture of Mycenaean Greece]. Moscow-Leningrad.

Marx, Karl
1931 "Letter of Marx to Engels, March 8, 1855." In K. Marx and F. Engels, *Sochineniia* [Works], Vol. XXII, Moscow-Leningrad.

1940 *Formy, predshestvoiushchie kapitalisticheskomu proizvodstvu.* [Pre-Capitalist Forms of Production.] Moscow.

1950 *Kapital* [Capital], Vol. III, Moscow.

Marx, K., and Engels, F.
1948 *Izbrannye pis'ma* [Selected Letters]. Moscow.

1955 *Sochineniia* [Works] Moscow.

Mavrodin, V.
1946 *Drevniaia Rus'.* [Ancient Rus.] Moscow.

Melikishvili, G. A.
1951 "Nekotorye voprosy sotsial'no-ekonomicheskoi istorii Nairi-Urartu." [Some questions of the socioeconomic history of Nairi-Urartu."] VDI, No. 4.

1958 "K voprosu o khetto-tsupaniiskikh pereselentsakh v Urartu." ["A contribution to the question of Hitto-Tsupanian immigrants in Urartu."] VDI, No. 2.

Menabde, E. A.
1956 *Nekotorye voprosy razvitiia instituta rabstva v Khettskom gosudarstve.* [Some questions of the institution of slavery in the Hittite state.] Tbilisi: author's abstract of dissertation.

1961 "O rabstve v Khettskom gosudarstve." ["On slavery in the Hittite state."] *Peredneaziatskii sbornik.* [Asia Minor Collection]. Moscow.

1963 "K voprosu ob ekonomicheskom razvitii khettskogo

tsarstva." ["A contribution to the question of the economic development of the Hittite Empire."] *Problemy sotsial'no-ekonomicheskoi istorii drevnego mira.* [Problems of the Socio-economic History of the Ancient World]. Moscow.

1965   *Khettskoe obshchestvo.* [Hittite Society]. Tbilisi.

Nikol'skii, N. M.
1937   "Nekotorye osnovnye problemy obshchei i religioznoi istorii Izrailia i Iudei." ["Some basic problems of the general and religious history of Israel and Judea."] In A. B. Ranovich, *Ocherk istorii drevneevreiskoi religii.* [Outline of the History of Ancient Jewish Religion.] Moscow.

1938   "Obshchina v drevnem Dvurech'e." ["The commune in ancient Mesopotamia."] VDI, No. 4, 72-98.

1939   "K voprosu o rente-naloge v drevnem Dvurech'e." ["A contribution to the question of tax-rent in ancient Mesopotamia."] VDI, No. 2.

1948   *Chastnoe zemlevladenie i zemlepol'zovanie v drevnem Dvurech'e.* [Private Landownership and Land Tenure in Ancient Mesopotamia.] Minsk.

1953   "Znachenie problemy obshchinnogo byta v Assirii dlia izucheniia sotsial'no-ekonomicheskoi istorii narodov drevnego Vostoka." ["The importance of the problem of communal life in Assyria for the study of the socioeconomic history of the peoples of the ancient East."] *Uchenye Zapiski Belorusskogo Gosudarstvennogo Universiteta,* No. 14, (Historical Series), 379-394.

1959   *Kul'tura drevnei Vavilonii.* [The culture of Ancient Babylonia.] Minsk.

Osipov, A.
1948   *Kratkii ocherk istorii Indii do X v.* [A Brief Outline of the History of India up to the Tenth Century.] Moscow.

Parain, Charles
1964   "Une étape nouvelle dans une discussion fondamentale." *La Pensée,* No. 114.

Perelomov, L. S.
1962   *Imperiia Tsin'.* [The Ch'in Empire.] Moscow.

Perikhanian, A. G.
1952   "K voprosu o rabovladenii i zemlevladenii v Irane parfianskogo vremeni." ["A contribution to the question of slaveholding and land tenure in Iran of the Parthian period."]

VDI, No. 4, 13-27.

1959 *Khramovye ob"edineniia Maloi Azii i Armenii.* [Temple Unions of Asia Minor and Armenia.] Moscow.

Pershits, A. I.
1961 "Khoziaistvo i obshchestvenno-politicheskii stroi Severnoi Aravii v XIX-pervoi treti XX vv." ["The economy and socio-political structure of Northern Arabia in the 19th century and the first third of the twentieth."] *Trudy Instituta ethnografii,* Vol. 69.

Pigulevskaia, N. V.
1940 *Mesopotamiia na rubezhe V-VI vv. n.e.* [Mesopotamia at the Turn of the Fifth Century C.E.] Moscow-Leningrad.

1956 *Goroda Irana v rannem srednevekov'e.* [The Cities of Iran in the Early Middle Ages.] Moscow.

Pokora, T.
1963 "Existierte in China eine Sklavenhaltergesellschaft?" *Archiv Orientalni,* Vol. 31, No. 3.

Postovskaia, N. M.
1947 "Nachal'naia stadiia razvitiia gosudarstvennogo apparata v drevnem Egipte." ["The initial stage of the development of the state apparatus in ancient Egypt."] VDI, No. 1.

1961 *Izuchenie drevnei istorii Blizhnego Vostoka v Sovetskom Soiuze (1917-1959 gg.).* [The Study of the Ancient History of the Near East in the Soviet Union]. Moscow.

Ranovich, A. B.
1947 "Zavisimye khrest'iane v ellinisticheskoi Maloi Azii." ["Dependent peasants in Hellenistic Asia Minor."] VDI, No. 2.

1950 *Ellinizm i ego istoricheskaia rol'.* [Hellenism and Its Historical Role.] Moscow.

Reder, D. G.
1950 "Voennaia demokratiia v stranakh drevnego Vostoka." ["Military democracy in the countries of the ancient east."] *Uchenye zapiski Moskovskogo oblastnogo pedagogicheskogo instituta* [Department of the History of the Ancient World], *14,* No. 1, 117-127.

Rubin, V. A.
1955 "Diskussiia o periodizatsii drevnei istorii Kitaia" ["The debate on the periodization of the ancient history of China"], VDI, No. 4.

1959   "Rabovladenie v drevnem Kitae v VII-V vv. do n.e."
["Slaveholding in ancient China in the VII-V centuries
B.C.E."], VDI, No. 3.

1960   "Narodnoe sobranie v drevnem Kitae v VII-V vv. do
n.e." ["The popular assembly in ancient China in the seventh
to fifth centuries B.C.E."] VDI, No. 4, 22-40.

1965   "Diskussiia o periodizatsii drevnei istorii Kitaia." ["A
discussion on the periodization of the ancient history of
China."], VDI, No. 4.

Sarkisian, G. Kh.
1953   "O gorodskoi zemle v Selevkidskoi Vavilonii." ["On
city land in Seleucid Babylonia."] VDI, No. 1, 59-73.

1960   *Tigranakert.* Moscow.

1952   "Samoupravliaiushchiisia gorod Selevkidskoi Vavilonii."
["The self-governing city of Seleucid Babylonia."] VDI,
No. 1, 68-83.

Savel'eva, T. N.
1962   *Agrarnyi stroi Egipta v period Drevnego Tsarstva.*
[The Agrarian Structure of Egypt in the Period of the Old
Kingdom.] Moscow.

Semenov, Iu. I.
1957   "K voprosu o pervoi forme klassovogo obshchestva,"
["A contribution to the question of the first form of class
society."] *Uchenye zapiski krasnoiarskogo pedagogicheskogo
instituta,* Vol. 9, No. 1.

1960   "V. I. Lenin o kategorii 'obshchestvenno-ekonomicheskii uklad." ["V. I. Lenin on the category of 'socioeconomic
system.'] *Uchenye zapiski krasnoiarskogo pedagogicheskogo
instituta,* Vol. 18.

1964   "Kategoriia 'obshchestvenno-ekonomicheskii uklad' i ee
znachenie dlia filosofskoi i istoricheskoi nauk." ["The category 'socioeconomic system' and its significance for philoso-
phical and historical scholarship."] *Filosofskie nauki,* No. 3.

1965   "Problema sotsial'no-ekonomicheskogo stroia drevnego
Vostoka." ["The problem of the socioeconomic structure of the
Ancient East."] NAA, No. 4. [See pp. 575-604 of this collection.]

Sergeev, U. S.
1948   *Istoriia drevnei Gretsii* [History of Ancient Greece].
Moscow.

Simanovskaia, L. V.
1940 "Vozniknovenie i razvitie gosudarstva v drevnem Kitae." ["Origin and development of the state in ancient China."] *Istoricheskii Zhurnal*, No. 7, 71-83.

Simon, J.
1962 "Stages in social development," *Marxism Today*, Vol. 6, No. 6.

Stepugina, T. V.
1950 "K voprosu o sotsial'no-ekonomicheskikh otnosheniiakh v Kitae v XIV-XII vv. do n.e." ["A contribution to the question of socioeconomic relationships in China in the fourteenth to twelfth centuries B.C.E."] VDI, No. 2, 56-76.

Struve, V. V.
1919 "Novye dannye ob organizatsii truda i sotsial'noi strukture obshchestva Sumera epokhi III dinastii Ura." ["New data on the social structure and organization of labor in Sumerian society in the period of the Third Dynasty of Ur."] SV, Vol. VI, 149-184.

1934a "Eshche raz o rabovladel'cheskoi latifundii Sumira III dinastii Ura." ["More on slaveholding latifundia in Sumer in the Third Dynasty of Ur."] PIDO, No. 718, 211-222.

1934b "Khettskoe obshchestvo kak tip voennogo rabovladel'cheskogo obshchestva." ["Hittite society as a type of military slaveholding society."] IGAIMK, No. 97.

1934c "Ocherki sotsial'no-ekonomicheskoi istorii drevnego Vostoka." ["Outlines of the socioeconomic history of the ancient East."] IGAIMK, No. 97.

1934d "Problema zarozhdeniia, razvitiia i upadka rabovladel'cheskikh obshchestv drevnego Vostoka." ["The problem of the origin, development and decay of the slaveholding society of the ancient east."] IGAIMK, No. 77.

1934e "Rabovladel'cheskaia latifundiia v Sumire III dinastii Ura." ["The slaveholding latifundia in Sumer in the Third Dynasty of Ur." *Sb. v. chest' S. F. Ol'denburga*. [Essays presented to S. F. Ol'denburg]. Moscow, 495-507.

1934f "Rabstvo v drevneishem Sumire" ["Slavery in most ancient Sumer"], IGAIMK, No. 97.

1940 "Marksovo opredelenie ranneklassovogo obshchestva." ["Marx's definition of early class society."] SE, No. 3.

1941   *Istoriia drevnego Vostoka* [History of the Ancient East]. Moscow-Leningrad.

1947a   "Obshchestvennyi stroi Iuzhnogo Mezhdurech'ia v epokhu III dinastii Ura." ["The social structure of southern Mesopotamia in the Third Dynasty of Ur."] *Iubileinyi sbornik, posviashchennyi 30-letiiu Velikoi Oktiabr'skoi sotsialisticheskoi revoliutsii* [Anniversary Symposium Dedicated to the Thirtieth Anniversary of the Great October Socialist Revolution.] Vol. II, Moscow.

1947b   "Sovetskoe vostokovedenie i problema obshchestvennogo stroia drevnego Vostoka." ["Soviet Oriental studies and the problem of the social structure of the ancient East."] *Vestnik LGU*, No. 1.

1948   "Naemnyi trud i sel'skaia obshchina v Iuzhnom Mezhdurech'e." ["Hired labor and the rural commune in Southern Mesopotamia."] VDI, No. 2, 13-33.

1949   "Novye dannye ob organizatsii truda i sotsial'noi strukture obshchestva Sumera epokhi III dinastii Ura." ["New data on the organization of labor and the social structure of Sumerian society of the period of the third dynasty of Ur."] SV, Vol. VI.

1953   "K voprosu o spetsifike rabovladel'cheskikh obshchestv drevnego Vostoka." ["A contribution to the question of the specific nature of the slaveholding societies of the ancient East."] *Vestnik LGU*, No. 9, 81-91.

1959   "Bor'ba s rabstvom-dolzhnichestvom v Vavilonii i Palestine." ["The struggle against debt-slavery in Babylonia and Palestine."] *Palestinskii sbornik,* No. 3 (66), 5-17.

1960   "Udel'nyi ves rabskogo truda v. Khramovom Khoziaistve dosargonovskogo Lagasha." ["The proportion of slave labor in the temple economy of pre-Sargonic Lagash."] VI, No. 2.

1961a   *Gosudarstvo Lagash v XXV-XXIV vv. do n.e.* [The State of Lagash in the 25th and 24th Centuries B.C.E.] Moscow.

1961b   Review of I. M. D'iakonov, *"Obshchestvennyi i gosudarstvennyi stroi drevnego Dvurech'ia. Shumer."* NAA, No. 2.

1961c   "Udel'nyi ves rabskogo truda v khramovom khoziaistve dosargonovskogo Lagasha." ["The proportion of slave labor in the temple economy of pre-Sargonic Lagash."] VI, No. 2.

1963   "Obshchina, khram i dvorets." ["Commune, temple and palace."] VDI, No. 3.

1965   "Poniatie 'aziatskii sposob proizvodstva.'" ["The concept 'Asiatic mode of production.'"] NAA, No. 1. [Translated in SA&A, Fall 1965, Vol. IV, No. 2.]

Stuchevskii, I. A.
1958a   "K tolkovaniiu dannykh papirusa Vil'bura o zemlepol'zovanii i nalogooblozhenii v Egipte vremeni Ramessidov." ["A contribution to the interpretation of the data of the Vilbour Papyrus on land tenure and taxation in Egypt of the Ramesside period."] VDI, No. 1.

1958b   Review: A. E. Bakir, *Slavery in Pharaonic Egypt.* Cairo: 1952. VDI, No. 2, p. 204.

1960   "O spetsificheskikh formakh rabstva v drevnem Egipte v epokhu Novogo tsarstva." ["On specific forms of slavery in ancient Egypt in the period of the New Kingdom."] VDI, No. 1.

1962   *Khramovaia forma tsarskogo khoziaistva Drevnego Egipta.* [The Temple Form of the Royal Estate in Ancient Egypt.] Moscow.

Suleikin, D. A.
1949   "Osnovnye voprosy periodizatsii istorii drevnei Indii." ["Basic questions of the periodization of the history of ancient India."] *Uchenye zapiski Tikhookeanskogo instituta,* Vol. II.

Suret-Canale, Jean [Siure-Kanal', Zh.]
1965   "Traditsionye obshchestva v Tropicheskoi Afrike i marksistskaia kontseptsiia 'aziatskogo sposoba proizvodstva.'" ["The traditional societies of Tropical Africa and the Marxist conception of 'the Asiatic mode of production.'"] NAA, No. 1. [Translated in SA&A, 1965, Vol. IV, No. 2.]

Ter-Akopian, N. B.
1965   "Razvitie vzgliadov Marksa i Engel'sa na aziatskii sposob proizvodstva i zemledel'cheskuiu obshchinu." ["The development of the views of Marx and Engels on the Asiatic mode of production and the agricultural commune."] NAA, Nos. 2 and 3.

Tiumenev, A. I.
1946   "O formakh zemel'noi sobstvennosti po nadpisiam obeliska Manishtusu." ["On the forms of landed property according to the inscriptions of the Manishtusu obelisk."] VDI, No. 4, 33-40.

1948a "Imel li termin 'gurush' ('kal'') sotsial'nuiu
znachimost'?" ["Did the term 'gurush' (kal) have social significance?"] VDI, No. 2.

1948b "Khoziaistvennyi personal khrama Bau v Lagashe
vremeni Urukaginy." ["The estate personnel of the temple of
Bau at the time of Urukagina."] VDI, No. 1.

1950 "K voprosu o naemnom trude v tsarskom khoziaistve
vremeni III dinastii Ura." ["A contribution to the question of
hired labor in the royal estate of the Third Dynasty of Ur."]
VDI, No. 1, 48-52.

1954 "Proizvoditeli materialnikh blag v tsarskom khoziaistve
vremeni III dinastii Ura." ["Producers of material goods in
the royal estate of the period of the third dynasty of Ur."]
VDI, No. 1.

1956 *Gosudarstvennoe khoziaistvo drevnego Shumera.* [The
State Economy of Ancient Sumer.] Moscow-Leningrad.

1957 "Perednyi Vostok i antichnost." ["The Near East and
the Classical World."] VI, Nos. 6 and 9.

Tokarev, S. A.
1933 "Rodovoi stroi v Melanezii." ["The clan system in
Melanesia."] SE, Nos. 3 and 4.

1945 *Obshchestvennyi stroi iakutov v XVII-XVIII vv.* [The
Social Structure of the Yakuts in the 17th and 18th Centuries.] Yakutsk.

Tōkei, Ferenc
1964 "Les vues de Marx et d'Engels," *La Pensée,* No. 114.

Tolstov, S. P.
1934 "Genezis feodalizma v kochevykh skotovodcheskikh
obshchestvakh." ['The genesis of feudalism in nomadic pastoral society."] IGAIMK, No. 103.

1935 "Voennaia demokratiia i problema 'geneticheskoi
revoliutsii.'" ["Military democracy and the problem of the
'genetic revolution.'"] PIDO, Nos. 7 and 8.

Tolstov, S. P., and Tokarev, S. A., eds.
1956 *Narody Avstralii i Okeanii.* [Peoples of Australia and
Oceania.] Moscow.

Utchenko, S. L., and Shtaerman, E. M.
1960 "O nekotorykh voprosakh istorii rabstva." ["On some
questions of the history of slavery."] VDI, No. 4.

Varga, E. S.

    1962   *Ocherki po problema politekonomii kapitalizma*
[Essays on Problems of Capitalist Political Economy.]
Moscow.

Vasil'ev, L. S.

    1961a   *Agrarnye otnosheniia i obshchina v drevnem Kitae.*
[Agrarian Relationships and the Commune in Ancient China.]
Moscow.

    1961b   "Problema *tszin tian'.*" ["The *Ching T'ien* problem."]
Kitai. Iaponiia. Istoriia i Filologiia. K 75-letiiu N. I. Konrada.
[China. Japan. History and Philology. Papers Presented to
N. I. Konrad on his Seventy-fifth Birthday.] Moscow, 24-38.

Vasil'ev, L. S., and Stuchevskii, I. A.

    1966   "Tri modeli vozniknoveniia i evoliutsii dokapitalist-
icheskikh obshchestv." ["Three models for the origin and
evolution of pre-capitalist societies"], VI, No. 5.
[Translated in *Soviet Studies in History*, 1966-1967, Vol. 5,
No. 3, 24-37.

Vestnik drevnei istorii

    1947   "K izucheniiu istorii krest'ianstva v drevnosti."
["Toward the study of the history of the peasantry in ancient
times."] Editorial, VDI, No. 1.

    1951   "Za glubokoe ovladenie teoreticheskim naslediem
Lenina." ["For a profound mastery of Lenin's theoretical
heritage."] VDI, No. 1.

    1953   "K itogam obsuchdeniia prospekta I i II tomov
'Vsemirnoi istorii'." ["Toward the results of the discussion
of the prospectus of vols. I and II of the 'World History.'"]
VDI, No. 2.

    1963   "Diskussiia po probleme rodovoi i sel'skoi obshchiny
na Drevnem Vostoke." ["Discussion of the problem of the
clan and rural communes in the ancient East."] VDI, No. 1.
[Translated in SA&A, Vols. II (No. 4) and III (No. 1).]

Vid'ialankar, S.

    1959   "Rabstvo v drevnei Indii." ["Slavery in ancient
India."] VDI, No. 3.

Vsemirnaia istoriia. [World History]

    1955-   Akademiia Nauk SSR, pub., Moscow.

Walther, A.

    1917   *Das altbabylonische gerichtswesen.* Leipzig: 1917.

Wolf, K.

    1947   "Traces of primitive democracy in ancient Israel."
Journal of Near Eastern Studies, VI, No. 2, 98-108.

Zel'in, K. K.

    1937   "Khetty i khettskaia kul'tura." ["The Hittite and
Hittite Culture."] *Istoricheski zhurnal,* Nos. 3-4, 187-201.

    1953   "Osnovnye cherty ellinizma."["The basic features of
Hellenism."] VDI, No. 4.

    1964   *Bor'ba politicheskikh gruppirovok v Afinakh v VI v.
do n.e.* [The Struggle of Political groupings in Athens in the
6th Century B.C.E.] Moscow.

PART VI

ETHNOGRAPHY OF FOREIGN AREAS

PART VI. ETHNOGRAPHY OF FOREIGN AREAS

Introductory Note

The two items translated in this section have been included on an ad hoc basis, in an effort to shed light on an area which is as yet inaccessible to Western scholars and whose "native ethnography" has not yet been translated to an adequate extent.[1] If this collection were being edited now, China would probably be de-emphasized in favor of other parts of Southeast Asia (for example, Kosikov 1970+, Girenko 1972+, and Guseva 1969+). However, the number of Soviet works concerning the ethnography of foreign areas, and based on firsthand experience, is still relatively small, and it seems fair to say that such studies occupy a fairly minor place in the Soviet ethnographic program. China has been and remains an exception to this rule, accounted for primarily by the theoretical importance of questions relating to the social orders of ancient and modern China from a Marxist point of view (see Introductory Note to Part V, pp. 449 – 453). The literature on ancient and modern China by Soviet scholars is quite considerable and has not to our knowledge been brought to the attention of non-Soviet readers in any systematic way (see, for example, L. S. Vasil'ev 1972 and Volkova 1972).

S. I. Bruk is a prominent Soviet demographer and cartographer, most of whose current work deals with the demography of the Soviet Union and Eastern Europe (Bruk 1972*, 1973). He serves on the editorial board of the journal *Sovetskaia etnografiia*, and during 1971 appears to have served as assistant director of the Institute of Ethnography, Academy of Sciences, USSR, in Moscow.

G. G. Stratanovich has been active for many years as researcher and editor in the field of Asian ethnography. Before the deterioration of Sino-Soviet relations, he worked extensively in China, and both at that time and later made scholarly trips to North Vietnam, Burma, and Japan, in connection with the publication of the volume on non-Soviet Asia in the *Narody mira* [Peoples of the World] series. Most of his recent publications in the journal *Sovetskaia etnografiia* have been brief (see for example, Komarovskii and Stratanovich 1966; Bruk and Stratanovich 1968). It seems likely that Stratanovich spends a great deal of his time in editorial work (see Nikonov and Stratanovich, eds. 1971) as well as in teaching.

* * *

NOTE

1.   A journal, *Chinese Sociology and Anthropology,* has appeared since 1968 in the series published by International Arts and Sciences Press, White Plains, New York, which also brings out *Soviet Sociology* and *Soviet Anthropology and Archeology.*

REFERENCES CITED

Bruk, S. I.
1973   "Istoriko-etnograficheskoe kartografirovanie i ego sovremennye problemy" ["Historical-ethnographic cartography and its contemporary problems"], SE, No. 3, 3-18.

Bruk, S. I., and Stratanovich. G. G.
1968   "K VIII Mezhdunarodnomu kongressu antropologicheskikh i etnograficheskikh nauk" ["Toward the VIIIth International Congress of Anthropological and Ethnological Sciences"], SE, No. 3, 124-128.

Komarovskii, G. E., and Stratanovich, G. G.
1966   "Risovodcheskaia obriadnost' i ee mesto v kul'te prirody" ["Rice-growing ritual and its place in the cult of nature"], SE, No. 2, 131-135.

Nikonov, V. A., and Stratanovich, G. G., eds.
1971   *Etnografiia imen* [The Ethnography of Names]. Moscow.

Vasil'ev, L. S.

    1972   *Rol' traditsii v istorii i kul'ture Kitaia* [The Role of Tradition in the History and Culture of China]. Moscow.

Volkova, L. A.

    1972   *Izmenenie sotsial'no-ekonomicheskoi struktury kitaiskoi derevni, 1949-1970 gg.* [Changes in the Socio-Economic Structure of the Chinese Village, 1949-1970]. Moscow.

DISTRIBUTION OF NATIONAL MINORITIES
IN THE PEOPLE'S REPUBLIC OF CHINA

S. I. Bruk

The People's Republic of China is a multinational
state. In addition to the Chinese [Hans], approximately
50 other nationalities inhabit its territory. And although
the latter number a bare 6% of the entire population, they
occupy more than half the entire land area of the country
and play a key role in its life.

Prior to the triumph of the people's revolution in
China, a system of national oppression prevailed, leading
to mutual hostility and mistrust among nationalities. Many
national minorities did not even sense their ethnic unity,
or else attempted to conceal their nationality to avoid discrimination. Following a policy of great-power chauvinism,
China's reactionary rulers not only suppressed small peoples, but even officially denied their very existence. The
policy of discrimination and suppression set back the economic and cultural advancement of ethnic minorities and
doomed them to poverty and slow extinction.

All this could not but influence the extent to which
the many peoples of China were studied. Until recently,
clarity was lacking on many problems associated with the
ethnic composition of the country. Even the names of
some peoples, particularly in Southwest China, became
known only in recent years. Lack of a census[1] in China
for a long period prevented the formation of even the
most general notion of the distribution and size of the
ethnic minorities.

The picture changed decisively after the revolution

was won in China. Much effort was expended on the study of ethnic minorities by the People's Government of China in connection with the tasks of national construction. It was found particularly difficult to resolve the question of whether a given group was a separate people or part of a larger people. This question was vitally important for regions in Southwest China where many peoples were in early stages of social and economic development, and where a number of ethnic groups still retained remnants of clan-tribal division. Thus, upwards of 40 distinct groups bearing their own names exist among the I-tsu people in Yunnan Province.

The ethnic composition of China was first determined with adequate scientific validity and reliability by the general census of 1953. In contrast to many capitalist countries where, in census-taking, the question of ethnic self-consciousness is replaced by that of mother tongue, resulting in underestimation of the size of ethnic minorities, in the Chinese People's Republic a question on ethnic affiliation is included on the census sheets. This has resulted in also determining those national groups which have lost their mother tongue to a significant extent, but have still preserved other ethnic characteristics that distinguish them from the Chinese (for example, the Manchus).

Based on census data as of June 30, 1953, 590,195,000 persons[2] inhabited the territory of China, including 554,675,000 Chinese. The remaining 35,520,000 inhabitants (6.02% of the total population) constituted the ethnic minorities.[3] About 40 peoples were differentiated by the census. Later, through much exploratory work by Chinese scientists and the activity of local agencies of the people's authority, several more peoples were found. Linguistically, the peoples of China can be grouped as shown in Table I; the numbers of the peoples are given as of mid-1953.[4]

The differentiation of certain peoples in this table is subject to dispute owing to the lack of adequate study of them. For several peoples (Tu-lung, Lo-hui, and others), there is no information at all, save for references to their areas of settlement. Several small and poorly studied groups are omitted from the table — such groups as the

Mo-lao, Ko-lao, Mao-nan, P'u-la, Chia-jung, Pu-lo-tse (tz'u), and others, which for the most part have not been differentiated as independent peoples. Also unstudied is the problem of whether to distinguish as an individual people the group of Tan living in the districts of Canton and Shantou, who are distinct from the Chinese in a number of ethnic characteristics.

The distribution of the peoples of China can be seen from the attached ethnic map (Figure 1). Ethnic minorities inhabit the entire western half of the country, as well as several areas in the south and north of China. Peoples belonging to the Sino-Tibetan language family and constituting roughly 70% of the total population of the ethnic minorities live in the south and southwest — in the provinces of Kiangsi, Yunnan, Kweichow, and Szechuan, and in Tibet. These peoples are intimately related to peoples of Southeast Asia by origin, language, and economic-cultural characteristics. About 25% of the total population of the ethnic minorities is made up of peoples of the Altaic language family, living in the north and northwest of China, in the autonomous areas of Sinkiang, Inner Mongolia, and Tungpei. They share many features with the peoples of Central Asia and Siberia. Peoples of these two language families are contiguous to each other only in northern Tsinghai Province, where up to ten peoples are concentrated in a single small region. Everywhere else, areas populated by Chinese, or mountainous deserts with no population at all, separate these two groups of peoples.

Southwest China is the most complex region in the ethnic sense. Here, 25 nationalities — Tibetans, I-tsu, Miao, Pai, Thai, Pui, Na-hsi, K'a-wa, and others — live in a fairly small area forming part of the three provinces of Yunnan, Kweichow, and Szechuan. Peoples are particularly intermixed in the north of Sinkiang.

Compact groups of ethnic minorities are found only in Tibet and in the semidesert regions of Inner Mongolia. They have also been preserved in the remote oases of Sinkiang. In all other areas the population is heavily intermingled. Chinese inhabit river valleys and the land along roads, and ethnic minorities occupy watersheds and mountainous areas. For example, a clear vertical zonality is observed in the distribution of peoples in the provinces of Yunnan and Kweichow. Mountainous areas are occupied by the Miao and Yao; then come the Chinese; and the low-lying floodplains are settled by peoples of the Chuang-Thai group.

China's cities are marked by a distinctive ethnic composition. As in many other countries, representatives of peoples at a higher stage of social and economic development predominate among city dwellers. The great bulk of the population in the cities of China (except for Tibet and southern Sinkiang) consists of Chinese, interspersed with small numbers of Dungans and (in Northeast China) also Manchus. The percentage of Dungans rises sharply in cities of the provinces of Kansu, Tsinghai, and Sinkiang. The cities of southern Sinkiang (Kashgaria) are almost exclusively settled by Uighurs; the cities of Tibet, by Tibetans. In recent years, a trend has been noted in the direction of a larger proportion of representatives of small peoples among city dwellers, especially in the centers of ethnic-minority settlement.

When we describe the distribution of ethnic minorities, we cannot fail to underscore the obvious disparity between the land area they occupy and their ratio to the total population. Population density in the ethnic areas is many times less than in areas settled by Chinese. The reason for this is as follows. Ethnic minorities are settled in the western (or Middle Asian) continental part of China, which differs greatly in physico-geographical conditions from the eastern. The western part is occupied by high plateaus and depressions intersected by the world's highest peaks. Here the climate is of the desert and semi-desert type; precipitation in most parts of the area does not exceed 100 mm a year; rivers are of low volume and often dry up. Much of the territory of Western China is poorly suited for economic exploitation. Large expanses of the Gobi and Takla-Makan Deserts are completely uninhabited, and this is also true of the vast area of mountainous cold desert in northwest Tibet, and of mountain ranges with elevations higher than 5,000 meters. Most of the territory of the autonomous areas — Inner Mongolia and Sinkiang, and also Tibet and Tsinghai — due to low

TABLE I

People	Population in thous.
Sino-Tibetan family	
Chinese Group	
Chinese (Han)	554,675
Dungans (Huei)	3,559
Total	558,234
Chuang-T'ai Group	
Chuang	6,611
Pung	1,248
Nung[5]	196
Sha[5]	180
T'ai	479
T'ung (Tung)	713
Shui	134
Li	361
Total	9,922
Tibeto-Burman Group	
Tibetans	2,776
Ch'iang	36
Nu	13
Tulung	2
Lo-yui	50
Chingpo	101
I-tsu	3,254
Hang-i	481
Li-su	317
Na-hsi	143
La-hu	139
A-ch'ang	18
Pai (Min-chia)	567
Tu-chia (Bi-se-ka)	94
Total	7,991
Miao-Yao Group	
Miao	2,511
Yao	666
Shē	151
Total	3,328

People	Population in thous.
Altaic Family	
Turkic Group	
Uighurs	3,640
Uzbeks	14
Tatars	7
Yuiku (Sara-Uighurs)	4
Kazakhs	509
Kirgiz	71
Salars	31
Total	4,276
Mongolian Group	
Mongols	1,463
Tung-hsiang	156
T'u (Mongors)	53
Pao-an	5
Dahurs	44
Total	1,721
Tunguso-Manchurian Group	
Solons	7
Evenki (Orochony, Birary, Manegry)	7
Manchus	2,419
Si-po	19
Nanays (Ho-che)	1
Total	2,453
Koreans	
Koreans	1,120
Mon-Khmer Family	
K'a-wa	286
Palaun	3
Pu-man	35
Total	324
Austronesian Family	
Kao-shan	200
Indo-European Family	
Mountain Tadjiks	14
Others	612
Grand Total	590,195

precipitation, lack of sizeable rivers, and mountainous terrain, can be used only for cattle-raising. Thus, at the present level of development of the productive forces, only certain parts of Western China can be used for agriculture, which predetermines the sparse settlement pattern of this entire region. Only 2.3% of the population live in the four border provinces and autonomous regions — Tibet, Sinkiang, Inner Mongolia, and Tsinghai — which account for 52% of the territory of the country; the mean population density here is 2.7 persons per square kilometer (23 times less than the average for the country as a whole, and almost 50 times less than the density in eastern China).

In spite of the vast area occupied by pastoralists — Mongols, Kazakhs, Kirgiz, etc. — they constitute a small proportion (only about 10%) of the ethnic minorities. Farming is the main occupation for all the rest; animal husbandry is of subsidiary importance (though more important than among the Chinese).

The ethnic characteristics of given groups of peoples can be seen more clearly when the distribution of various religions in China is examined. The Chinese proper follow Buddhism of the northern [Mahayana] branch, Taoism, and Confucianism (the latter, although not a religion in the proper sense of the word, has in recent times adopted several ceremonials of a religious character).[6] All these religions are so intermixed that it is not possible even to delimit the range of their adherents, let alone to localize the areas of their distribution. In quite a few cases, the population of a single village attends temples of various faiths. The religious situation among ethnic minorities is more clear-cut. Among peoples of the Chuang-Thai group, and also among the Miao, Yao, and some other peoples of Southwest China, Buddhism of the southern [Hinayana] branch is practiced. Lamaist Buddhism is the religion of the Tibetans and Mongols. Dungans and Turkic-group peoples follow Islam,[7] which penetrated Western China as far back as the 7th to 8th centuries. Shamanism, along with Buddhism and Taoism, is widespread among several peoples of the Tunguso-Manchurian group, and also in part among the Dakhurs and Koreans. Tribal religions are found among many peoples, particularly in Southwest

China. Some of the religions cited, especially Islam and Lamaist Buddhism, strongly permeate the life and culture of various peoples.

Before going on to characterize the distribution of ethnic minorities, we should dwell briefly on the distribution of the *Chinese*. The Huangho basin was the center of the formation of the Chinese people. From here Chinese spread south, north, and west, and by degrees assimilated the peoples of the Mon-Khmer, Chuang-Thai, Tibeto-Burman, Mongol, Tunguso-Manchurian, and other groups who were living there. At present, Chinese are settled in small numbers in only two areas — Tibet and Sinkiang (less than 10%). In all other major areas they constitute the absolute majority of the population. In provinces such as Yunnan and Kweichow — centers in which various groups of ethnic minorities were formed — as an outcome of Chinese colonization, more than two-thirds of the inhabitants are now Chinese. Inner Mongolia and Tungpei, the homeland of Mongol and Tunguso-Manchurian peoples, are 90% populated by Chinese, although large-scale Chinese colonization of these areas began only in the last quarter of the nineteenth century. Thus, even in areas of compact settlement by ethnic minorities, the Chinese population is usually very sizable.

The Chinese group also includes the Dungans (Huei), who do not differ in language from the Chinese. They are classed as a separate people owing to their differences from the Chinese in way of life and economy, especially their religious distinctness. In religious allegiance, the Dungans are Sunni Muslims of the Arzamite persuasion. In rural localities they rarely mix with the Chinese and in most cases form independent settlements; in cities they occupy districts (blocks) separate from the Chinese.

Various theories of the origin of the Dungans exist. Liu Chen-yui maintains that their ancestors were ancient Turks who settled the northwest of China in the 5th-6th centuries C.E. Lin Kan hypothesizes that the bulk of the Dungan nationality was formed from Muslims who migrated to China during the Yuan dynasty (1280-1368) from Persia, Arabia, and Central Asia; the Iranian-speaking and Arabic-speaking migrants in the course of time acquired the Chinese language, script, and culture as a whole. S. P. Tolstov and M. G. Levin believe them to be Chinese colonists who settled in a Turkic-speaking environment on the northwest border of China as early as the 2nd century B.C.E. and were later converted to Islam. Other theories of the origin of Dungans derive them from the Kidans, Togons, and other peoples living in North China in the 7th-11th centuries C.E.[8] It is highly probable that the Dungans are a mixed group, and that the various theories of their origin mutually supplement each other.

The principal Dungan population is concentrated in the provinces of Kansu, Tsinghai, and Sinkiang. Large groups of Dungans are also encountered in the provinces of Honan, Hopei, Shantung, etc. A chain of Dungan settlements stretches along the main roads on the northern borders of China, from the western part of Sinkiang to Peking. In all these areas they live mainly in cities and adjoining villages, where they engage in truck gardening, orchardry, crafts, and trade.

Peoples of the *Chuang-T'ai group* inhabit a sizeable territory, extending southward to the Gulf of Siam, northward to the southern borders of Szechuan, in the west to Assam, and easterly to Hainan Island. Over all this territory Thai peoples speak languages differing but little and most closely related (within the Sino-Tibetan language family) to Chinese. Peoples of this group are settled in China in the provinces of Kiangsi, Kweichow, Yunnan, and Hunan, and on Hainan Island, where they live intermingled with other peoples.

Roughly two-thirds of the total population of the Chuang-T'ai group is made up of Chuang, settled in a compact mass over the entire western half of the Kiangsi Autonomous Region; here they number upwards of 70% of the total population. Some Chuang, living close to Chinese, have been strongly influenced by them. Accordingly, prior to the 1953 census, many investigators severely underestimated the numbers of the Chuang in Kiangsi (instead of 6.5 million, the figure of 2-2.5 million persons was given). The Chuang living north of the Hung-shui-ho River, who are to a large extent Chinese-speaking, had been enumerated among the Chinese.

Closely related to the Chuang are two small nationalities: the *Sha* and the *Nung*, settled in the southeastern
part of Yunnan Province, northeast of the city of Malipo.
The Sha live in the districts of Chiu-pei, Kuang-nan, and
Shi-ch'iung. The Nung are located west of them, in the
districts of Wen-shan and Fu-ning. Both these peoples inhabit wooded uplands, while river valleys are populated by
Chinese.

The *Pui*, or Chung-chia (some Pui groups bear the
names of Shui-hu, T'u-pien, Jao-chia), inhabit the southwest of Kweichow Province. The Pui live adjoining the
Miao in the central parts of this province. They have settled mainly the counties of Tu-yun, An-shun, Kuei-ting,
Hsin-i, and Pi-chieh. The Pui also constitute the majority
surrounding the main city of Kweichow Province — Kuei-
yang.

The *T'ai (Thai)* — related to the Shan of Burma — are a
nationality settled in the southern half of Yunnan Province. They are divided into two branches: the Thai-Hsi-
shuang-pan-na and the T'ai-Te-hung. They live in small
groups adjoining other peoples (Chinese, Chingpo, Li-su,
Hang-i, K'a-wa) and occupy the swampy, malarial river
valleys.

The *T'ung*, or Tung, have settled in a continuous
mass in a territory that is part of three provinces: southeastern Kweichow, northern Kiangsi, and the western part
of Hunan. For a long period they have been in close proximity with the Chinese and have been strongly assimilated
by them. This nationality is close to the Shui people. The
Shui are settled in the southeast corner of Kweichow — in
the districts of Li-po, Du-shan, and San-tu.

The *Li* are the aborigines of Hainan island. They live
in the mountainous region of Wu-chih-shan and the adja-
cent regions of Pai-sha and Mei-fu. The Li are divided into
four groups: the Pen-ti-li, Mei-fu-li, Ki, and La. The
Pen-ti-li live in the wild mountainous regions in the south
and center of the island; economically, they have lagged
behind the other Li groups, who have been subject to
strong Chinese influence.

Most of the peoples in the Chuang-T'ai group are
engaged in farming; they cultivate paddy field rice. Among

these people, as among the Chinese, animal husbandry is of limited importance. Only in the economy of the Li people, living on Hainan Island and occupying a separate position in the T'ai group of peoples, does animal husbandry, especially buffalo-raising, play a major role.

The principal area of settlement of peoples of the *Tibeto-Burman group* is Tibet and three provinces of Southwest China: Szechuan, Kweichow, and Yunnan. Tibetans also live in the more northerly provinces of Tsinghai and Kansu. The composition of this group within China comprises (linguistically) three subgroups: Tibetan, Chingpo, and I-tsu.

The Tibetan subgroup includes, in addition to the Tibetans proper, small peoples: the Ch'iang, Nu, Tu-lung, and Lo-yu. Peoples of this subgroup occupy the vast territory of the Tibetan highlands, extending 1300 km from north to south and 2000 km from east to west. The highland is bounded on all sides by the world's highest mountains: the Himalayas, the Karakorum, and the Kun-lun. The sources of the longest rivers in Asia — the Yangtze, the Huangho, the Mekong, the Brahmaputra, etc. — are at the edges of the highland. The Tibetan highland is marked by severe climate with intense frosts and sharp contrasts between day and night temperatures. The northern and western part of the Tibetan highland, due to the sharp rise in climatic severity, is detrital-gravel high-altitude desert, almost devoid of life. A large number of Tibetans have settled outside China, along the southern and western slopes of the Himalayas in Nepal, and also in Sikkim, Bhutan, Ladakh, and Baltistan, part of India.

The *Tibetans* are the vast majority of the population in Tibet. In addition, Chinese also live here in small numbers (in the cities), as well as Gurkhas, and representatives of several peoples of the Himalayan group — emigrants from Nepal and India. At times Uighur pastoralists from Sinkiang roam into the northwest part of Tibet.

Tibetans in Tsinghai Province have settled more than 70% of the territory, and only in two areas — near the Tsaidam Basin and in the Hsi-ning Basin — do other people in addition to Tibetans (Chinese, Kazakhs, Mongols, T'u or Mongors, Tung-hsiang, Salars, etc.) reside. In

Szechuan, Tibetans occupy all the western, mountainous part, almost half the area of the province; their eastern border is the lower course of the Yalunchiang River, the city of Kang-ting, and the Minchiang River. In Kansu, Tibetans have settled southwest of Lanchou. They have also populated the Yunlingshan mountains in the most northwesterly part of Yunnan Province.

Remnants of tribal division have been preserved among Tibetans. Until recently, the basic features of a feudal order were retained in Tibet. The chief pursuit of most Tibetans is farming,[9] almost always combined with animal husbandry. Farming is conducted in southern Tibet, in the valleys of the Ts'angpo River and its tributaries, where a fairly dense sedentary population is concentrated. The greater part of the population lives in villages, here situated at elevations up to 4,500-4,800 meters above sea level. The most important grain in Tibet is mountain barley.

Nomads and seminomads constitute not more than one-fifth of total population. They migrate with their herds over moderate distances; their mode of life differs only slightly from that of the settled peoples. The pastoralists chiefly raise yaks, sheep, and long-haired goats. In contrast to Mongols, Tibetan cattle breeders almost always have fields.

Tibetans practice Lamaism, a variety of Buddhism, which penetrated into Tibet as far back as the 7th century C.E. All political power came into the control of the Lamaist clergy in the 17th century. At present, several monasteries and tens of thousands of lama-monks are found in Tibet.

The remaining peoples of the Tibetan subgroup have been poorly studied. Under the name Lo-yui are subsumed several nationalities living on both sides of the Chinese-Indian border in the area of a bend of the Brahmaputra River, southeast of Lhasa. These include the Dafla, Mir, Abor, and Mishmi.[10] The Dafla and Mir live within the bend of the Brahmaputra on both sides of its tributary, the Subansiri. The Abor and Mishmi are settled in the mountainous area northeast of the city of Sadiya, on the left bank of the Brahmaputra. All these peoples are engaged in mountain farming and hunting. The Nu and

Tulung live in the Lu-chiang (Sa-luen) valley, in the mountainous region of northern Yunnan Province. Finally, the Ch'iang, Tibetan by language, are found in Ssu-ch'uan, east of the city of Ta-chiang-lu. The Ch'iang are evidently the aboriginal population of this area, having adopted the Tibetan language and culture.

The I-tsu subgroup includes, besides the I-tsu proper, several smaller peoples: Hang-i, Li-su, Na-hsi, La-hu, Pai, A-ch'ang, and T'u-chia. All these people are so intensely intermingled that different authors classify individual subdivisions of them with different peoples. Along with farming, animal husbandry and hunting are quite developed among these peoples.

The I-tsu are scattered over an enormous territory encompassing three provinces: Szechuan, Yunnan, and Kweichow. Their present-day center of settlement is the mountainous country of Ta-liang-shan, located at the junction of these three provinces. Along with the peoples of the Chuang-Thai group and the Miao-Yao, the I-tsu are the most widespread nationality of Southwest China. To the north they extend as far as 30° N. (the city of K'ang-ting in Szechuan Province); to the south, as far as 20° N. L. (near Ssu-mao in Yunnan) and farther, with the transition into Vietnam and Laos; eastward, deep within Kweichow Province to 105° E. L.; and westward to the border with Tibet.

Until recently, a feudal order with significant survivals of slaveholding existed among the I-tsu, with prisoners of war working as slaves. Survivals of tribal organization have been preserved. Some tribes are hostile toward each other. The largest group of I-tsu is the Nosu, living in the largely inaccessible mountainous country of Ta-liang-shan, who were almost independent of Chinese authority (the Nosu were called "independent I-tsu").

The principal pursuit of the southern I-tsu is hoe farming; mountain rice, corn, and wheat are the main crops grown. Among the northern and western I-tsu, in addition to farming, animal husbandry is also developed — the breeding of cattle, sheep, goats, and horses. Hunting and fishing are of subsidiary importance.

Recently a fairly numerous group of Tu-chia (or

Bi-se-ka) has been found in Hunan Province, closely related to the I-tsu, but living among the Miao and the Chinese, and strongly influenced by them.

Hang-i, or Woni, is the general name for numerous tribes settled in the south of Yunnan Province, along the right bank of the Red River. The biggest of these tribes include the Ma-hei, Kato, Pu-t'a, Pio, San-su, Kanun, and A-ka (the latter now live within the limits of northeast Burma). All these peoples speak a language close to that of the I-tsu.

The *Li-su* have settled in the Sa-luen River valley in Yunnan Province. To the east they extend to the Mekong, and westward to the Nmaika River, a tributary of the Irrawaddy. In the main they live in Fu-kung Uyezd in the Li-chiang Area. The Li-su are divided into individual tribes, the chief of which are the Wopa, Nopa, Lama, Tsepa, Wapa, Lapa, Nurra, P'yapa, Lipa, and Shopa. They are closely related to the Chingpo, who, however, belong to another subgroup of the Tibeto-Burman languages.

The Na-hsi, or Moso, inhabit the northwest of Yunnan Province, in the area of the loop formed here by the Yangtze River; to the west their settlements extend to the Mekong River. The language of the Na-hsi is close to the language of the I-tsu, but it also has many similarities to the language of the Tibetans who are their neighbors.

The La-hu, or Lo-hei, live in the area of Pu-erh in Yunnan Province. They inhabit the rocky gorge between the Sa-luen [Salween] and Mekong rivers, south of 23° 30' N.; small groups have settled also in the northern areas of Thailand and Burma. The La-hu speak one of the dialects of the I-tsu language. In several elements of material culture, and by physical type, they are closely related to the Wa (or K'a-wa), part of the Mon-Khmer group of peoples. According to Roce (1910), the La-hu are derived from a mixture of I-tsu tribes with Wa tribes.

The *A-ch'ang* are a small ethnic group living in the valley of the Maynthi River in Yunnan Province. By language, they are part of the I-tsu subgroup. In their customs and material culture, they have much in common with the neighboring T'ai and Chingpo nationalities.

The *Pai* (Min-chia) constitute a sizeable and compactly

settled group living in the area of Lake Er-hai (Yunnan Province). In contrast to other national minorities of the province who inhabit mainly mountainous areas, the Pai live in large valleys and engage in farming and trade. The Pai, like other peoples of the I-tsu subgroup, follow Buddhism of the southern branch, but those living in the northern area have begun, under the influence of the nearby Tibetans, to follow Lamaism (they are known as Lama-jen — that is, Lamaists).

The Chingpo (called Kachin in Burmese) and the closely related Tsai-wa group form the main bulk of the population in the far north of Burma. In China they have settled the mountainous areas in the western and southwestern part of Yunnan Province, where they live together with the Thai and K'a-wa nationalities. Lachi tribes related to the Chingpo live along the China-Burma border, on both sides. The principal pursuit of the Chingpo is slash-and-burn agriculture (raising rice and corn); animal husbandry and hunting are secondary.

The Miao and Yao peoples have recently been differentiated by Chinese investigators as an independent group within the Sino-Tibetan language family (they were previously considered part of the Mon-Khmer language family). [11] They live in South China and in the northern areas of Vietnam, Laos, and Thailand, occupying the mountainous regions of those countries.

The Miao are scattered in separate groups over the entire vast expanse of South China. They live in the provinces of Kweichow, Hunan, Yunnan, Szechuan, and Kiangsi, and on Hainan Island. However, only in two localities do the Miao constitute sizable compact groups: the east of Kweichow Province and the southwest of Hunan Province. In Kiangi they are settled in small groups in the province's center. In Szechuan, Miao live in the southwest of the province, along the border with Kweichow. In Yunnan they have settled in isolated groups in the districts of E-shan, I-liang, Hsien-pin, Kun-ming, Ang-nin, and Wu-ting. On Hainan, individual Miao villages[12] are scattered over the entire central area of the island. In almost all areas the Miao have been displaced deep into the mountains and live surrounded by Chinese and peoples of the Chuang-

Thai group.

In mode of life, culture, and language, the Miao are not a homogeneous mass. They have come under strong Chinese influence in several areas, for example, in Hunan. Until recently, the Miao retained survivals of tribal relationships. In various areas several dozens of tribal groups have been found. The largest of these are the Hung-miao, Hei-miao, Pai-miao, Ch'ing-miao, and Hua-miao.

The Miao chiefly pursue mountain farming (rice, wheat) — irrigated on terraces — and slash-and-burn on mountain summits. Animal husbandry, hunting, and felling and rafting of timber are secondary.

The *Yao* are a nationality related to the Miao and live in the mountainous regions of the provinces of Kiangsi, Kwantung, and Hunan. Smaller groups are found in Kweichow and Yunnan. The principal settlement area of the Yao is located along the borders of three provinces: Kwantung, Kiangsi, and Hunan. In Kwantung Province their settlements are also found in the districts of Sin-ning, Lo-tung, and Liang-chou. In Kiangsi they inhabit compactly the mountainous region of Yao-shan in the center of the province; some Yao villages are scattered over the entire province. In Hunan, the Yao occupy the southernmost region of the province. Only one-third of this nationality speaks the Yao language, and two-thirds the languages of the Miao, the Tung, and the Chuang *(Druzhba* [newspaper], August 23, 1957).

The Yao are engaged in farming (dry-rice cultivation, maize), and also in hunting, felling, and hauling timber.

The *Shē* are a little-studied ethnic group scattered in mountainous terrain in Fuchien and Chekiang provinces, and also in the provinces of Chiangsi and Kwantung. About half of all Shē live in the district of Ching-ning of Chiekiang Province. They regard themselves as migrants from Kiangsi; they speak a language similar to the language of the Yao, but strongly Sinicized.

Nationalities of the *Turkic group* are located in the western areas of China: Sinkiang, Kansu, and Tsinghai.

We have already given characterizations of the Turkic nationalities living in Sinkiang (Uighurs, Kazakhs, Kirgiz, Uzbeks, and Tatars) (Bruk 1956). Only the Salars and the

Yuiku (Sara-Uighurs) live outside Sinkiang, as well as a number of Kazakhs who in 1936 (after the suppression of an uprising begun by them in Sinkiang) were resettled by the Kuomintang in Tsinghai Province, in an area west and south of the Tsiadam Basin.

The *Salars* are the most easterly of the Turkic-speaking groups of China. They occupy a mountainous locality on the right bank of the Huangho River in the area of the city of Hsun-hua in Tsinghai Province and in the districts of Lin-hsia and Lin-tan in Kansu Province. The Salars live in large settlements, not mixing with neighboring nationalities. They have preserved the legend that they came from Samarkand in 1370 (Rockhill 1901: 86). Other sources state that they are originally from Serakhs (Lin Kan 1954). Their language is close to Uighur, but has a considerable admixture of Tibetan, Mongolian, and Chinese words. The main pursuit of the Salars is farming. Like all other Turkic nationalities of China except the Uighurs, the Salars are adherents of Islam.

The *Yuiku*, or Sara-Uighurs, live in Kansu Province, south of the Suchou-Hanchou Road, along the northern spurs of the Nan-shan Mountains. Their western group (Sara-Uighur) speak Mongolian; the eastern (Kara-Uighur), one of the Turkic languages (closely related to ancient Uighur). All Yuiku are engaged in pastoralism and follow a nomadic mode of life. By religion, most Yuiku are Lamaist Buddhists.

Peoples of the *Mongol* group inhabit the vast areas of the steppes and semideserts north of the Great Chinese Plain. Westward, Mongol nomads extend to the western borders of Sinkiang, and eastward to the Nong-ni River and the so-called Willow Wall, which served as a border between the Mongols and the Manchus. Through protracted processes of colonization, a sizeable territory north of the Great Plain has been occupied by Chinese settlers. Small groups of Mongols are distributed southward in Tibet and the northern areas of Yunnan Province.

The great dispersion of Mongol population is to be accounted for historically. As is well known, in the early 13th century a powerful alliance of nomadic Mongol tribes conquered many countries of Central Asia and

Eastern Europe. By the mid-13th century the Mongol state extended from the shores of the Pacific Ocean to Central Europe. In 1368 the Mongol empire disintegrated, and individual Mongol groups were left isolated from each other, separated from their homeland. In the early 15th century Mongols were divided into western and eastern, and, in the mid-16th century, the latter were in turn divided into northern and southern.

At present, the following peoples of the Mongol group have been differentiated in China: the Mongols proper, the Tu (Mongors), the Tung-hsiang, Pao-yang, and the Dahurs. The *Mongols proper* occupy the autonomous region of Inner Mongolia, northern Sinkiang, and also the provinces of Liaoning, Kirin, Heilungkiang, and Tsinghai. They lead mainly a nomadic way of life and have retained remnants of tribal division up to the present. Former tribes occupying a definite area have become fairly stable groups, almost completely distinct from each other. The largest of these groups are as follows: Gorlosy, Dzhalayty, Khorchiny, Naymany, Tumuty, Chakhary, Khuchity, Utszumchiny, Torgouty, Khozhouty, Elety, and others. In China, five dialects have been distinguished among the Mongols: eastern, central (closely related to the Khalkhask), Bargu-Buryat, western, and Oirat (Sinkiang).[13] The Dahurs live in Heilungkiang, Inner Mongolia, and in small numbers in Sinkiang; in origin, they are evidently Mongolized groups of Tunguso-Manchurians. The *T'u, Tung-hsiang,* and *Pao-yang* inhabit the regions of Lanchou and Sining along the border of Kansu and Tsinghai provinces; they have been subject to the strong influence of the Chinese, Dungans, and Tibetans.

The main pursuit of most Mongols is animal husbandry. They raise sheep and goats, and, to a lesser extent, cattle, horses, and camels. The population migrates with its herds and flocks over distances from 10 to 25 km (sometimes the distances of migration amount to 50 km and longer). In certain areas — for example, in the Chakhar steppes and on the Kuei-sui Plain — some Mongols have given up nomadic cattle-breeding and cultivate the land like the Chinese. In several localities, hunting is important. The Dahurs, Pao-an, and Tun-hsiang, in contrast to other Mongols, are sedentary and pursue farming.

Most Mongols practice Lamaist Buddhism, which penetrated into Mongolia from Tibet in 1586. Lamaist monasteries possessed much of the livestock and land, and engaged in trade and moneylending. The higher lamas concentrated in their control not only spiritual but secular power. Only with the victory of the people's revolution was the power of the Lamaist monasteries undermined. The Pao-an and the Tun-hsiang, living among the Dungans, are Muslims.

Peoples of the *Tunguso-Manchurian group* — Manchus, Si-po, Nanays, Solons, and Evenki — live in separate dispersed groups in Northeast China, in Tungpei (formerly Manchuria). The population of Tungpei, where the historical routes traveled by peoples of Central Eastern, and where those of Northeast Asia have crossed, has long been multitribal in character. In addition to aboriginal Tunguso-Manchu tribes, peoples of other groups — Chinese, Mongol, and Korean — have penetrated here from all sides. Chinese colonization from the south was especially vigorous.

The more advanced Chinese culture had an enormous influence on the backward Tunguso-Manchurian tribes. In the localities of the greatest penetration by the Chinese, these tribes were strongly assimilated and lost their own language and way of life. Therefore, the Tunguso-Manchurian nationalities are very dispersed at present, and survive mainly in the mountainous and taiga areas of Tungpei.

Considerable changes in the ethnic makeup of the population of Tungpei are connected with the actions of the Manchu rulers in resettling large groups of Manchus in the inner regions of China; at the same time, Dahurs, Solons, and Bargu-Buryats moved from the Transbaikal and other localities of Eastern Siberia to Tungpei. At the close of the 19th century, the influx of Korean settlers from the southeast increased.

The main pursuit of the Manchus and the Si-po is farming. The Nanays engage in fishing and partly in hunting. The main occupation of the Solons is animal husbandry (raising horses and dairy cattle). Evenki are chiefly hunters, but animal husbandry of the same type is developed, and in part also reindeer breeding.

The Manchus are the aborigines of Tungpei. At the close of the 16th century, Manchu tribes headed by Nurhach'i established their state in the Ch'ang-pai-shan mountains. Owing to a strong military organization, the Manchus succeeded, in the mid-17th century, in conquering all of China, and the Tai-ch'ing (Manchu) dynasty ruled there until 1911. To keep conquered China in submission, garrisons of Manchu forces were established in Chinese cities. Gradually, sizeable Manchu colonies were formed outside Tungpei, principally in the cities.

In Tungpei, Manchus inhabit the valleys of the Nong-ni (north of Chichikar) and Amur (southeast of Aykun) rivers in Heilungkiang Province, and also the basin of the upper Sungari River and the valley of the Mu-tan-chiang River in Kirin Province. In all these areas they inhabit villages located around cities. Outside Tungpei, sizeable groups of Manchu remain in the Peking area. They also live in the cities of Shan-hai-kuang, Mi-yung, Chi-kou, Sian, Nan-chou, and others.

It must be noted that of the 2.4 million persons who called themselves Manchu in the 1953 census, only a small number, in remote villages near Chichikar and Kirin, and also in Sinkiang, retained features of national way of life and language. In all the other regions, they have been assimilated under the influence of the more advanced Chinese culture and have lost their own mode of life (including language and script).

The *Si-po*, or Si-pings, live in the northwestern part of Sinkiang, in the valley of the Ili River near Kuldja; a small group of Si-po has settled in Tungpei on the lower course of the Nongni River. In Sinkiang, they became military settlers as part of the "bannered"[a] Manchu forces in the middle of the eighteenth century, after the defeat of the Djungarian Khanate. The Sipo have retained their language, closely related to Manchu.

The Nanays (Ho-che), like the Manchus and the Si-po, are part of the southern subgroup of the Tunguso-Manchurian group of peoples. They occupy wooded and marshy expanses at the confluences of the Sungari and the

Ussuri with the Amur; the area is centered on Fugdin.

The Solons and the Evenki are part of the northern (Tungus) subgroup of the Tunguso-Manchurians. The *Solons* were resettled from the Transbaikal to Manchuria in 1732. In Tungpei they live on the right bank of the Nongni River near the city of Chichikar in the upper reaches of the river, and also in the area of Haylar; they are also found in the Ili Territory of Sinkiang, where they were resettled together with the Dahurs in 1764. The Solons were part of the Manchu bannered forces. Therefore, some of them live in cities where there were Manchu garrisons, such as Chich'ikar, Hailar, Butha, Mergen, and Aigun. The language of the Solons has a sizeable admixture of Mongol words.

The *Evenki* live in the taiga regions of northern Tungpei. Due to their dispersion over the enormous territory, individual territorial groups ov Evenki took form, differing from each other in way of life and partly in language. Such groups here include the Manegry, Birary, and Orochony. The Manegry live in the area of the Ilhuri-Alin Range (in the basin of the Humaerhe River). The Birary live along the northern spurs of the Lesser Hingan. The Orochony (meaning "reindeer-herders") are settled along both slopes of the Greater Hingan. However, reindeer Orochony have survived only in a small group north of the Nu-er-he (Bystraia) River;[14] all other Orochony are horse breeders. The Evenki live a seminomadic life (more precisely, they engaged in seasonal migrations).

Koreans began settling in China on free land in southeastern Tungpei as far back as several centuries ago. The main reason for this was the poverty and landlessness of the Korean peasantry. A strong impetus to resettlement was given by the unprecedented famine caused by drought in Korea in the 1870s. However, the massive resettlement of Koreans in Northeast China began after Japan occupied Korea in 1910.

The bulk of the Korean population lives in areas bordering Korea, on the north bank of the Tumyn River, in the Yan-chi Basin, and along the banks of the Yalu Rivers. In these regions Koreans constitute upwards of 70% of the total population (Chinese here live in cities).

Smaller groups of Koreans are settled throughout Tungpei. To the south, their settlements extend to Ying-k'ou; to the north, to the lower Sungari; to the west, as far as Hailar. Here small chains of Korean villages extend mainly along rivers (especially the Mu-tan) and railways — the routes along which the Koreans advanced.

Koreans engage mainly in growing paddy rice,[15] and in lumbering, charcoal burning, and various crafts.

Of the *Mon-Khmer peoples* within China, the K'a-wa (related to the Wa in Burma and the Lawa in Thailand), the *Pu-man*, and the *Palaun* have survived. They are all settled in small groups within the southern part of Yunnan Province, chiefly in the valleys of the Lu-chiang and Lan-tsang-chiang rivers. The main occupation of the K'a-wa and Pu-man is slash-and-burn agriculture, cattle breeding, and hunting. In contrast, the Palaun are engaged in field farming.

Of peoples in other language families, the following should be mentioned.

The *Kao-shan* (in Chinese, "mountaineers") are the aboriginal population of Taiwan Island, related to the Malays.[16] Their villages are scattered in the mountainous areas which occupy more than half the island's territory. Most Kao-shan have preserved their customs and their language, which belongs to the Indonesian group of the Austronesian family of languages. Only a part of this nationality, living on the plain and in hilly areas, is being gradually assimilated due to prolonged contact with the Chinese.

The Kao-shan retain a number of suvivals of the primitive-communal order. They are divided into tribes, distributed as follows: the Amei and the Emei live to the east along the coast, the T'ai-yeh-erh and the Shaisty in the north; the Paiwan in the south; the Chuo and the Punung in the center of the island.

Most Kao-shan are engaged in pastoralism, but some of them, living in lowland areas, have changed over to farming. Also developed are hunting and fishing.

The Tadjiks of China are part of the group of so-called Mountain Tadjiks. They live in the southwest of Sinkiang, in the Tashkurgan area, and in the valley of the

Tiznaf and its tributaries, in remote inaccessible mountain localities. Most Tadjiks lead a nomadic way of life and are engaged in pastoralism, while a minority pursue mountain farming and are sedentary. Sinkiang Tadjiks, or Sarykoltsy, are related to the Vahantsy, Shughantsy, and Roshantsy who inhabit the Pamirs in the Soviet Union and Afghanistan. They speak one of the dialects of the Shugnan language, belonging to the eastern subgroup of the Iranian group of languages. [17] Their language has a sizeable admixture of Turkic words.

Moreover, representatives of other peoples also live within the Chinese People's Republic.

In Sinkiang, in the inaccessible mountains on the northern slope of the Karakorum, on the border with Kashmir, there are small groups of the so-called *Kanzhuts*, who have not been studied at all; these are evidently the Burishki, most of whom are located in Kashmir. Here there are also small numbers of *Kashmiris*, *Afghans*, and *Gypsies*.

Vietnamese, *Malays*, *Arabs*, and others are encountered in small numbers in the south of China.

The number of *Russians* who have lived in China, in Tungpei and Sinkiang, is quite sizeable. Russians began settling in Tungpei with the construction of the Chinese Eastern Railroad (at the close of the 1890s). The total number of Russians amounted to 250,000 here. They lived in Harbin, in station settlements of the Chinese Eastern Railroad, and also in the area of the Trekhrech'e (the valleys of the three right-hand tributaries of the Argun River: the Haul, the Derbul, and the Ken-he). With the exception of the Russians of the Trekhrech'e, who engaged in agriculture, the rest worked on the railroad and in various branches of industry, engaged in trade, etc. In Sinkiang, Russian Old Believers began to settle at the close of the 19th century; here they set up a number of settlements in the north of the Altai District. Russians lived also in the cities of Urumchi, Kuldja, and Chuguchak. Recently, the Russians for the most part have been repatriated to the Soviet Union.

* * *

All peoples enjoy full equality in the Chinese People's Republic. According to the Constitution, all nationalities "enjoy the freedom of use and development of their own language and script, and freedom to retain or change their customs and practices." In the course of economic and cultural construction, the state has shown concern for the needs of all nationalities, and has taken full account of the characteristics of their development in matters of socialist transformations.

In all localities where ethnic minorities live compactly, territorial autonomy is exercised, and autonomous regions, districts, and counties have been established. Their borders have been established by taking account of historically developed relationships among the ethnic minorities living here, and also of local economic conditions. Some territory with Chinese population is included in non-Chinese autonomous areas. This promotes the most rapid elimination of the economic backwardness of small peoples.

In a number of localities, ethnic minorities are scattered in small groups over the entire territory. In this case, ethnic townships have been formed within the uyezds. If, however, ethnic minorities live dispersedly and autonomous ethnic areas cannot be set up, democratic unified organs of self-government for the various ethnic groups are formed.[18]

In consonance with these principles, four autonomous regions, 30 autonomous districts, and about 50 autonomous counties have been established in places of compact settlement by ethnic minorities, according to data as of the end of 1957 (cf. the map of non-Chinese administrative areas of China, Figure 2). In addition, a preparatory committee has been formed, and in the very near future establishment of the Tibetan Autonomous Region, including Tibet proper and the territory of Chamto, part of the abolished province of Sikang, will be officially announced. Thirty of the largest ethnic minorities have their own autonomous units.

The Chinese People's Government has consistently implemented a policy of a differentiated approach to transformations carried out among ethnic minorities at

651

different stages of social and economic development. Of the 35.5 million persons constituting ethnic minorities, socialist transformations are essentially complete among 30 million. Democratic transformations are now under way in areas with a population of approximately three million. In Tibet, the western areas of Szechwan, the northwestern and western areas of Yunnan, where these transformations are planned for a later time, a number of measures are being implemented to improve the life of the peoples and to raise their cultural level. The Communist Party of China believes that in regard to transformations among minorities, hasty actions must not be taken, and that in some cases the schedules for their implementation must be extended.

* * *

EDITORS' NOTE

a. The Manchu "banners" were organizations based on kinship (to some extent fictive) which fulfilled military-political functions.

NOTES

1. Partial censuses were conducted in China in 1908-1911 and in 1928, but they almost completely omitted areas populated by ethnic minorities.
2. This figure does not include Chinese living outside China, the number of which has been determined to be 11,743,000 persons.
3. The officially published population figure for ethnic minorities *(Jenmin Jihpao*, November 1, 1954) — 35,320,000 — does not include the ethnic minorities on the island of Taiwan, the Kao-shan, who number about 200,000 *(Kuangmin Jihpao*, March 26, 1957).
4. Approximately the same grouping is given by Lo Ch'ang-p'ei and Fu Mao-chi in the journal *Chinese Language*, March 1954 (in Chinese) and by Fu Mao-chi in the journal *Narodnyi Kitai*, 1956, No. 21. Some changes have been introduced in accordance with the grouping proposed by Ma Hsueh-liang *(China Reconstructs*, 1954, No. 3).

5. Recently, the Nung and the Sha have been included among the Chuangs.

6. It must be noted that in present-day China we can speak of the distribution of these religions only in a very limited sense. Today, adherents of these religious world views are not very numerous, especially in the cities.

7. In addition to these, Islam is adhered to by the Tadjiks and by some peoples of the Mongol group (Tung-hsiang, Pao-an).

8. All these theories are examined in Lin (1954) and G. G. Stratanovich (1954).

9. It is incorrectly stated in many studies that the main pursuit of Tibetans is pastoralism. Thus, the well-known geographer P. Gourou writes: "The inhabitants of Tibet know no means of livelihood other than nomadic pastoralism" (1956: 44). This error stems from the fact that small nomadic Tibetan tribes are scattered over a vast territory of mountainous desert, while the great mass of Tibetans inhabit river valleys.

10. These names are given by Indian authors.

11. The languages of the Miao and Yao have been very poorly studied, which accounts for the lack of agreement on their origin. Several scholars have based themselves on the investigations of Davies (1909), who was not a specialist in linguistics.

12. The nationality calling itself Miao on Hainan Island speaks the Kuangsi dialect of the Yao language.

13. Ethnic-tribal differentiation has proceeded further in the Mongolian People's Republic than in China. There the Oirats are listed among the ethnic minorities.

14. Reindeer-breeding Orochony belonging to the tribes of the Ainaks and Nakagyrs left Yakutia in the 1820s and therefore call themselves "Yakuts." On this basis, several authors have erroneously groups them with the Yakuts.

15. It is interesting to observe that paddy rice is almost never cultivated by Chinese in Tungpei. About 90% of the plantings of this crop here are maintained by Koreans.

16. Some authors relate them to the Mon-Khmers.

17. In our article on the ethnic composition of Sinkiang (Bruk 1956), it is erroneously stated that the Mountain Tadjiks speak the Shugnan dialect of the Tadjik language.

18. Such organs are formed where ethnic minorities constitute as little as 10% of the total population (and in some cases even where they number less than 10%, but where there are clearly expressed ethnic relationships).

LITERATURE CITED

Bruk, S. I.
  1956   "Etnicheskii sostav i razmeshchenie naseleniia v Sin'tszianskom uigurskom avtonomnom raione KNR" ["Ethnic composition and distribution of the population in the Sinkiang Uighur Autonomous District of the Chinese People's Republic"], *Sovetskaia etnografiia*, No. 2.

Davies, H. R.
  1909   *Yunnan: The Link Between India and [the] Yangtze.* London.

Gourou, Pierre
  1956   *Aziia* [Asia]. Moscow.

Lin Kan
  1954   "Ob etnogeneze dungan" ["On the ethnogenesis of the Dungans"], *Sovetskaia etnografiia*, No. 1.

Roce, A.
  1910   "Lisu (Yavyin) tribes of the Burma-China frontier," *Memoirs of the Asiatic Society of Bengal*, Vol. III, No. 4.

Rockhill, W.
  1901   *V strane lam. Puteshestvie po Kitaiu i Tibetu* [In the Country of the Lamas. A Journey in China and Tibet]. St. Petersburg.

Stratanovich, G. G.
  1954   "Vopros o proiskhozhdenii dungan v russkoi i sovetskoi literature (spravka)" ["The question of the origin of the Dungans in the Russian and Soviet literature (an informational report)"], *Sovetskaia etnografiia*, No. 1.

(Sovetskaia etnografiia, 1958, No. 1)

ECONOMIC AND SOCIAL RELATIONSHIPS
AMONG THE CHINGPO

G. G. Stratanovich

The Chingpo are one of the nationalities scattered throughout the region where the boundaries of India, China, and Burma meet. The total population of the Chingpo exceeds 400,000. In the People's Republic of China, the Chingpo (101,558 as of the 1953 census) are found chiefly in the districts of Lun-ch'uan, Lu-hsi, Jui-li, Lien-shan, Chan-hsi, Ying-chiang, and Liang-he of the Te-hung T'ai-chingpo Autonomous Region, and also in the district of Keng-ma of the special region of Lin-ts'ang (see Anon. 1956). Most numerous and relatively compactly settled are the Chingpo (Kachin) who live in the Burmese Union. From the calculations of E. R. Leach (1954: 309), most of them — 205,000 — live in the Kachin region (Chingpo Autonomous Region); these include Chingpo proper — 165,000; Aszi — 5,000; Maru — 20,000; and Lashi — 15,000. About 60,000 Chingpo have been settled, according to the same source, in the northern part of the Shan Autonomous Region, including Chingpo proper — 39,000; Aszi — 8,000; Maru — 12,000; and Lashi — 600. Official data for the Union of Burma are still very imprecise: the data of the 1941 census were burned in a fire, and the reports of spot censuses of 1953, 1955, and 1958 are incomplete for several reasons; reference material of 1955 gives the Chingpo (Kachin) population as 0.3 million. A total of 1,500 Chingpo (Hsingpo) are registered by the latest censuses in India (the district of Lakhimpura in the state of Assam), where formerly various investigators and travelers had cited a figure closer to 100,000.

By linguistic origin, the Chingpo, in the opinion of most Chinese linguists (Fu Mao-chi, etc.), are part of a special group of the Tibeto-Burman branch of the Sino-Tibetan linguistic family.

Anthropologically, the Chingpo are southern Mongoloids. However, the percentage of wavy-haired, high- and narrow-faced, and also narrow-nosed individuals, with raised nasal bridge, which is higher than usual for peoples of the South Asiatic race, may show the significant presence among the Chingpo of the so-called "warrior type," which has been distinguished among the Eastern Tibetans.

The Chingpo distinguish four main subdivisions in their social composition: (1) Chingpo proper, settled mainly in the Union of Burma; (2) Tsai-wa, the main bulk of whom live in the Chinese People's Republic; (3) Lang-so, or Lang-vo; and (4) Cha-shan (La-ch'i).

In the works of Chinese, Burmese, Indian, and Western European travelers and investigators, we encountered more than 100 names used as ethnyms of the Chingpo. This is due to the fact that neighboring peoples name each of the subdivisions of the Chingpo differently, usually without considering their names for themselves. The relationship of the main names is shown in Table 1.[1]

In addition, in ancient Chinese literature we sometimes also find names given the Chingpo in feudal China: *"yeh-jen"* (literally, "savage") and *"shan-t'ou"* (that is, inhabitants of mountain peaks). In the old Burmese and European literature the following names are found: *"khka-khku"* (living upriver, in contradistinction to *"khka-nam"* — living downriver), and *"tkheinbo"* — phonetically an imprecise transcription of the word "Chingpo." Finally, the use of tribal names as ethnyms for Chingpo has introduced confusion. There were five main tribes: Marip (with 15 clan subdivisions); Lakhtaun, or Lakhtoo (18 clans); Lepai, or Lakhpai (17 clans, each of which is in turn divided into two); Nkhkum (8 clans); Maran, or Maram (4 clans). It is hardly desirable to list the clan names here.[2]

Within the territory of the Chinese People's Republic

TABLE 1

Name

Subdivision	Self-designation	In dialects				In languages			
		Chingpo	Tsai-wa	Lang-so	Cha-shan	Chinese	Thai	Burmese	Others
Chingpo proper	Chingpo (Singpo, in Assam)	Chingpo	Shitung	Pova, Puman, Pok'e	Po (from the Thai Khpok)	Tashan Chingpo	Kan, Khpoo (Khpon, Khpok)	Kachin (more correctly, Kkhak'-yen)	Apu, Laokang Kaiku
Tsai-wa	Tsai-wa	Ach'i, Aszi, Szi	Tsai-wa	----	----	Hsiao-shan Chingpo	Acha	----	----
Cha-shan	Lach'i	Lahsi (Lashi)	----	----	Lach'i (Lashi)	Chashan	----	Laszi (Lashi)	----
Lang-so	Lang-wo	Mala, Maru, Malu	Lalung	Lang-wo	Lan, Man'wa	Lanso Lansung	Acha	Maru	----

the Tsai-wa Chingpo predominate; and in the Union of Burma, the Chingpo proper. The dialects of the Chingpo proper and the Tsai-wa Chingpo differ substantially; the dialects of the Cha-shan and Lanso are close to that of the Tsai-wa. From the data of Chinese investigators, differences can be traced most clearly in the vocabulary (up to 80% of the words differ), but there are also purely phonetical and grammatical differences. In the Union of Burma, the linguistic differences between the Chingpo proper and the Tsai-wa (Aszi, or Szi) and also the Lanso (Maru) have been erased in the "triangle" (the region formed by the confluence of the Nmaika and Malika rivers). In the Chinese People's Republic, Chingpo live in close proximity with peoples belonging to the same linguistic branch — to the I-tsu group: the Lisu, Achan, and others — and also close to peoples in the Thai group: the Thai Na — the Thai population of the Thai-Chingpo autonomous region (Burmese: Shan Tarok); and Thau Hyn (that is, the Shan of the northeast of the Union of Burma); the Nung (one of the subdivisions of the Chuang); the Nu and the Tulung. Here the Chingpo also live close to the Chinese. In the Union of Burma, the Chingpo are in contact with the Achan, the Lisu, the Shan, and the Burmese.

The linguistic classifications of the Chingpo in a special group of the Tibeto-Burman branch of the Sino-Tibetan linguistic family allows us to suggest that like all peoples who are bearers of languages of this branch, they can be regarded as the aboriginal stratum in their present places of settlement only in a very relative sense. However, the Thais and the Burmese, with whom the Chingpo were forced to wage a struggle during their advance southward, also were not the first settlers of these areas. The neolithic relics about which E. R. Leach (1954: 230) wrote probably belong neither to the Chingpo, nor to the Thai, nor to the Burmese. The Chingpo are rightly considered the most recent stratum of newcomers, who moved here from the mountainous plateau regions of northwestern China. The comparative recency of the period in which this ethnic stratum shifted southward permits us to reconstruct this route with confidence. The Chingpo until recently had no written language; however, in this case, reconstruction is made easier not only by the very detailed nature of their traditions, but also by the ceremonial associated with this kind of oral history (primarily with the ceremony of "seeing off the soul") and with the patrilineal "sequence of names." This ceremony has been described by Li Chih-ch'un (1955: 68). When one of the men dies, a ceremony is performed of "seeing off the soul" to the places where the remote ancestors of all the Chingpo were born and founded the clan. As if mentally journeying together with the spirit, the *"chai-wa"* — the keeper of traditions — or one of the old men recounts to the assembly how the soul passes through the stages of this journey (a chain of mountains, many broad rivers, high peaks, ravines, and bridges) until finally the soul reaches the high plateau (Chinese: *"ping-ting-shan";* Chingpo: *"machoi tingra").* Considering the order of details of this journey as proof of the relative veracity of the entire report, Li Chih-ch'un attempts to represent the movement of the Chingpo from the Sikan-Tibetan range to the south through the region of the headwaters of the Huang-ho, the Yangtze, the Saluen, and the Nuchiang to the headwaters of the Nmaika and Malika rivers, and further westward as far as the mountain ranges of the Hukong River valley and the Assam Mountains. Encountering resistance from the Akhom (Thai of Assam), the Chingpo retreated to the southeast toward the Irrawaddy along the valleys of its tributaries. However, at that time the valley of the Irrawaddy River was already settled by Burmese and Shan. Thus, the Chingpo, partially displacing and partially skirting the latter, were compelled to move from the city of Bhamo eastward, and again enter the boundaries of Yunnan Province in the district of Lien-shan and Lu-hsi, and farther to the south, toward Lants'an, up to the limits of the Shan principality of K'entung. (A number of Chinese authors, in contrast to Li Chih-ch'un, hold that the Chingpo appeared in the southern part of their present-day ethnic territory directly from the Chashan Mountains, without entering Burma.)[3] The time of these movements has been approximately established by means of the "sequence of names" (which is as follows: if the name of the grandfather was Yaun-sau, then the name of the father will be Sau-chang, the name of the son Chang-lang, the name of the grandson Lang-pau, etc.). Li Chih-ch'un (1955; see map) has established that the Chingpo have lived in the region of the headwaters of the Nmaika and Malika rivers for almost fifty generations now[4] — that is, about a millennium; in the regions of Chiang-sinpo and the valley of the Khukong (Sinpinyang) — about forty generations, or roughly 800 years; in the area of the cities of Myitkyna and Bhamo — only 8-10 generations, or 160-200 years; in the vicinity of the settlements of Luhsi and Genma — 4-6 generations, or 80-120 years. Thus, it can be held that the Chingpo settled the mountainous zone of northwestern Yunnan Province at the beginning of the second millennium of our era. In northern Burma their advance occurred in the 17th-18th centuries, with a new advance into Yunnan at the close of the 18th century and the beginning of the 19th.

In their movement toward the south, the Chingpo waged battles against the Shan. Ethnic islands of the Shan, formerly subject to the Chingpo, remain even today in the Khukong River valley and in other regions of the mountainous northern area of the Union of Burma (they were encountered by the present author in February 1957). In plains areas or in the foothills of the northeastern part of the Union of Burma, the Chingpo themselves were forced to occupy the middle or upper zone of hills, placing themselves in a subordinate status to the Shan feudal lords but, in so doing, displacing the Palaun and the Wa. The only group to move southward later than the Chingpo (according to the data of Li Chih-ch'un 1955: 66) were the Lisu, who were not about to displace their predecessors, and were forced to occupy the highest zone — the mountain peaks. It must be noted that the Burmese-Chinese border has not been an obstacle to the advance of the Chingpo.

* * *

Social relationships among the Chingpo in Burma

prior to the declaration of independence, and in China before Liberation (that is, before 1948-1949), were marked by considerable complexity. Leach, in writing on social relationships among the Kachin (Chingpo of Burma), considers these relationships so distinctive that they do not fall under any of the criteria adopted in ethnology, and therefore represent an unsolved riddle (Leach 1954: 6, 8).

It must be kept in mind that the social development of the Chingpo of different regions was not the same. Both the administrative methods and the nature of the administrative system applied to the Chingpo varied. In Burma the British introduced indirect administration for the Kachin; in China, direct administration prevailed. In the first case the apex of the administrative system was represented by rulers of feudal type — *"duva,"* called princes in the literature (literally, representatives of the *"du"* aristocracy) — subordinate to the British resident. In the latter case the Chingpo were governed by *"t'u-hsi"* and *"shankuan"* ("administrator" and "mountain head," respectively) — representatives of the Chinese administration, often not even ethnically Chingpo, but Chinese (Han) or Thai.

The historical conditions of the formation of the Chingpo as a nationality were determined ultimately by contact with neighboring peoples, more highly developed in a social sense. Ties with feudal China were limited to trade, owing to the underdeveloped means of communication; contacts with the feudal societies of the Burmese, Shan, and Assamese were more intimate in terms of social ties, while economic relations amounted only to the export of raw materials from the areas inhabited by the Chingpo. It is likely that this accounts for the presense of the so-called democratic (in the Chingpo language — *"gumlao"*) and "aristocratic" *("gumsa")* tribes. In describing a Chingpo society of the *gumsa* type, Leach takes it to be intermediate between the feudal (comparatively developed — G. S.) societies of the Shan and Khontai (Thailand Thai, Siamese) and the "democratic" societies of the Chinese Chingpo, and also the Lisu and other peoples. Hence, evidently, the conclusion as to the low

661

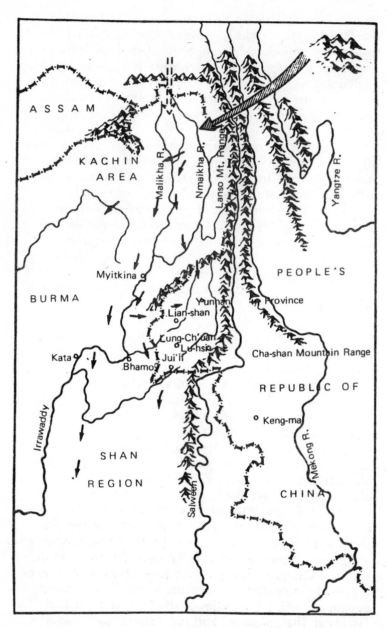

FIGURE 1. Route of the Chingpo to the locales of their present-day settlement (according to Li Chih-ch'un).

degree of feudalization of Chingpo society (Leach 1954: 9). Feudal relationships were comparatively well-developed among the Chingpo of the Burmese lowland (Bhamo, etc.) and more poorly in the mountainous regions. Gumlao-type societies predominated in the high-altitude zone of the Khukong River valley and the headwaters of the Nmaika and Malika rivers.

The colonial seizure of Burma by Great Britain (this process begain from 1825 and was officially held to be completed by 1876, but it actually lasted almost until this present century) led to contradictory results. On the one hand, the British were in need of dependable support to keep the colony under their control. In the outlying border regions "scheduled" for indirect administration, the tribal and feudal aristocracy was chosen by the colonizers as the source of this support from among the local population. In order to strengthen the positions of this stratum of Chingpo society in every way, the colonizers, formally confirming the "prince" as the new leader, established the principle of direct inheritance of the authority of the "deceased prince" by the "prince of the blood" (here the eldest son; whereas among the Chingpo and most of their neighbors, ultimogeniture prevails). On the other hand, the colonizers were interested in weakening the solidarity of the Chingpo, and also in dispersing the population of north Burma over its entire area. Large Chingpo villages were broken up; dozens of small mountain settlements of free commune members were formed. The authority of the Kachin feudal lord — the *"duva"* — extended over several such settlements *("kakhtaun")*, from two or three to several dozen.

The administration of old China also rested on tribal aristocracy and was interested in breaking up the Chingpo groups, but, as in other areas of China, fiscal policy was based on a system of mutual responsibility of commune members. The smallest tax-paying unit was a group of households, a settlement *("ka")*.

In reinforcing the positions of the aristocracy within Chingpo society, the British colonial authorities, independently of their aims, at the same time undermined the economic foundations of a considerable number of *duva* by forbidding them to receive tribute from the settled

FIGURE 2: Chief of one of the Lashi groups in festive dress.

farming population of the valleys (generally these were Thai, but the population also included Burmese and Chinese living in valleys controlled by warlike Chingpo) and by abolishing slavery.

Chingpo society as a whole did not know the slaveholding formation, although rudiments of slaveholding did exist among them. Some authors cite evidence that slaves — *"mayyam"* — often amounted to more than half of the total number of inhabitants in certain villages (Leach 1954: 160, 301; Barnard 1930: 180, 185). However, data personally collected by the present author (1957), and information in the literature, throw doubt on these reports. There were two types of slaves among the Chingpo: those who were originally captives of war *("tinun-mayyam")* and debt-slaves *(ngon-mayyam").* Most of those captured during raids against neighboring groups (for example, the Assamese, the Burmese officials) became slaves of the *duva*. Men were used in his operations; women were often given as part of the dowry of a *duva's* daughter or as payment for her. The status of slaves differed from that of free commune members in that the former could be sold and resold, and did not own property. In Chingpo customary law, it is firmly established that the children of a slave couple, and of a slave and a free woman, are slaves, but the children of a freeman and a slave woman are free (Leach 1954: 160-161), provided their father pays the owner of the slave woman a bride-price. (It must be noted that the children of a free couple became their father's "legitimate" children only after he made the usual bride-payment — *"num shalai"* — or a payment for each illegitimate child in turn *["sumrai khaka"].)* In striving to break free of the restrictions imposed by tribal ties, a strong chief was forced to rely on the slaves (Leach 1954: 185); "the slave is closer to his lord than is the kinsman," the Chingpo observe. Information on the large number of debt slaves among all subdivisions of Chingpo is possibly explained by the broad concept of debt *("khka")* among the Chingpo: it embraced all forms of debt dependency and of obligations. Thus, a youth working in his father-in-law's household for two to three years to pay off the bride-price regarded himself as a debtor. All young men held themselves to be potential debtors — *mayyu*, the clan of the son-in-law — in relation to the *damà*, the clan of the father-in-law; but since marriage, according to tradition, encompassed a circle of three clans, "debt" relationships in this case cancelled each other out. Anyone receiving a gift considered himself a debtor (since he must, according to custom, reciprocate); this included everyone who received something of real or symbolic value during exchanges in festival periods (a kind of potlatch). Loans of grain (against the harvest or with deferred payment in installments) or livestock (especially water-buffalo, the principal sacrificial animal) led to direct debt obligations, and to debt slavery if the debtor was unable to pay back what he owed, including (in Burma) a percentage of interest. The status of the debt slave sometimes depended on his prospects of repaying the debt. The debt slave could never be sold. He could have his own home and other property. The "master" was empowered to appropriate the payment obtained for the daughter of a debt slave, but could not claim his wife or daughter.

Slavery was abolished by the British administration in Burma as early as the 1880s *("mayyan"* — intertribal wars, the source of replenishment of *duva* households with captured slaves — were also restricted). Later, ransoming of slaves was practiced: thus, according to League of Nations data, in 1925-1928 almost 9,000 slaves were ransomed in the valleys of the Khukong, Nmaika, and Malika rivers (Barnard 1930: 185). In fact, however, debt slavery and the ownership of inherited slaves persisted until the end of the 1940s. In China, the campaign against slavery among the Chingpo began right after liberation.

Thus, three main strata can be distinguished in Chingpo-Kachin society: *"du"* (aristocracy), *mayyam* (slaves), and *darat* (free commune members). In each of these strata, sublayers can be distinguished.

In the milieu of the aristocracy, the sublayers were determined by descent, size of territory controlled, and "profession" (more precisely, role in society). The most noble, and consequently the most powerful under the

Chingpo customary law, was the *tuva* — the head of the cadet line of the main clan of the Chingpo. We must state here that the tribal structure has been preserved among all Chingpo until the present, chiefly in the sphere of regulation of marital relationships, as well as in the realm of religious practices. Some idea of the highly developed tribal pedigree, and the interrelationships of its branches, can be obtained from the following diagrams compiled by Li Chih-ch'un and Leach.

As Diagram I shows, the first ancestor of all Chingpo, Vach'eyva (his immediate brothers and cousins were heads of the subdivisions of Lanso, Chashan, Lashi, or Laszi), had, according to tradition, five sons, who became the ancestors of five tribes — the *"am'yu"* (in Leach's opinion, seven or eight main tribes had settled in Burma [1954: 128 n]). The head of the youngest of these tribes became the first ancestor of the Lakhpai line, and his four sons founded four brother clans (the youngest of these was the head of the largest clan, the Shatang). Generations that had no offshoots (i.e., remained undivided) did not produce special lines, and remained in a single household *(khtingoo)*, the head of which was the *"uma"* — the youngest son of the household founder (or the *uma* of the oldest generation of those living in the house).

Employing the right of the chief to offer sacrifices to Madai-natu, the god of heaven, or to Shadip-natu, the god of the earth, the *umdau* (the head of the Khpanroo line) prepared a festival *(manau)*; formally, this required the sanction of the *umadu* of the senior line (the Layaun, the Kadau, or, directly, the Lakhtoo). However, neither in China nor in Burma did the head of the senior line (in Diagram II — tribe of the Lakhtoo), in contrast to the senior Shan feudal lord *("zao," "zaopilo"* — senior *"zao")*, enjoy economic privileges relative to other *duva*. His high descent gave him noble status; his words and deeds were evaluated, with account taken of the prestige due his noble status. It was held that the authority of the aristocracy was not dependent on wealth, but the actual economic position of the *duva* determined to a large extent his social standing. Actually, his authority and power depended on the territory he controlled, and on the number of villages *(kakhtaun)* or groups of related villages *(mare)* subordinate to him (at the close of the 1940s a group of isolated farmsteads was called a *mare)*. The Shankuan and other aristocratic sublayers of the Chingpo of China usually controlled one or two to three settlements. In the valley villages of Burma, prior to the declaration of independence, the number of households *(khtingoo)* often exceeded 100. However, in the mountainous parts of China and Burma, villages consisted of 20-30 *khtingoo*, often belonging to two or three *am'yu*. The *duva* held the offices of judge, military leader, organizer of economic enterprises, and head of the functioning executive, and was also one of the religious functionaries.

Court procedure among the Chingpo consisted of a public hearing of a case by a council of elders — the *"salang khpoon."* The council of elders comprised *salangy* — heads of the Chingpo subdivisions living in a given region; as the head of the oldest line, the *duva* was only the chief of these. Also participating in the council were the elders of the village — *"m'it su"* (wise people). The *"kasa"* (Leach 1954: 184) — orators — spoke in behalf of the plaintiff and the defendant. Punishment usually amounted to a fine in favor of the victim, and the judges (the fine was usually set in terms of various edible provisions and animals — hogs, buffalo, and poultry; all this went to entertain the participants in the court). Thus, the authority of the court was consolidated by the "wisdom of decisions."

The *duva* emerged as military leader during vendettas *(banglat khka)* or raids on neighbors — that is, open military actions *(khp'en gazat)*. However, these duties were fulfilled by the *duva* only in local wars. Relatives of the *duva* (but not he himself) served on his recommendation in the British colonial army, where there were individual Chingpo military units, and also in the police during the colonial period, where Chingpo were quite numerous.

The functions of the *duva* included, above all, taking tribute from the settled valley population and from the trade caravans passing along the roads over territory controlled by a given *duva*. The word of the *duva* had great

DIAGRAM I (Li Chih-ch'un 1955: 72)

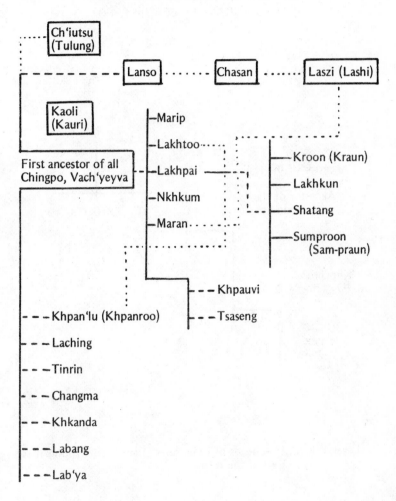

Legend: ☐ main subdivisions; ─ ─ ─ verifiable ties; ···· reconstructed
ties

DIAGRAM II (Leach 1954: 131)

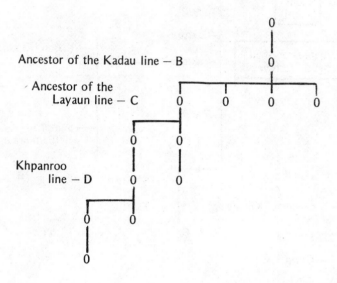

A first ancestor of
the Lakhtoo clan
(tribe).

Ancestor of the Kadau line — B

Ancestor of the
Layaun line — C

Khpanroo
line — D

Legend: B, C, D — heads of cadet lines *("uma˙tu"* — youngest sons
of the ruler).

weight in resolving land questions. Under customary law, the *duva* and the *salangi* were the *"madu"* — landowners. Rank-and-file commune members only used its fruits (literally *"sha,"* ate, or *"lu,"* drank the earth [Leach 1954: 155]). Disputes over land, transfer of a village, etc., were considered and resolved by the *duva* in Burma and by the eldest members of the community in China.

In contrast to the usual idea that Chingpo leaders combined secular and religious functions, our inquiry confirmed Leach's view that their significance in the religious life of the community was restricted to holding festivals *(manao)* or to granting others the right to hold these festivals in return for an appropriate consideration. During the period of the celebration of the *manao* in honor of Madai-nata or Shadip-nata by the *duva* himself (and only he had this right), the priest *(tumsa)* officiated. In the Burmese Chingpo society, various aspects of religious life were served by a highly specialized staff of clergy. They included the following: the *"chzhayva"* — reader, teller of legends, traditions, and exhortations; the *"tumsa"* — priest in charge of the rituals (ceremonial of the festivals); the *"khkinchuang"* — diviner-soothsayer; the *"m'ikhtoi"* — summoner of spirits (the middleman between the spirits of the departed and their living progeny; he was also a healer) (Huang Shao-huai and Yeh Yung-hua 1958: I, 88); etc. As a rule, attainment of these posts was determined by experience or inherent abilities, but the posts were not hereditary (except for the *"m'ikhtoi,"* who among the Chingpo of China, were usually women who transmitted their "gift" in a family). This ramified priestly aristocracy, together with the hereditary tribal aristocracy, constituted the main exploiting stratum of Chingpo society. In the mountain zone of Chinese Chingpo settlement, the religious functions were commonly combined with the secular; the hierarchy of religious leaders was less specialized, but influence was more profound and took in all areas of Chingpo life.

The general masses, the main layer of Chingpo society — *"darat daroi,"* that is, free commune members — clearly regarded themselves until very recently as members of a clan *(am'yu)* or of some line of descendants of the main

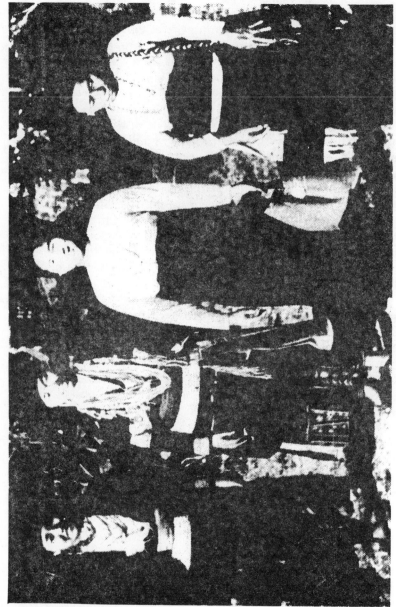

FIGURE 3. Lashi and Kachin women.

tribes. Everyone knew that people of one specific tribal subdivision stood in the relation of *"damà"* to him — that is, they gave their women to his kinsmen as wives; likewise, another tribal subdivision was bound to his kinsmen by the relationship of *mayyu* — that is, they took wives from his subdivision (compare the relationships of *"pela"* in the marital customs of southeastern Indonesia, or of *"dokha"* among peoples of the Amur). Each person had a more or less definite idea of his place in the "khtingoo" — family, household. Thus, a traditional *"kakhpukanau"* was established — a relationship between brothers in a single clan, or tribe *(am'yu)*, in a single subdivision *("lakun")*, and in a single household *("dap")*. However, other ties that are not tribal in character also exist among the Chingpo. Some of them were earlier. These were the age-grades: *"ma ni"*, (children), with attainment of sexual maturity, became *"shabran ni"* (youths) and *"makhkoon ni"* (young women); marrying at 20 or 18, respectively, they became *"madu ni"* — a married couple — and with their age-mates *"la"* (men) and *"num"* (women) emerge as the group of *"ka ni"* or workers (Leach 1954: 133). Other ties are relatively new: these include the neighborhood commune, the union of *"pu ni"* — inhabitants of the same village — who regard themselves as a unit, opposed to other *pu ni*. They have common local *naty* (spirits) of the earth, to whom they offer sacrifices on a common *"numshan."* This was the site of sacrifices and festivals, including a sacred grove, with the obligatory banyan tree and memorials of past festivals: bamboo altars *("khkunri")*, poles *("wutang")* in memory of the sacrificial immolation of domestic fowl, cross-pieces with engraved designs *("lapan")* in memory of the immolation of buffaloes, and also a cleared area for dancing during festivals.

The Chinese investigators Li Chih-Ch'un, I Chün, Huang Shao-huai, Yeh, Yung-hua, and others (I Chün 1958: 121) emphasize that, among the Chingpo, crafts had not yet separated out into a special branch of economic activity — that is, there was no special stratum of artisans in Chingpo society, just as there was no special stratum of traders from within the group. Theoretically, wealth per se

FIGURE 4. *Numshan* — site of prayers among the Chingpo; in the foreground a *khkunri*, an altar with bamboo tubes — "receptacles for spirits."

FIGURE 5. *Wutang* — poles with baskets at a Chingpo *numshan*.

did not bring honor in Chingpo society. The *"khpachzhi"* — one of the rank-and-file commune members who won authority by his wisdom or by holding festivals — was regarded as an honored person. But during these festivals, many sacrificial animals were consumed in such numbers that Chingpo were often compelled to purchase them from neighboring peoples (Huang Shao-huai and Yeh Yung-hua 1958: 88). Virtually all cattle were consumed in the sacrifices. The expression *"sut lu ay va"* — "rich person" — was used to designate the one who had much *"khpaga,"* property. Various articles associated with religious observances figured large in this category of property: bronze ritual drums; unusually high-quality, artistically executed *"nkhtu"* (swords), and *"nkhp'e"* (richly ornamented pouches); etc. The greatest value, however, was attached to parcels of irrigated rice land: *"khkau na."* Even accumulations in monetary form were sometimes encountered. Rich persons could engage in usury; however, grain (against the harvest) or cattle (the yield serving as the interest in this case) were loaned at interest; it was still considered reprehensible to receive interest in monetary form.

* * *

The territory occupied by the Chingpo was held to be divided between their subdivisions, and since the second half of the 19th century also among the *darat* communes. In Burma, as stated above, the *duva* and the *salang* were regarded as the owners of the land; in China, the land was deemed, as early as the Ming period, to be the property of the central Chinese regime, in whose name its representatives, the *t'u-hsi* and *shan-kuans,* ruled it (the Shankuanate of Ch'a-shan was established in the "second year of the rule of Yung-le," 1404; the Shankuanate of Lim "in the sixth year of Yung-le," 1408). Also established during the Ming dynasty were eight frontier posts, controlling mountain passes in the zone of the Burmese-Chinese border; most of the passes were in the ethnic territory of the Chingpo. Ordinary commune members were regarded as "using" the food products coming from the land. An ancient concept of tribal festivals of "eating the forest" or "drinking the earth" — that is, very early harvest festivals belonging partly to the hunting-and-gathering stage — was retained among the Chingpo, as already mentioned, in the terms describing land tenure: "to eat of the earth" *(sha ga)* or "drink of the earth" *(lyu ga)*. The right of land tenure within the territory of a given village was recognized for all its inhabitants, even though two or three tribal groups were represented in the village population. The neighborhood commune regarded the land alloted to it as its *"bu ga"* (a term often translated as "land of the fathers"). Each family in the village could clear a new section if its former land was exhausted. Although the communal territory was fairly extensive, rich mountain plowland — that is, untouched for more than 15 years and suitable for tilling — was not so plentiful. The farming level of the Chingpo was very low; it was considered easier to clear a new field than to fertilize old, exhausted land and work it better. In spite of this, the transfer of a village as a result of the exhaustion of its surrounding land was very rare; this is accounted for by a clear awareness of the danger of "taking alien land," which would entail its passage under the control of another *duva, salang,* or *shankuan,* and, in addition, an expense beyond the capacity of the commune, for the ceremony of "establishing relations" with him.

The clearing of a new plot or the laying out of terraced fields, as well as basic farming procedures — planting and sowing, harvesting (and also the building of a new house) — were operations often executed through "work-bees" (by kinsmen or members of a neighboring commune) or, in other words, collectively, especially among the Chinese Chingpo.

In economic-cultural type, the Chingpo until recently were hoe farmers. Only in some places, mainly in the low-land areas of Burma, was a small plow used. The principle farming implements were the hoe and the sword.[5] Until recently, the areas of land worked by hoes after burning-over, by the slash-and-burn method, represented more than 70% of all land worked. By amount of rainfall and character of the natural plant cover, the arable lands of the

Chingpo are divided into two types. The first type includes lands on densely forested slopes facing the wet monsoons, which is more fertile, but requires considerable outlay of labor to clear the fields. Fields of this type remain fertile for two to four years, and up to ten years with annual burning of trunks and stumps. Restoration of soil fertility here requires 12-15 years. The second type includes land on slopes facing northwest, whose exposure to monsoons is blocked by mountains. The plant cover here is grass and scrub. Fallowing is necessary here after one or two years, and return to fallow land is possible only in 15-16 years. That is all the more reason why artificially irrigated land is valued. Food crops grown by the Chingpo include paddy rice (usually the pink glutinous varieties), dry rice, millet, sorghum *(kaoliang)*, corn, buckwheat, various legumes, potatoes, and sweet potatoes; technical crops include short-staple cotton, flax, and the opium poppy. In recent years, tea plantations have been expanded. Bananas, tangerines, durian fruits, squash, etc., are raised by the Chingpo on garden and orchard plots.

Animal husbandry, judging from traditions, was very advanced in the past among the Chingpo; in recent years it has been confined to the raising of hogs, draft animals, and domestic fowl (chiefly chickens). The draft animal is usually the water buffalo; less often, oxen and cows are used. But generally large horned cattle (especially water buffaloes) are sacrificial animals. Therefore, the Chingpo had very few draft animals.

The Chingpo also engaged in fishing in mountain rivers and in hunting, and in part in food-gathering. Hunting — a male pursuit — was more collective and ceremonial than directed toward subsistence.

Recently, many Chingpo have been engaged in lumbering (incidentally, one of my informants — the Burmese Lashi Mating Hsao-ying, a young ethnographer — reported that his clan was from ancient times linked economically with the Chinese [Han], since its chief occupation was felling trees and shipping to China logs used to make coffins). Lumbering was the main form of migrant labor for Chingpo.

Both in the principal and the auxiliary pursuits of the

FIGURE 6. Fence across a river, with a gate for trapping fish in the high-water season.

Chingpo, a sexual division of labor was clearly expressed. The main burden lay on the woman; besides working in the home and tending the children, the obligations of women include spinning and weaving, sewing clothes and embroidery, gathering reeds and plaiting mats from them, making utensils from bamboo, tending livestock, keeping up the orchard and garden plot, and doing most of the field work. The man bore the obligation of protecting the village and the women working in the field, and participated in clearing fields (among the Chingpo, the principal implement used in felling trees, and in several other activities, was the sword), in plowing (if draft animals were used), and in harvesting (chiefly in carrying the harvest to the granary), etc. Everything related to the use of wood (felling trees, laying in and splitting bamboo and liana, collecting lacquer, and painting strips of pressed bamboo and liana red and black), and also the jeweler's art, were the men's province. Children (boys and girls) began participating quite early in the adult work appropriate to their sex.

Property relationships among the Chingpo were fairly complex. Thus, among the Chingpo in pre-Liberation China, three types of property prevailed (I Chün 1958: 120): (1) ownership of domestic livestock, farm implements and utensils, and the dwelling — this property can be freely disposed of, transferred to progeny, or given as a gift; (2) ownership of irrigated fields, orchard and garden plots, bamboo groves (with the owner's mark), and tea plantations — this ownership could also be transferred to heirs, and used as security for loans, but if the owner abandoned the village, or died without leaving heirs, the ownership of this property passed to the Shan-kuan (in some regions, this property could be sold, but the fellow commune members — the ka ni — of the owner had the right of first refusal); (3) property in fallow land, which had been worked and abandoned, pastures, mountain forest, formerly in communal ownership (as already noted above, in Burma these lands were under the duva's jurisdiction).

Recently, a certain intensification of the development of private property has been observed, primarily by expansion of the number of land parcels planted to paddy rice. A still very weak stratum of landowners from among the

FIGURE 7. Houses of Chingpo near the city of Mogaung.

rank-and-file peasantry is becoming distinguishable;
Chinese investigators call their farms of "kulak type."
Some shifts are under way among the aristocracy. In
Burma the clan-tribal aristocracy is fortifying its positions
through marital ties with the Shan aristocracy and the
Burmese bureaucracy. In China, where kin ties between
the Chingpo and representatives of the administration were
infrequent, reinforcement of the positions of the aristocracy (Shan-kuans, religious practitioners, and village
elders) has proceeded through acquisition of the best land
parcels by them. The size of an eminent Shan-kuan's
parcel was frequently more than four times that of the
maximum plot of families of rank-and-file commune members. In this way farms of the "estate type" (again using
the terminology of Chinese investigators) are formed.
Small Shan-kuans participated personally in farm work.

We must remember at the same time that the level of
economic development as a whole is very low among the
Chingpo. Suffice it to say that among the Chingpo of
China, when the harvest was apportioned, there was a bit
more than four months' supply of farm produce for each
person (I Chün 1958: 120). In addition, inhabitants of
remote mountain settlements of the Chingpo of Burma
suffered greatly from lack of salt. There was no local salt
industry. Salt was brought from afar. Even in 1957 a salt
caravan we met had been traveling toward settlements of
the P'u-t'ao region for five or six weeks.

* * *

The end of the 1940s brought the peoples of Burma
and China independence. The establishment of the Union
of Burma was proclaimed on January 4, 1948. Under the
constitution already drawn up in 1947, the Kachin
(Burmese Chingpo) received an autonomous national territory (the Kachin Autonomous Province) embracing the
territory of Myitkina and Bhamo — that is, the principal
areas of Chingpo settlement. On January 10, 1952, this
decision was made operative. Government measures to
improve the economic position of the country's provinces
and to raise the cultural level of the population envisaged

the laying of roads and improvement of existing highways, the development of agriculture and industry, and the betterment of the status of public education and public health. Road construction, which was stepped up in 1955-1957 in one of the territories in Myitkina District, was continued along the previously adopted course of building strategic highways leading to the northern border region. However, these highways were also vital for the development of the economy of the mountain people (thus, the traveling time of trade caravans was cut to one-half or one-third). It is remarkable that small Chingpo villages — almost of farmstead type — were once more unified, after the declaration of independence, into large settlements with access to highways and rivers. Agricultural and soil stations established in the Kachin Autonomous Province assist Chingpo peasants in becoming acquainted with advanced methods of farming. In 1957, construction of a large, sophisticated sugar plant (near the city of Mogaung) intended for seasonal processing of local raw material, which naturally required development of the most water-demanding crop — sugar cane — was completed in the province. (Unfortunately, very little attention has been paid to irrigation work, although the key to the development of the economy of the local population lies in irrigation.) Government forest operations in the province have also been developed.

Improvement of medical service to the provincial population has been directed primarily at combatting venereal diseases — the onerous heritage of the Japanese occupation, and also of the concentration of American military units along the southern borders of China during the Second World War.

Public education has also made marked gains in the province. Not only in the cities the number of which in the province is small, but also in large villages, primary schools are now operating. Incomplete and complete secondary schools [high schools], previously nonexistent among the Chingpo, have been built. A larger number of Chingpo have begun to receive higher education in the universities of Rangoon and Mandalay. Young ethnographers, doctors, and technicians from "Mass Education" teams play a large role in instructing adults in literacy and trades.

The end of the 1940s was marked by the proclamation of the People's Republic of China. The life of the Chingpo in China was radically altered. Making allowance for the specific features of Chingpo social relationships, the Communist Party and the People's Government of the People's Republic of China included the region of Chingpo settlement among those where agrarian reform will not be executed in the usual manner. The first goal of the people's regime in areas of the most compact settlement of Chingpo was to raise the level of production of food crops. During the first years after Liberation, the government annually issued more than 300,000 yuan in loans to the Chingpo of Teh-hung Region alone. However, this still left up to 60% of Chingpo peasants for whom foodstuffs were sufficient only for six months a year. At the beginning of 1952, the goal of raising Chingpo farm productivity was set. Chingpo peasants are being organized for construction of water-supply systems, the building of dams, and the expansion of plowland. The graphic example of Chinese agricultural cooperatives showed the Chingpo peasants the advantages of producer cooperatives and of the mechanization of farming processes. In 1954 there were four farming cooperatives in Teh-hung Region, in three of which labor productivity had already been increased 2.5 times in the first year of its existence. Labor productivity in the "Mans" producing cooperative of Wen-chiang District of the Teh-hung T'ai-Chingpo Autonomous Region rose by another 80% in 1955. It is interesting to compare the increase in income of members of this cooperative, expressed in money: in 1954, 1955, and 1956 each able-bodied person received 200, 350, and more than 500 yuan, respectively. The number of Chingpo members of producer cooperatives in 1956 exceeded 12,000; in 1957 more than 70 new cooperatives were set up; more than 4,000 Chingpo peasant families were part of cooperatives based on virgin lands. Since the start of the Great Leap Forward, the Chingpo peasantry have won new successes. In 1958 the harvest was inceased twofold as compared to 1957 in Lu-hsi District of Teh-hung

684

FIGURE 8. Chingpo school in a suburb of Mogaung.

FIGURE 9. Group of Chingpo and Lashi of Putao (Union of Burma) — participants in a protest meeting against the so-called "anti-Chinese movement" inspired by imperialist agents in early 1957.

Autonomous Region, where up to 500 Chingpo farms are located. Each able-bodied person received 1,200 chin of grain (higher than the national average). At the close of 1958 the "San T'ai Shan" (Three Great Mountains) people's commune was established here. Soon thereafter Chingpo peasants began to set up people's communes in their other settlement areas. As is known, people's communes are combined farms, including small and medium-size industrial enterprises. Thus, the Chingpo, on a par with other peoples of the region, participate in the work of these enterprises: they make steel, prepare construction materials for houses and farm buildings and build electric power stations. The cultural level of the Chingpo rose as never before. Many of their settlements were electrified and supplied with radios. The newspaper "Unity" is being published in Chingpo and Chinese in the Teh-hung Autonomous Region. Expansion of the school network, and the adoption, in March 1957, of a new, scientifically prepared script for the Tsaiwa, Chashan, and Lanso, and also improvements in the old script kept for use by the Chingpo proper, have promoted a rapid rise in the literacy not only of children, but also of the adult population. Enormous successes have also been won in public health.

The life of the Chingpo in the People's Republic of China is a glowing example of Marxist-Leninist nationality policy. Owing to the wise leadership of the Communist Party and the people's government of China, and due to the enormous assistance of its elder brother, the Chinese people, the Chingpo nationality, previously a suppressed ethnic minority, and now a full-fledged member of the multinational family of peoples of China, is progressing toward socialism directly from the early feudal stage, having bypassed the capitalist order.

Peoples historically connected with the Chingpo see in the example of Chingpo life the path to a brilliant future, and no attempts by imperialists and their agents will succeed in upsetting the fraternal relationships of these peoples, just as agents of American imperialism failed in attempts to use the Chingpo of the Union of Burma for attacks on the People's Republic of China or to alienate them from the Chingpo of new China.

NOTES

1. Cited in Anon. 1956: 68; supplemented by the author of the present article, with account taken of questionnaire materials and data of Li Chih-chun (1955).
2. Cf. A. Grierson 1902, Vol. III, Part II, tables; Li Chih-chun 1955: 72.
3. Data of Sung Shu-hua and Yang Yui-hsiang, from whose materials the section on Chingpo in I Chun, 1958, was written.
4. Taking into account the early marriages of Chingpo in ancient times and the possibility of two or three generations coexisting, the period of activity of one generation is taken as 20 years.
5. The role of the sword as a universal implement is emphasized by all Chinese investigators writing on the Chingpo.

LITERATURE CITED

Anon.
   1956   *Yun-nan shen shao-shu Min-chu Kai-k'uang* [Brief Reports on the Position of National Minorities of Yunnan Province].

Barnard, J.
   1930   "The frontier of Burma," *Journal of Royal Central Asian Society,* Vol. XVII, 180, 185.

Grierson, G. A.
   1902   *Linguistic Survey of India,* Calcutta, Vol. III, Part II.

Huang Shao-huai and Yeh Yung-hua
   1958   *Wo-kuo shao-shu min-tsu-ti Tsu-chiao ho fêng-hsu* [Beliefs and Rituals of Ethnic Minorities of Our Country], Peking, Vol. I.

I Chün
   1958   *Wo-kuo shaoshu minchu chien che* [Brief Description of the Ethnic minorities of Our Country], Peking.

Leach, E. R.
   1954   *Political Systems of Highland Burma*, V, London.
Li Chih-chun
   1955   "Chingpo-chu chin-kuang" [Status of the Chingpo],
   Chung-kuo min-tsu wên-ti yan-chiu ch'i kan, No. 2.

(Sovetskaia etnografiia,
1959, No. 4)

PART VII

APPENDICES

GLOSSARY

Artel' — In prerevolutionary Russia, a group of workers which received pay as a unit and distributed it among themselves, either in equal shares or according to some agreed-upon formula. Under Soviet law, the same term is applied to a producers' cooperative in the strict sense, such as a kolkhoz or a craft association.

Aul — A village in the Caucasian region, or in those parts of Central Asia formerly inhabited by nomads; in prerevolutionary times, a group of families nomadizing jointly.

Chastushka (plural: chastushki) — One of the best known forms of Russian folk song: a four-lined rhymed verse of humorous and satirical, or sometimes romantic, content.

Devishnik — A gathering of girls at the bride's house on the eve of the wedding, marked by various ritualized games, ceremonies, and singing, comparable to a bachelor supper.

El' (variant: elat) — In the sedentary parts of Central Asia, a community based on kinship; the *el'* continues to exist parallel to and independent of more modern forms of community, such as the kolkhoz and its subsidiary units.

Far North — A part of the Soviet Union comprising the Arctic region of Siberia, and extending from the northern Urals to Bering Strait. The Far North has a special status in Soviet law and economic planning, in that work there entitles one to special cash allowances and to special retirement and vacation privileges.

Five Year Plan — The unit of time within which Soviet economic development is planned, goals set, etc. The first Five Year Plan began in 1928; the ninth is currently in progress.

Front-rank (Russian: *peredovyi)* — The expression applied in the Soviet Union to persons who act consistently accordingly to standards approved by the regime.

Hectare — A metric unit of area: 2.47 acres.

Intelligentsia — In Soviet usage, a group including all persons with higher education or with specialized secondary (paraprofessional) training.

Kalym — In Central Asia and the Caucasus, a fee formerly paid (and sometimes still paid in hidden form) by the bridegroom's family to that of the bride.

Kamlanie (from an Altai root, meaning "to jump") — The ceremony performed by the shaman, comparable to a spiritualist seance.

Kan — The typical Chinese system for house heating, consisting of a stove with hot air ducts which serve to warm sleeping benches; also used by the peoples of the Soviet Far East.

Kishlak — A village in the sedentary part of Central Asia.

Kolkhoz (plural: kolkhozy) — Collective farm.

Kolkhoznik — Member of a collective farm.

Komsomol — Short for Communist League of Youth (in Russian); the youth division of the Communist Party, including people between 18 and 26.

Kopek — A unit of coinage; the hundredth part of a ruble.

Krai — A territorial-administrative unit, generally used for sparsely settled and underdeveloped parts of the Soviet Union.

Kungasa (plural: kungasy) — A type of flat-bottomed boat with a square sail, used in Soviet Far Eastern rivers and sounds.

Makhalla (Arabic) — In Central Asia and other formerly Muslim parts of the Soviet Union, a quarter in a town or city, usually inhabited by people who are or consider themselves to be related. The makhallas have recently been given some civil functions, utilizing the prestige of elderly men and women.

Mal'chishnik — Bachelor supper; the male counterpart of the *devishnik*.

MRS — (1) Motor-Fishing Station; the agency which supplied heavy equipment to fishing kolkhozy (until 1959, when the equipment was sold to the kolkhozy), and which even after 1959 continued to repair the equipment; (2) Machine Repair Station, the agency which, in agricultural regions, until the 1960s, had charge of repairing farm equipment.

Oblast — A Soviet territorial-administrative unit, comparable in size, though not necessarily in powers, to a state in the U.S. The Autonomous Oblast is a form of political organization used for small ethnic groups which are not considered advanced enough to have their own Union Republics or Autonomous Republics.

Okrug — A territorial-administrative unit ranking below the oblast. The National Okrug ranks in size and degree of autonomy below the Autonomous Oblast.

Posidelka — Literally, a sitting party. In prerevolutionary Russia, a gathering of young people for singing, dancing, sewing, spinning or basket-weaving, and conversation; part of the traditional courting pattern. In places where entertainment facilities are inadequate, the *posidelka* continues to exist.

Pridanoe — What is "given along with" the bride, comparable to a trousseau in the West, but including such items as bicycles, typewriters, and so forth, nut usually found in a trousseau.

Primak — A son-in-law living with his wife's parents.

Raion — The basic territorial-administrative unit, ranking below the oblast.

Red yurt — An institution for agitation and propaganda of the early Soviet period, still used in nomadic areas. The *yurt* is a tent.

Ruble — A unit of currency, formally equivalent to approximately one dollar. In this book, prices are usually given in "old rubles," ten of which make one ruble.

Sagene — An old Russian unit of measurement, 2.134 meters.

Shariat — Collection of Muslim laws and rules based on the Koran.

Small peoples of the North — A group of 25 to 26 small ethnic units in Siberia and the European North which collectively enjoy certain privileges in terms of education and self-government. The Nivkhi are one of the small peoples.

Soviet — Literally, "council," the basic governing body at various levels under the Soviet system.

Sovkhoz (plural: sovkhozy) — State farm, where the Soviet government makes all investments and assumes all risks. Workers on sovkhozy have a status identical to that of industrial workers and are represented by a trade union, whereas kolkhozniks have a special status.

Stoibishche — A nomadic camp of the primitive Siberian peoples.

Taiga — The Siberian forest, made up of coniferous and deciduous trees.

Tekhnikum — A specialized secondary school which trains para-professional personnel.

Trudoden' (plural: trudodni) — A unit of payment on the kolkhoz, worth a specified amount in money and goods, now replaced by a guaranteed annual wage.

Tsentner — A unit of measurement: 100 kilograms; 220 pounds.

Union Republic — The largest and most powerful territorial-administrative unit in the Soviet Union; there are 15 Union

Republics. The Autonomous Republic ranks below the Union Republic in size and ethnic development, in the Soviet sense.

Uyezd — A prerevolutionary territorial-administrative unit, roughly equivalent to the raion.

Volost — A small prerevolutionary territorial-administrative unit including a number of neighboring villages.

Waqf (Arabic) — A charitable foundation under Moslem law, consisting of a plot of land or other property, the income from which supports a religious, educational, or eleemosynary institution.

Yukola — Air-dried fish, put up in bundles, widely used by the Siberian and Far Eastern peoples.

ZAGS — Vital Statistics Bureau, where births, deaths, marriages, and divorces are registered.

RECOMMENDED READINGS

SS = Soviet Sociology
SS&A = Soviet Anthropology and Archeology
IJS = International Journal of Sociology

Abramzon, S. M.
1962 "Reflection of the Process of the Coming Together of
Nations in the Family Life and Daily Habits of the Peoples of
Central Asia and Kazakhstan, " SS, I, No. 2, 41-52.

Aglarov, M. A.
1965 "Forms of Marriage and Certain Features of Wedding
Ceremonial Among the 19th Century Andii (Based on Field
Data of 1959-1960)," SA&A, III, No. 4, 51-59.

Alekseenko, E. A.
1968 "The Cult of Bear Among the Ket (Yenisei Ostyaks),"
in Diószegi, 1968a, 175-192.

Allworth, Edward, Editor
1973 *The Nationality Question in Soviet Central Asia,*
New York [especially Dunn, Ethel, and Dunn, Stephen P.,
"Ethnic Intermarriage as an Indicator of Cultural Convergence
in Soviet Central Asia," 45-60].

Ambroz, A. K.
1967 "On the Symbolism of Russian Peasant Embroidery of
Archaic Type," SA&A, VI, No. 2, 22-37.

Andronikova, I. M.
1972 "Evolution of the Dwellings of the Russian Gypsies,"
SA&A, XI, 3-28.

Annaklychev, Shikhberdy
1966-1967 "The Life of the Oil Workers of Nebit-Dag and
Kum-Dag, SS, III, No. 3, 12-40; No. 4, 36-43; IV, No. 1,
3-18; No. 2, 34-57; No. 3, 16-31.

Anokhin, G. I.
1968 "Communal Traditions Among the Contemporary
Norwegian Peasantry," SA&A, VI, No. 3, 50-60.

Anokhina, L. A., Krupianskaia, V. Iu., Shmeleva, M. N., Dunn,
Stephen P., and Dunn, Ethel
1973 "On the Study of the Russian Peasantry," *Current
Anthropology,* 14, 143-157.

Aptekman, D. M.
1966 "Causes of the Vitality of the Ceremony of Baptism

Under Modern Conditions (On the Basis of the Results of a Concrete Sociological Investigation)," SS, IV, No. 2, 10-16.

1970 "A Preliminary Characterization of the Contemporary Status of the Religious Temperance Movement," SS, VIII, 329-342.

Arutiunian, Iu. V.
1971 "A Preliminary Socioethnic Study," SS, IX, 401-423.

1971-1972 "A Preliminary Sociological Study of a Village," SS, X, 3-45, 153-190, 289-328, 411-435.

1973a "A Concrete Sociological Study of Ethnic Relations," SS, XI, 328-348.

1973b "Culture and Social Psychology of the Soviet Rural Population," IJS, III, 119-136.

1973c "Social Mobility in the Countryside," IJS, III, 320-354.

1973d "The Distribution of Decision-Making Among the Rural Population of the USSR," IJS, III, 106-118.

Babaeva, R.
1967 "Materials for the Study of Marriage Ceremonies on the Apseron Peninsula in the Past," SA&A, VI, No. 2, 3-11.

Belova, V. A.
1972 "Family Size and Public Opinion," SS, XI, 126-144.

Benet, Sula, Translator and Editor
1970 *The Village of Viriatino*. Garden City, N.Y.

Bobrinskii, A. A.
1963 "Materials for the Study of Marriage Ceremonies on the Apsheron Peninsula in the Past," SA&A, VI, No. 2, 3-11.

Boiko, V. I.
1971 "Direction and Motivations of Potential Migration of the Peoples of the Lower Amur," SS, IX, 567-578.

Borzykh, N. P.
1973 "The Prevalence of Ethnically Mixed Marriages in the Central Asian Republics and Kazakhstan in the 1930s," SS, XI, 394-411.

Bromlei, Iu. V.
1969 "Major Trends in Ethnographic Research in the USSR," SA&A, VIII, 3-42.

Bruk, S. I.
1972 "Ethnodemographic Processes in the USSR (On Materials From the 1970 Census)," SS, X, 331-374.

Butkiavichius, I. P., Terent'eva, L. N., and Shlygina, N. V.
1968 "Peasant Settlements of the Baltic Area (History, Present Condition, and Prospects for Development)," SA&A, VI, No. 3, 3-22.

Cheboksarov, N. N.
1970 "Problems of the Typology of Ethnic Units in the Works of Soviet Scholars," SA&A, IX, 127-153.

Chizhikova, L. N.
1966 "Dwellings of the Russians," SA&A, V, No. 1, 32-55.

Daniliauskas, A.
1963 "A Contribution to the Study of the Culture and Mode of Life of Lithuanian Workers," SS, II, No. 1, 47-51.

Danilova, L. V.
1971 "Controversial Problems of the Theory of Precapitalist Societies," SA&A, IX, 269-328.

Diószegi, V., Editor
1968a *Popular Beliefs and Folklore Tradition in Siberia,* The Hague.

1968b "The Three-Grade Amulets Among the Nanai (Golds)," in Diószegi, 1968a, 387-406.

Djabbarov, I. M.
1973 "Crafts of the Uzbeks of Southern Khorezm in the Late Nineteenth and Early Twentieth Centuries (A Historical-Ethnographic Sketch)," SA&A, XII, 34-64, *et seq.*

Djarylgasinova, R. Sh.
1968 "On the Question of Cultural Convergence of the Koreans of the Uzbek SSR with Neighboring Peoples (The Traditional and the New in the Economy and Material Culture)," SA&A, VII, No. 1, 26-35.

Djunusov, M. S.
1963 "Soviet Autonomy and the Vestiges of Nationalism," SS, II, No. 1, 11-25.

Dunn, Ethel
1968 "Educating the Small Peoples of the Soviet North: The Limits of Culture Change," with an appendix, "Notes Toward a Medical Sociology of the Small Peoples of the Soviet North," *Arctic Anthropology,* V, No. 1, 1-31.

1970 "Education and the Native Intelligentsia in the Soviet North: Further Thoughts on the Limits of Culture Change," *Arctic Anthropology,* VI, No. 2, 112-122.

1971 "The Importance of Religion in the Soviet Rural Community," in Millar, James R., Editor, *The Soviet Rural Community*, Urbana, Ill., 346-375.

Dunn, Ethel, and Dunn, Stephen P.
1964 "Religion as an Instrument of Culture Change: The Problem of the Sects in the Soviet Union," *Slavic Review*, 23, 459-478.

Dunn, Stephen P.
1966 "Cultural Processes in the Baltic Area Under Soviet Rule," Research Monograph No. 11, Institute of International Studies, Berkeley.

1969a "Some Reflections on Ways of Looking at Primitive Religion, in Reply to S. A. Tokarev," SA&A, VII, No. 3, 37-44.

1969b "Sovietology Old and New," *Canadian Slavic Studies*, 3, 565-574.

1971 "Structure and Functions of the Soviet Rural Family," in Millar, James R., Editor, *The Soviet Rural Community*, Urbana, Ill., 325-345.

Dunn, Stephen P., and Dunn, Ethel
1963 "Transformation of Economy and Culture of the Soviet North," *Arctic Anthropology*, I, No. 1, 1-28.

1965 "Talks with Soviet Ethnographers and Some Reflections," *American Anthropology*, 67, 985-997.

1967a *The Peasants of Central Russia*, New York.

1967b "Soviet Regime and Native Culture in Central Asia and Kazakhstan: The Major Peoples," *Current Anthropology*, 8, 147-208.

1972 "The Peoples of Siberia and the Far East," in Vucinich, Wayne S., Editor, 289-312.

Dyrenkova, N. P.
1968 "The Protection of Children Among the Shors," in Diószegi, 1968a, 235-238.

Editorial [From *Sovetskaia Etnografiia*].
1963 "The Teaching of Social, Cultural, and Physical Anthropology in Secondary Schools and Higher Education Institutions," SA&A, II, No. 1, 3-7.

Efremova, L. S., Luts, A. A., and Chivkul', E. P.
1964 "Changes in Fishing Technology and in the Culture and Daily Life of the Fishermen of Soviet Latvia and Estonia,"

SS, III, No. 2, 20-25.

Esbergenov, Kh.
1964 "On the Struggle Against Survivals of Obsolete
Customs and Rites (The Karakalpak *As* Memorial Feast),"
SA&A, III, No. 1, 9-20.

Evstigneev, Iu. A.
1973 "Ethnically Mixed Marriages in Makhachkala, " SS,
XI, 369-381.

Gagarin, Iu. V.
1970 "The Abandonment of Sectarianism in the Komi
ASSR," SS, VIII, 358-382.

Gagen-Torn, N. I.
1971 "The Leningrad Ethnographic School in the 1920s
(The Origins of Soviet Ethnography)," SA&A, X, 146-167.

Gagen-Torn, N. I., and Vasina, A. I.
1973 "The Retrospective Method of Analysis in the Works
of D. K. Zelenin," SA&A, XI, 306-323.

Gantskaia, O. A., and Debets, G. F.
1968 "On the Graphic Representation of the Results of a
Statistical Survey of Inter-Ethnic Marriages," SS, VI, No. 4,
45-55.

Gantskaia, O. A., and Terent'eva, L. N.
1968 "Ethnographic Studies of Ethnic Processes in the
Baltic Area," SA&A, VI, No. 3, 23-38.

Gardanov, V. K., Dolgikh, B. O., and Zhdanko, T. A.
1962 "Major Trends in Ethnic Processes Among the Peoples
of the USSR," SA&A, I, No. 1, 3-18.

Gur'ianov, S. T.
1967 "The Intellectual Interests of the Soviet Worker," SS,
V, No. 3, 7-29.

Gurvich, I. S.
1962 "Directions to Be Taken in the Further Reorganization
of the Economy and Culture of the Peoples of the North,"
SA&A, I, No. 2, 22-30.

1964 "Russian Old Settlers Along the Kamchatka River
Valley (A Contribution to the Question of the History and
Ultimate Destiny of the Russian People in Siberia)," SA&A, II,
No. 3, 39-48.

Hajdu, P.
1968 "The Classification of Samoyed Shamans," in Diószegi,
1968a, 147-174.

Ianovskii, V.
1969 "Man in the North," SS, VII, No. 4, 16-26.

Il'inykh, N. I.
1972 "Peculiarities of the Organization and Activity of Mennonite Congregations," SS, XI, 145-159.

Iusupov, G. V.
1968 "Survivals of Totemism in the Ancestor Cult of the Kazan Tatars," In Diószegi, 1968a, 193-204.

Kalits, V. Ia.
1962 "New Features in the Life of the Peasants of Kihnu Island," SA&A, I, No. 1, 27-36.

Kálman, B.
1968 "Two Purification Rites in the Bear Cult of the Ob-Ugrians," In Diószegi, 1968a, 85-92.

Kaloev, B. A.
1969 "M. M. Kovalevskii (On the 50th Anniversary of His Death)," SA&A, VIII, 145-167.

Kapustin, N. S.
1971 "Specific Features of Certain Survivals of Religion in Everyday Life," SA&A, X, 37-56.

Katunskii, A. E.
1964 "The Reactionary Nature of the Contemporary Old Believer Ideology," SS, III, No. 2, 39-43.

Kharchev, A. G.
1967 "Marriage in the USSR," SS, V, No. 4, 3-25.

Kholmogorov, A. I.
1973 "International Traits of Soviet Nations," SS, XI, 211-327; XII, 3-33, et seq.

Klibanov, A. I.
1965 "The Dissident Denominations in the Past and Today," SS, III, No. 4, 44-60.

1970a "Fifty Years of Scientific Study of Religious Sectarianism," SS, VIII, 239-278.

1970b "Sectarianism and the Socialist Reconstruction of the Countryside," SS, VIII, 383-411.

1971 "Problems in the Psychology of Religious Sectarianism," SS, IX, 505-566.

Kobychev, V. P., and Robakidze, A. I.
1969 "Basic Typology and Mapping of Dwellings of the Caucasian Peoples (Materials for the Caucasian Historical-

Ethnographic Atlas)," SA&A, VII, No. 4, 13-28.

Konstantinidi, S. S.
1971 "On Public and Governmental-Legal Measures for Improving Conservation in the Kazakh Soviet Socialist Republic," SS, IX, 579-592.

Kosven, M. O.
1964 "Who is the Godfather?," SA&A, II, No. 4, 3-14.

Kozenko, A. V., and Monogarova, L. F.
1973 "A Statistical Study of the Indices of Monoethnic and Mixed Marriages in Dushanbe," SS, XI, 412-422.

Kozlova, K. I.
1970 "Experience Gained in Studying the Molokans of Armenia," SS, VIII, 318-328.

Kriukov, M. V.
1972 "Types of Kinship Systems and Their Historical Inter-relationship," SA&A, XI, 107-150.

Krupianskaia, V. Iu., and Rabinovich, M. G.
1964 "The Ethnography of the City and Industrial Settle-ment," SS, III, No. 2, 13-19.

Lebedev, A. A.
1973 "The Secularization of the Population of a Socialist City," SS, XII, 77-105.

Levin, M. G. and Potapov, L. P., Editors
1964 *The Peoples of Siberia.* Chicago.

Lipset, S. M.
1973 "Commentary: Social Stratification Research and Soviet Scholarship," IJS, III, 355-392.

Lobacheva, N. P.
1969 "On the Shaping of New Marriage Ceremonial Among the Peoples of Uzbekistan," SA&A, VII, No. 4, 3-12.

Lunin, B. V.
1970 "The Life and Works of Academician Vasilii Vladimirovich Bartol'd," SA&A, IX, 91-126.

Maslova, G. S.
1968 "Changes in the Traditional Folk Costume of Riazan During the Soviet Period (Based on Data of the Interdisciplin-ary Expedition, Institute of Ethnography, Academy of Sciences, USSR)," SA&A, VII, No. 1, 36-48.

Maslova, G. S., and Saburova, L. M.
1962 "An Ethnographic Study of the Russian Collective-

Farm Peasantry of Eastern Siberia in 1957-59," SA&A, I, No. 1, 19-26.

Melik-Pashaian, K. V.
1966 "The Life and Work of Ervand Lalaian," SA&A, V, No. 2, 35-43.

Menovščikov, G. A.
1968 "Popular Conceptions, Religious Beliefs and Rites of the Asiatic Eskimos," in Diószegi, 1968a, 433-450.

Michael, Henry, N., Editor
1963 *Studies in Siberian Shamanism,* Toronto [includes articles by Chernetsov, V. N., Vasilevich, G. M., Anisimov, A. F., and Prokofyeva, Ye. D.].

Min'ko, L. I.
1973 "Magical Curing (Its Sources and Character, and the Causes of Its Prevalence)," SA&A, XII, 3-33, *et seq.*

Monich, Zinaida I.
1973 "The Professional and Paraprofessional Component in the Structure of the Rural Population (Based on Data from the Belorussian SSR) (Part 1)," SS, XII, 56-76; *et seq.*

Nahodil, O.
1968 "Mother Cult in Siberia," in Diószegi, 1968a, 459-478.

Naulko, V. I.
1964 "The Present Ethnic Composition of the Population of the Ukrainian SSR," SS, III, No. 1, 12-23.

Nosova, G. A.
1970 "A Preliminary Ethnographic Study of Habitual Orthodoxy (Based on Data from Vladimir Oblast)," SS, VIII, 343-357.

Okhrimenko, G. I.
1967 "Russian Decorative House-Painting of the Transbaikal," SA&A, VI, No. 2, 38-51.

Ostapenko, L. V.
1971 "The Village of Gadyshi Today," SS, X, 46-63.

Panian, A. E.
1969 "The New Life of the Kolkhozniks of the Village of Mrgavan, Artashat Raion, Armenian SSR," SA&A, VIII, 123-144.

Perevedentsev, V. I.
1967 "On the Influence of Ethnic Factors on Geographical Population Shifts," SA&A, VI, No. 2, 12-21.

1970-1972   "Population Movement and Labor Supply in
Siberia," SS, VII, No. 3, 33-56; No. 4, 27-43; VIII, 24-67,
129-158; IX, 424-474; XI, 31-56, 107-125.

Pimenov, V. V.
1964   "Life of Karelian Lumberjacks on the Job," SS, II,
No. 3, 13-20.

Pivovarov, V. G.
1970   "The Religious Group of Parishioners in the System of
a Church Parish (A Preliminary Model)," SS, VIII, 279-317.

Popov, A. A.
1968   "How Sereptie Djaruoskin of the Nganasans (Tavgi
Samoyeds) Became a Shaman," in Diószegi, 1968a, 137-146.

Potapov, L. P.
1963   "Ethnographic Study of the Socialist Culture and
Mode of Life of the Peoples of the USSR," SA&A, I, No. 3,
3-16.

Porshnev, B. F.
1969   "Attempts at Synthesis in the Field of the History of
Religion," SA&A, VII, 20-36.

Saburova, L. M.
1970   "The Literature on New Rituals and Festivals Published
in 1963-1966 (Basic Questions and Tendencies in the Field),"
SA&A, VIII, 283-303.

Sanarov, V. I.
1970   "Elements of Ancient Beliefs in Gypsy Religion,"
SA&A, VIII, 187-213.

Sarkisyanz, Manuel
1972   "Russian Conquest in Central Asia: Transformation
and Acculturation," in Vucinich, Wayne S., Editor, 313-337.

Savoskul, S. S.
1973   "Socioethnic Aspects of the Intellectual Culture of the
Rural Population of the Tatar ASSR," SS, XI, 349-368.

Selivanov, V. I.
1966   "Primary Rural Collectives and Their Influence on the
Formation of Personality," SS, V, No. 2, 3-10.

Semenov, Iu. I.
1965   "The Doctrine of Morgan, Marxism, and Contemporary
Ethnography," SA&A, IV, No. 2, 3-15.

Sergeeva, G. A., and Smirnova, Ia. S.
1973   "A Contribution to the Question of the Ethnic Self-

Identification of Urban Young People," SS, XI, 382-393.

Shlygina, N. V.
1968 "The Role of Economic Activities in the Assimilation of the Vod' and Izhora Population: Late 19th and Early 20th Centuries," SA&A, VI, No. 3, 39-49.

Smirnova, Ia. S.
1962 "Avoidance Customs Among the Adygei and Their Disappearance During the Soviet Era," SA&A, I, No. 2, 31-39.

1964 "Some Religious Survivals Among the Black Sea Adygei," SA&A, III, No. 2, 3-8.

Snesarev, G. P.
1963 "Pachiz (An Ethnographic Relic of Ancient Ties Between India and Khorezm)," SA&A, II, No. 1, 8-14.

1971 "In the Ruins of Ancient Kiat," SA&A, X, 135-145.

1971-1973 "Remnants of Pre-Islamic Beliefs and Rituals Among the Khorezm Uzbeks," SA&A, IX, 204-225, 329-352; X, 3-36, 253-289; XI, 219-253, 331-380.

Sokolova, Z. P.
1962 "Certain Ethnic Processes Among the Sel'kups, Khanty, and Evenks of Tomsk Oblast," SA&A, I, No. 2, 50-56.

Studenetskaia, E. N.
1963 "Contemporary National Dress (On the Occasion of the Arrangement of a New Exhibition by the State Museum of the Ethnography of the Peoples of the USSR)," SA&A, II, No. 2, 3-14.

Taksami, C. M.
1968 "Features of the Ancient Religious Rites and Taboos of the Nivkhi (Gilyaks)," in Diószegi, 1968a, 407-422.

Terent'eva, L. N.
1973 "Ethnic Self-Identification by Adolescents in Ethnically Mixed Families," SS, XII, 34-55.

Tokarev, S. A.
1966 "Principles of the Morphological Classification of Religions," SA&A, IV, No. 4, 3-10; V, No. 1, 11-25.

1969 "Rejoinder to Dunn," SA&A, VII, No. 3, 44-46.

Tolstov, S. P., and Zhdanko, T. A.
1965 "Directions and Problems of Soviet Ethnography," SA&A, III, No. 3, 3-20.

Trofimova, A. G.
1964 "Types of Settlements and Houses of the Oil Workers of Baku," SS, II, No. 3, 21-33.

Tudorovskaia, E. A.
1967 "On the Classification of Fairy Tales," SA&A, VI, No. 1, 23-31.

Tugolukov, V. A.
1963 "The Vitim-Olekma Evenki," SA&A, II, No. 2, 15-40.

Vacheishvili, A. Sh., and Menabdishvili, E. S.
1972 "Ethnic Relations in the Social Structure of an Industrial Work Force," SS, XI, 3-30.

Vasil'ev, V. I.
1966 "The Forest Entsy (An Essay on Their History, Economy, and Culture)," SA&A, IV, No. 3, 3-32.

Vasil'ev, V. A., Simchenko, Iu. B., and Sokolova, Z. P.
1966 "Problems of the Reconstruction of Daily Life Among the Small Peoples of the Far North," SA&A, V, No. 2, 11-21.

Vasil'eva, E. K.
1971 "An Ethnodemographic Characterization of Family Structure in Kazan in 1967," SS, X, 64-80.

Vasilevič, G. M. [Vasilevich]
1968 "The Acquisition of Shamanistic Ability Among the Evenki (Tungus)," in Diószegi, 1968a, 351-372.

1972 "Preshamanistic and Shamanistic Beliefs of the Evenki," SA&A, XI, 29-44.

Verbov, G. D.
1968 "Funeral Rites Among the Enets (Yenisei Samoyeds)," in Diószegi, 1968a, 123-124.

Vishniauskaite, A. I.
1965 "Family Life of Lithuanian Collective Farmers," SA&A, III, No. 4, 51-59.

Volkova, N. G.
1966 "Changes in the Ethnic Composition of the Urban Population of the North Caucasus During the Soviet Period," SS, IV, No. 2, 17-33.

Vucinich, Alexander
1971 "The Peasants as a Social Class," in Millar, James R., Editor, *The Soviet Rural Community*, Urbana, Ill., 307-324.

Vucinich, Wayne S., Editor
1972 *Russia and Asia: Essays on the Influence of Russia on the Asian Peoples,* Stanford.

Wasson, R. Gordon
1968 *Soma: Divine Mushroom of Immortality,* New York.

Yanowitch, Murray, and Fisher, Wesley A., Eds. and Trs.
1973 *Social Stratification and Mobility in the USSR,* White Plains, N. Y. (IJS, III, Nos. 1-2).

Zadykhina, K. L.
1963 "Ethnographic Data on the Mode of Life of the Uzbek Workers of Tashkent and Andizhan," SS, I, No. 4, 10-18; II, No. 1, 36-46.

Zel'in, K. K.
1968 "Principles of Morphological Classification of Forms of Dependence," SS, VI, No. 4, 3-24.

Zhdanko, T. A.
1962 "Mode of Life of Members of Fishing Cooperatives on Islands of the South Aral," SA&A, I, 40-49.

LIST OF ABBREVIATIONS USED

EO — *Etnograficheskoe obozrenie*

IGAIMK — *Izvestiia Gosudarstvennoi Akademii istorii material'noi kul'tury*

IJS — International Journal of Sociology

Izv. AN — *Izvestiia Akademii nauk*

KSIE — *Kratkie soobshcheniia Instituta etnografii*

NAA — *Narody Azii i Afriki*

PIDO — *Problemy istorii dokapitalisticheskikh obshchestv*

SA&A — Soviet Anthropology and Archeology

Sb. MAE — *Sbornik Muzei antropologii i etnografii*

Sb. ORIaS — *Sbornik Otdeleniia russkogo iazyka i slovestnosti (Akademii nauk)*

SE — *Sovetskaia etnografiia*

SS — Soviet Sociology

SV — *Sovetskoe vostokovedenie*

TIE — *Trudy Instituta etnografii*

UZLGU — *Uchenye zapiski Leningradskogo Gosudarstvennogo universiteta*

VDI — *Vestnik Drevnei istorii*

VI — *Voprosy istorii*

VIMK — *Vestnik istorii mirovoi kul'tury*

XXV MKV — *XXV Mezhdunarodnyi kongress vostokovedov. Doklady sovetskoi delegatsii.* [Papers of the Soviet delegation to the 25th International Congress of Orientalists] Moscow, 1960.

ZhS — *Zhivaia starina*